5, 6, 9.
ch 3

Women and Men at Work

Dec 17

next monday Law Review 6:00 oris 20a

+20 00

29.00

Sociology for a New Century

A PINE FORGE PRESS SERIES

Edited by Charles Ragin, Wendy Griswold, and Larry Griffin

Sociology for a New Century brings the best current scholarship to today's students in a series of short texts authored by leaders of a new generation of social scientists. Each book addresses its subject from a comparative, historical, global perspective, and, in doing so, connects social science to the wider concerns of students seeking to make sense of our dramatically changing world.

- *How Societies Change* Daniel Chirot
- *Cultures and Societies in a Changing World* Wendy Griswold
- *Crime and Disrepute* John Hagan
- *Racism and the Modern World* Wilmot James
- *Gods in the Global Village* Lester Kurtz
- *Constructing Social Research* Charles C. Ragin
- *Women, Men, and Work* Barbara Reskin and Irene Padavic
- *Cities in a World Economy* Saskia Sassen

Forthcoming:

- *Social Psychology and Social Institutions* Denise and William Bielby
- *Global Transitions: Emerging Patterns of Inequality* York Bradshaw and Michael Wallace
- *Schools and Societies* Steven Brint
- *The Social Ecology of Natural Resources and Development* Stephen G. Bunker
- *Ethnic Dynamics in the Modern World* Stephen Cornell
- *The Sociology of Childhood* William A. Corsaro
- *Waves of Democracy* John Markoff
- *A Global View of Development* Philip McMichael
- *Health and Society* Bernice Pescosolido
- *Organizations in a World Economy* Walter W. Powell

Women and Men at Work

Barbara F. Reskin
The Ohio State University

Irene Padavic
Florida State University

PINE FORGE PRESS
Thousand Oaks ◆ *London* ◆ *New Delhi*

For information, address:

 Pine Forge Press
A Sage Publications Company
2455 Teller Road
Thousand Oaks, California 91320
(805) 499-4224
Internet:sdr@pfp.sagepub.com

Production: Scratchgravel Publishing Services
Designer: Lisa S. Mirski
Typesetter: Scratchgravel Publishing Services
Cover: Lisa S. Mirski
Print Buyer: Anna Chin

Printed in the United States of America

94 95 96 97 98 10 9 8 7 6 5 4 3 2

Library of Congress Cataloging-in-Publication Data

Reskin, Barbara F.
    Women and men at work / Barbara Reskin, Irene Padavic.
        p.   cm. — (Sociology for a new century)
    Includes bibliographical references and index.
    ISBN 0-8039-9022-7 (pbk. : alk. paper)
    1. Sex discrimination in employment—United States. 2. Women-
-Employment—United States. 3. Men—Employment—United States.
I. Padavic, Irene.   II. Title.   III. Series.
HD6060.5.U5R47   1994
331.13'3'0973—dc20   93-47612
                                                             CIP

 This book is printed on acid-free paper that meets
Environmental Protection Agency standards for recycled paper

For our mothers,
Verna Smith and Ann Padavic,
from whom we learned that
women's jobs are real work
and whose sacrifices gave us
opportunities they never had

Contents

ABOUT THE AUTHORS

Barbara Reskin is Professor of Sociology at The Ohio State University. She has had more clerical jobs than she cares to remember, including switchboard operator, freight-bill typist, and grant accountant. Her research examines how workers' sex and race affect their work opportunities, and she has written several articles and books on these topics—most recently, *Job Queues, Gender Queues: Explaining Women's Inroads into Male Occupations*, with Patricia Roos. She is former Vice President of the American Sociological Association and chairs the American Association of University Professors Committee on Women.

Irene Padavic is Associate Professor at Florida State University. Her research has been in the areas of gender and work, economic restructuring, and the labor process. Before becoming a professor, she had been a candy seller at a movie theater, a cocktail waitress, a telephone solicitor, a door-to-door promoter of real estate, a paralegal, and a coal handler at a power plant.

ABOUT THE PUBLISHER

Pine Forge Press is a new educational publisher, dedicated to publishing innovative books and software throughout the social sciences. On this and any other of our publications, we welcome your comments, ideas, and suggestions. Please call or write to:

Pine Forge Press
A Sage Publications Company
2455 Teller Road
Thousand Oaks, California 91320
(805) 499-4224
Internet:sdr@pfp.sagepub.com

Foreword

Sociology for a New Century offers the best of current sociological thinking to today's students. The goal of the series is to prepare students, and—in the long run—the informed public, for a world that has changed dramatically in the last three decades and one that continues to astonish.

This goal reflects important changes that have taken place in sociology. The discipline has become broader in orientation, with an ever growing interest in research that is comparative, historical, or transnational in orientation. Sociologists are less focused on "American" society as the pinnacle of human achievement and more sensitive to global processes and trends. They also have become less insulated from surrounding social forces. In the 1970s and 1980s sociologists were so obsessed with constructing a science of society that they saw impenetrability as a sign of success. Today, there is a greater effort to connect sociology to the ongoing concerns and experiences of the informed public.

Each book in this series offers a comparative, historical, transnational, or global perspective in some way, to help broaden students' vision. Students need to be sensitized to diversity in today's world and to the sources of diversity. Knowledge of diversity challenges the limitations of conventional ways of thinking about social life. At the same time, students need to be sensitized to the fact that issues that may seem specifically "American" (for example, the women's movement, an aging population bringing a strained social security and health care system, racial conflict, national chauvinism, and so on) are shared by many other countries. Awareness of commonalities undercuts the tendency to view social issues and questions in narrowly American terms and encourages students to seek out the experiences of others for the lessons they offer. Finally, students also need to be sensitized to phenomena that transcend national boundaries, economies, and politics.

Women and Men at Work provides students with an in-depth examination of the world of work at the end of the twentieth century. Many books deal with women and men at work. Some focus on a single topic, context, or occupation; others are primarily historical; still others employ an economic perspective that discounts or ignores sociological insights; many focus almost exclusively on women; and a few focus on women of color. This book differs from other books by comparing women's and men's work status, addressing contemporary issues within a historical perspective, incorporating comparative material from other countries, recognizing differences in the experiences of women and men from different racial and ethnic backgrounds, drawing on both qualitative and quantitative data, and—most important—seeking to link social scientific ideas about workers' lives, sex inequality, and gender to the real-world workplace in which students will work for most of their lives. Throughout this book, we integrate theory and evidence—statistics that summarize work outcomes for women and men, research about the effects of workers' sex on their jobs, and accounts of the experiences of real workers. By putting evidence about the experiences of today's workers in a historical perspective, we highlight continuities with the past and illuminate change.

Preface

On October 7, 1993, ABC's *Prime-Time Live* broadcast a segment that compared the experiences of Chris and Julie, male and female "testers" whom ABC had hired to learn whether sex discrimination still existed in 1993. Because of their sexes, Chris and Julie were not perfect doubles, but both were trim, blonde, neatly dressed college graduates in their late 20s, and both were experienced professional testers. *Prime-Time Live* showed what happened when Julie and Chris, wired for sound and equipped with hidden cameras, went through the motions of getting settled in a new city.

Julie and Chris applied for two jobs advertised in the help-wanted columns. The first advertisement mentioned several positions, and the interviewer talked to Julie about a possible job answering phones. The same interviewer offered Chris a management job. After learning that the interviews had been taped, the interviewer commented off camera that he would never want a man answering his phone. The second advertisement was for territory managers for a lawn-care firm. Julie and Chris presented similar resumes, each showing managerial experience. The company's owner gave Julie a typing test, asked her about her fiance's business and even his name, and then offered her a job as receptionist that started at "about $6" an hour. In contrast, the owner chatted with Chris about how he keeps fit playing tennis, soccer, and softball; gave him an aptitude test, not a typing test; and offered him the job of territory manager, which would pay $300 to $500 a week. Later, the owner told *Prime-Time Live* that he thought Julie was applying for a different job and that women "do not do well as territory managers, which involves some physical labor." He also said he had hired a female receptionist and several male territory managers.

We provide this detailed account because it offers up-to-date evidence of sex inequality at work. Our students sometimes feel that the studies or statistics in their books are out of date and that sex inequality has disappeared. As a matter of fact, one of sociologists' most persistent findings on this issue is that sex inequality has eroded very, very slowly.

This is not to say that change does not occur. Also in October 1993, a *New York Times* article reported that an award-winning female agent of the Federal Bureau of Investigation was resigning after nine years' service (D. Johnston 1993:A7). During an undercover assignment, she charged, her supervisor grabbed her from behind, put her in a choke hold, and promised to promote her if she consented to sex. Another supervisor warned the female agent that a formal complaint could cost her job. As he and others had predicted, her career did stall after she complained. The FBI has long discriminated against women. It did not hire any female agents until 1972, and in 1993 still almost 90 percent of the agents were men. The highest-ranking woman ran a small field office in remote Anchorage, Alaska. However, a few days after the news story about the sexual harassment charge, the FBI announced that it was promoting the Anchorage woman to assistant director, along with a Hispanic man (also a first), an African-American man, and two white men.

Women and Men at Work addresses the same issues that appear in news stories: men's and women's everyday experiences on the job and their progress in the world of work. To these real issues we bring the evidence of history and the theories and data of sociologists and economists interested in work, inequality, and gender. A thorough account of women and men at work must address the questions implied in the above examples: Why doesn't an employer want a man to answer his phone? Why did the owner of the lawn-care firm offer Julie a low-paying job as a receptionist when her credentials were as good as Chris's? Why should a receptionist earn less than a territory manager? Why are women more likely than men to be sexually harassed at work and less likely to be promoted? Although we cannot answer all these questions in this book, we summarize scientists' findings that bear on them and evaluate the answers that their findings imply.

Chapter 1 focuses on what work is and the three components of what we call "gendered work": the sexual division of labor, the devaluation of women's work, and the construction of gender on the job—processes that we return to throughout the book. Chapter 2 provides a historical context for gendered work in the Western world. It examines the effects of industrialization and the evolution of the labor force and the sexual division of labor. Chapter 3 provides an overview of sex inequality in the workplace and introduces several general explanations for sex inequality that the following chapters employ.

Chapter 4 focuses on workers' segregation into different kinds of work on the basis of their sex, as well as their race and ethnicity. It examines the causes of segregation and mechanisms that can reduce it. Chapter 5 looks at two expressions of hierarchical sex and race segregation in the work-place—differences in opportunities to move up and exercise authority—and evaluates possible reasons for these differences. Chapter 6 focuses on the pay gap between the sexes. It shows how men of color and all women compare to white men in their average earnings, assesses trends in the earnings ratio, reviews explanations for the pay gap, and discusses strategies to reduce it.

Chapter 7 explores how and why employers and workers make gender salient in the workplace. Chapter 8 examines the connections between paid and family work for women and for men. It considers what governments and employers can do and are doing to deal with the problems that workers face in combining paid and family work. Chapter 9 concludes by speculating on the effects of recent trends in the organization of work on female and male workers in the twenty-first century.

This book is the product of many persons' efforts. We are indebted to all the scholars whose ideas helped to shape our own and whom we cite in the pages that follow; to our students and colleagues, who make our work fun; to the millions of women and men around the world whose experiences on the job provide the focus and the data for this book; and to our friends who offered encouragement when we were ready to abandon this project, assume new identities, and leave town. That these groups are too large for us to thank by name does not diminish our indebtedness or gratitude. Among the smaller group of people who helped materially in our finishing this book are Lynda Ames, Katharine Donato, Greg Draus, Anne Draus, Randy Earnest, John Felice, Larry Griffin, Wendy Griswold, Lowell Hargens, Jane Hood, Chiara Huddleston, the Institute for Women's Policy Research, Marcia Johnson, Gail McGuire, Wanda Mitchell, John Myles, the National Committee on Pay Equity, Victoria Nelson, Ann Padavic, J. Anthony Paredes, Mary Pohl, Cathy Rakowski, Carole Ray, Claire Robertson, Ruth Rosenblum, Steve Rutter, Rebecca Smith, Verna Smith, Marc Steinberg, and Ronnie Steinberg. We particularly thank soon-to-be full-fledged sociologists Naomi Cassirer, Michelle Fondell, and Laura Geschwender, whose not-very-well-paid labor was vital in our completing this book.

Barbara Reskin and Irene Padavic

Women and Men at Work

1

Work and Gender

Underpinning all human activity is work. We spend most of our lives preparing for work, working, or using the products of others' labor. Even when we are simply relaxing in front of the TV set watching *General Hospital*, the evening news, or Monday night football, we are enjoying the results of the labor of others. The workers who bring these television shows to millions of viewers include executives and administrators, personnel managers, advertising agents, writers and editors, producers and directors, newscasters and announcers, actors and musicians, production engineers, camera operators, electrical technicians, computer operators, clerks and typists, and maintenance workers. Fifty years ago, neither royalty nor oil barons could summon up the labor of so many thousands simply to entertain them.

Just as we take for granted the air we breathe, we take for granted the work that creates the world around us. This book aims to make work visible so we can examine the work that women and men do and explore the ways that workers, the workplace, and work become saturated with gendered meanings.

What Work Is

Although we use the term *work* in many ways ("working on a relationship," "working on a suntan"), its core meaning is activities that produce a good or a service—such as mowing the lawn, selling encyclopedias, testing silicon chips, and refueling military aircraft. In this book, we define **work** to include activities that produce goods and services for one's own use or in exchange for pay or support. This definition encompasses three kinds of work: *paid* work (also called **market work**), which generates an income; **coerced work**, which people are forced to do against their will and with little or no pay (for example, as slaves or prisoners);

Note: **Boldface** terms in the text are defined in the Glossary/Index.

and *unpaid* work (also called **nonmarket work**), which people voluntarily perform for themselves and others. An important form of nonmarket work in modern societies is **domestic work**—work that people do around their homes for themselves and members of their household. If you aren't convinced that unpaid work is really work, think of your experiences waxing your car, planning and cooking a meal that will impress your friends, or buying groceries or gifts on a limited budget during exam week.

This distinction between market and nonmarket work is fairly recent. For most of history, people did not see work as separate from the rest of their lives. Life was work, just as it was rest and recovery from work. The average person consumed all that she or he produced, and few people were paid for their labor. Only with the development of capitalism and industrial work did work come to be seen as paid activities. As more people became engaged in this new form of work, the terms *unpaid work, nonmarket work,* and *domestic work* came to refer to the plain, old-fashioned, unpaid work that people had always done.

As more workers took paid jobs, however, people increasingly treated paid work as the only "real" work; the unpaid work that people did in their own homes became devalued or invisible. Today economists and statisticians who monitor the size and productivity of the workforce in industrialized countries reserve the term *work* for activities that people do for pay. American economists, for example, estimate the nation's gross national product in terms of the output of its paid workers. Defining work in this way excludes much of the work done by people in developing countries as well as almost all the work that women—and sometimes men—perform at home for their families.

This book examines the roles that women and men play in paid and unpaid work. We show that workers' sex profoundly affects their work lives, although the way that it does so also depends on people's race, ethnicity, and class. We show too that the effects of sex have varied throughout history and around the world. However, before we discuss the ways that people's sex affects the kinds of work they do, the rewards it brings, and its effects on their family lives, we must clarify the terms *sex* and *gender* and introduce the concepts of sex differentiation and gender differentiation.

Sex and Gender

Although many people use the terms *sex* and *gender* as synonyms, they have different meanings. We use the term **sex** for a classification based on human biology. Biological sex depends on a person's chromosomes and is expressed in the person's genitals, internal reproductive organs, and hormones. **Gender,** in contrast, refers to a classification that societies construct to exaggerate the differences between females and males and to maintain **sex inequality.**

Sex Differentiation

All societies recognize the existence of different sexes and group people by their sex for some purposes. Classifying people into categories based on their sex is called **sex differentiation.** Because of the importance societies attach to sex, sex differentiation begins at birth. However, in our society each new baby is assigned to one of just two sexes on the basis of just one indicator, the appearance of the external genitalia.[1] The term *the opposite sex* reveals our society's preoccupation with the differences between males and females.

Sex differentiation usually exists as part of a system of sex inequality—**a sex-gender hierarchy**—that favors males over females. Although sex differentiation need not inevitably lead to sex inequality, it is essential for a system of inequality. Distinguishing females and males is necessary in order to treat them differently.

Gender Differentiation

To justify unequal treatment of the sexes, the differences between them must seem to be large and important. **Gender differentiation** refers to the social processes that exaggerate the differences between males and females and create new ones where no natural differences exist (West and Zimmerman 1987:137; Reskin 1988). Gender differentiation also distinguishes activities as male or female.

Together, sex differentiation and gender differentiation ensure that females differ from males in easy-to-spot ways. Clothing fashions, for example, accentuate physical differences between the sexes. At times, fashion has enhanced the breadth of men's shoulders or of women's hips and has called attention to women's or men's sexual characteristics. After trousers were introduced in the nineteenth century, it was several years before men gave up the skin-tight breeches that "showed off [their] sexual parts" (Davidoff and Hall 1987:412). Shoe styles, too, have contributed to gender differentiation by exaggerating the difference in the

---

[1]Biologically, most people are one sex or the other, although a few people have a combination of chromosomes, reproductive organs, and hormones that is not unambiguously male or female.

sizes of women's and men's feet. In prerevolutionary China, upper-class Chinese women had their feet bound so they could wear tiny shoes; in the United States in the early 1960s, the only fashionable shoes women could buy had narrow, pointed toes and 3-inch heels.

Clothing also creates differences between the sexes that have no natural basis. Disposable-diaper manufacturers now market different designs for girls and boys—for example, police cars and cement trucks on boys' diapers and frolicking teddy bears on girls'.[2] Until the beginning of the twentieth century, however, male and female infants were dressed alike—usually in white dresses. When Americans did begin to color code babies' clothing, they dressed boys in pink and girls in blue. Not until almost 1950 did the convention reverse, with blue becoming defined as masculine and pink as feminine—and hence taboo for boys (Kidwell and Steele 1989:24–7). Such shifts demonstrate that what is critical for maintaining and justifying unequal treatment between the sexes is not *how* cultures set the sexes apart but *that* they do it.

The Social Construction of Gender

The process of transforming males and females who differ rather minimally in biological terms into two groups that differ noticeably in appearance and opportunities is called the **social construction of gender.** As anthropologist Gayle Rubin (1975:178) said, "A taboo against the sameness of men and women [divides] the sexes into two mutually exclusive categories [and] thereby *creates* gender." Various rewards and punishments induce people to go along with the social construction of gender and thus conform to cultural definitions of femininity and masculinity.

A fable about a stranger who arrived at a village begging for food provides an analogy of the difference between sex and gender. When the villagers said they had no food at all, the stranger announced he had a magic stone with which he volunteered to make "stone soup." As the stone simmered in a pot of boiling water, the stranger told onlookers that the soup would be even more delicious if they could find just one onion to add to it. Someone admitted to having an onion, which was added to the pot. When the stranger said that the soup would be truly superb but for the lack of a carrot, another villager produced a carrot. The stranger got the villagers to add potatoes, turnips, garlic, and even bones with a

---

[2]When our research assistant was in the supermarket checking diapers, she overheard a mother ask a little girl which "pull-up" diapers she wanted. The little girl shouted, "Boys'!"

bit of meat. The "stone" soup the stranger eventually dished out to the villagers was hearty and delicious. Although we do not want to push the analogy too far, sex and gender resemble the stone and the soup. Like the stone, biological sex is the foundation on which societies construct gender. Like the soup, gender depends little on people's biological sex and mostly on how societies embellish it. And just as the stranger tricked the villagers into thinking that an ordinary stone was the essential ingredient in stone soup, cultures often deceive us into thinking that biological sex accounts for the differences between females' and males' behavior and life outcomes.

The emphasis that cultures place on sex blinds us to the far greater importance of gender differentiation in producing differences between men and women. Gender is a social construction, not a biological inevitability. This distinction is clear in the striking variability anthropologists have observed in male and female behavior across different cultures (Mead 1949).

In this book, we use the term *sex* when people's biological sex is the basis for how societies, organizations, or other people treat them. We use the term to stress the point that people's sex influences how others act toward them. For example, we refer to *sex discrimination* and *sex segregation*. In contrast, we use the term *gender* to refer to differences between the sexes that are socially constructed.

Societies produce and maintain gender differences—that is, engage in **gendering**—through several social processes: socialization, the actions of social institutions, and interaction among people (West and Zimmerman 1987). Thus gender is a system of social relations that is embedded in the way major institutions (including the workplace) are organized (Acker 1990; Lorber 1992:748). This conception of gender encourages us to examine the ways that social institutions embody gendered arrangements and at the same time create and maintain differences in their female and male members.

A primary reason for the gendering of human activities is to maintain male advantage. Gender roles and gendered organizations institutionalize the favored position of men as a group; in other words, organizations play a fundamental role in establishing a sex-gender hierarchy that favors men over women. Individual men then enjoy the benefits of being male without doing anything special to obtain those benefits. Most men are not even aware of the benefits they derive solely because of their sex.

Although sex is an important basis for differentiating people into categories, societies use other characteristics as well. Foremost are race and ethnicity; in many societies, religion, appearance, age, sexual orientation, and economic position are also important bases for sorting people. Just as societies magnify the minor biological differences between males and females, they elaborate small differences between persons of different ages or races. The discussion of the history of work in Chapter 2, for example, will show that just over 100 years ago, families and employers treated children as small adults, who worked alongside their parents in fields and factories. Some societies still do not legally differentiate children from adults: Children can enter into marriage or be tried for murder. Today, however, Americans differentiate children, adolescents, and "senior citizens" from everyone else. Thus childhood, adolescence, and "senior citizenship" have been socially constructed as special statuses. Some societies also engage in social differentiation on the basis of race and ethnicity. In the United States, for example, patterns of immigration and world affairs have created a strong tradition of racial and ethnic differentiation, and people's race and ethnicity may strongly influence their work lives. When we address the effects of such differentiation, remember that race and ethnicity may also have socially constructed meanings.

Gendered Work

To stress the fundamental role of gender differentiation in creating differences between men and women, some social scientists use **gender** as a verb to refer to the process of differentiating the sexes. They call the process of gender differentiation *gendering* and speak of activities that organizations or cultures have attached to one or the other sex as *gendered*. These terms signify outcomes that are socially constructed and give males advantages over females (Acker 1990:146). They describe the production of assumptions about gender as well as the institutions that are shaped by those assumptions. One such institution is gendered work, which is the subject of this book. This section focuses on three features of gendered work: the assignment of tasks based on workers' sex, the higher value placed on men's work than on women's work, and employers' and workers' construction of gender on the job.

The Sexual Division of Labor

The assignment of different tasks to women and men, or the **sexual division of labor,** is a fundamental feature of work. All societies delegate tasks in part on the basis of workers' sex, although which sex does exactly which tasks has varied over time and differs across the countries of the world. Tasks that some societies view as naturally female or male are assigned to the other sex at other times or in other places. In Muslim societies, for example, where religious law requires strict sex segregation, men hold such jobs as elementary school teacher, secretary, and nurse; Westerners think of these as women's work (Papanek 1973:310–1). In the United States, only one-fifth of physicians and less than 4 percent of street sweepers are female; in Russia, women are the majority in each of these occupations.

Within the same country and the same occupation, either sex may do a particular job. Although women were four times as likely as men to work as food servers in the United States in 1990 (U.S. Bureau of the Census 1992a), many restaurants—especially fancy ones—employ only waiters. Neither sex has a monopoly on the skills needed to serve food, but many restaurants create a sexual division of labor in which one sex cooks and the other serves. Race and age frequently figure into particular job assignments as well, and Chapter 4 will describe these divisions of labor.

The production of cloth illustrates how the sexual division of labor can shift. Up to the fourteenth or fifteenth century, producing silk was women's work. The delicate nature of spinning and weaving silk by hand might have explained this division of labor, but during the sixteenth and seventeenth centuries an all-male weavers' guild in London not only took over silk work but also prohibited members from teaching the trade to females (Kowaleski and Bennett 1989). In contrast, female silk workers in Paris, having formed their own guilds, were able to remain in the trade. Over the succeeding centuries, textile manufacturers have hired women or men—or sometimes both—at one time or another.

Changes in which sex does a task occur slowly, because the existing sexual division of labor shapes social expectations. Kinds of work become labeled in people's minds as belonging to one sex and inappropriate for the other (Oppenheimer 1968). In Gambia, for example, women have cultivated rice since the fourteenth century. During a desperate food shortage in the nineteenth century, the government tried to encourage men to help grow rice. The men refused, insisting that rice was "a woman's crop" (Carney and Watts 1991:641). Of course, there is nothing inherently female about raising rice: In parts of Asia, men have traditionally been responsible for growing rice (Schrijvers 1983).

For each example of a rigid use of sex to assign tasks, there is another in which the sexual division of labor is blurred. Consider an example from U.S. history. In colonial America , survival required that everybody work. The sexual division of labor made men primarily responsible for growing food and women for manufacturing the products their families needed. The sexes often cooperated, however, as in the family production of linen from flax plants. Boys pulled the flax and spread it out to dry. Then men threshed it to remove the seeds. After the stalks had been soaked, cleaned, and dried, men broke the flax with wooden daggers. Then women combed out rough material and wound the flax around a distaff, from which they spun linen thread. Women repeatedly washed, bleached, and "belted" the thread with a branch against a stone before they wove it into fabric. The sexual division of labor through which colonists survived made the sexes interdependent; when necessary, each sex did work usually done by the other (Earle 1896).

Nor did North American slave owners exhibit much regard for a conventional sexual division of labor. Instead, they used race as the primary basis for assigning tasks. Enslaved African-American women, men, and children were forced to work in factories, mills, and mines, as well as in fields. Women and children worked alongside men in processing iron, textiles, hemp, and tobacco; refining sugar; and lumbering. Half the workers who dug South Carolina's Santee Canal were women. Female and male slaves worked together maintaining railroad tracks. In iron mines and refineries, women lugged trams, loaded ore into crushers, and operated the furnaces and forges. Neither on plantations nor in factories did their sex spare female slaves from grueling work (Starobin 1970:165–8).

Societies gender work by labeling activities as appropriate for one sex or the other. These labels influence the job assignments of women and men, and they influence employers' and workers' expectations of who ought to perform various jobs. Across societies and over time, however, no hard-and-fast rules dictate which sex should do a particular task. What is crucial for preserving sex inequality is not the tasks performed by each sex but the fact that men and women do different tasks.

The Devaluation of Women's Work

A sexual division of labor need not lead to inequality between the sexes. Historians Joan Scott and Louise Tilly (1975:44–5) argued that, although women and men in preindustrial Europe had different spheres, neither sphere was subordinate. In practice, however, sex differentiation fosters the tendency to devalue female activities.

The devaluation of women and their activities is deeply embedded in the major cultures and religions of the world. For example, the Judeo-Christian religion, a strong influence on Western culture, ascribed to female servants three-fifths the value of male servants (Leviticus 27:3–7).

The devaluation of women's work has existed for so long that we cannot explain its origin. It continues to occur both because it is part of the ideology in many parts of the world and because it is in men's interest. Men, who assign value to human activities (as pay setters, for example), tend to take male activities as the standard and see other activities as inferior—regardless of the importance of these activities for a society's survival (Mead 1949; Schur 1983:35–48).

The devaluation of women and their work is a key factor in differential compensation for men and women. In the United States, for example, where most dentists are male, dentists are near the top of the income hierarchy; in Europe, where most dentists are female, dentists' incomes are much closer to the average. Generally, as you will see in Chapter 6, the more women in an occupation, the less both its female and male workers earn. Contemporary societies' devaluation of unpaid work—particularly housework—stems partly from the second-class status assigned to any work that is usually done by women.

Living in a culture that devalues female activities makes these practices seem natural. Consider 13-year-olds' after-school jobs. A neighbor pays a boy $10 for 45 minutes' work mowing the lawn, and a girl $4 for an hour's babysitting. Why does the babysitter accept this pay gap? She may not realize how much less she has earned, of course. In addition, she has probably already absorbed her society's attitude that girls' jobs are worth less than boys'. In a series of experiments, students assigned lower values to identical tasks when women students did them and judged women's performance as inferior to men's, although the female students worked more quickly and accurately than the men did (Major 1989:108–10). Students who were told that women usually did the job thought it deserved less pay than those who had been told that men usually did it (Major and Forcey 1985).

In sum, enduring cultural attitudes that devalue women are expressed in the lower value that employers, workers, and whole societies place on the work that women usually do. This devaluation of women's work reduces women's pay relative to men's. In this and other ways, which Chapter 6 will discuss, devaluation helps to preserve the sex-gender hierarchy.

The Construction of Gender on the Job

A byproduct of the ways that employers organize work and workers produce goods and services is their construction of gender on the job. Employers and workers bring gender into the workplace through sex stereotypes that fabricate or exaggerate actual sex differences and through policies and behaviors that highlight irrelevant sex differences. Such gender differentiation is prevalent in the workplace. However, gender differentiation is so fundamental in social organization and plays such a key role in sex inequality that we see it not only in the workplace but in every social institution.

Within the workplace, however, employers play a primary role in gendering. When they create new jobs, set pay levels, organize how work will be done, and settle on working conditions, employers often have a particular sex in mind. For example, machinery would be designed quite differently for workers averaging 5'11" and 175 pounds and workers averaging 5'4" and 125 pounds. Furthermore, if employers have male workers in mind, they assume their workers will accept shift work and overtime. In contrast, employers who plan to hire women workers often organize jobs as part time and create pay and benefit systems that discourage long-term employment.

Many modern jobs were created when most workers were male. The assumptions surrounding the creation of these jobs were gendered, and the consequences of those assumptions have survived. Until the late 1960s, for example, many states barred employers from putting women in jobs that could involve lifting more than 25 pounds. Ten years after the California Supreme Court struck down such laws as discriminatory, many employers continued to exclude women from such jobs. These employers did not consciously decide to ignore the court's decision; however, organizational practices resist change. Employers that do not wish to discriminate have higher priorities than examining the gendered assumptions that earlier generations built into jobs (Bielby and Baron 1986). In effect, the workplace remains gendered partly because of organizational inertia: Past decisions were based explicitly or implicitly on sex stereotypes, and effects of those decisions persist in today's places of work.

To be sure, many employers continue to introduce gender into the workplace through current actions or policies. Sometimes employers use gender to control workers, get more work out of them, or sell products. For example, when a male coal miner assigned to lift heavy steel rails remarked that it looked like a four-man job, his supervisor asked him, "Aren't you man enough?" (Yarrow 1987:9). Some employers emphasize workers' sex to prevent collective action by male and female employees or to divert workers' attention from bad working conditions. Silicon-chip factories in Southeast Asia, for example, sponsored makeup classes and beauty contests to distract young women from their physically punishing jobs (Grossman 1979:4). By orienting these young women to their appearance and to marriage, the company reduced the likelihood that the women would protest dangerous working conditions. Employers have also turned a blind eye to sexual materials in the workplace because such materials seem to make some male workers happy.

Workers, too, construct gender at work. They may do so in order to forge bonds with other workers of the same sex, to express their gender identity, or to amuse themselves. Workers also use gender to control one another, to exclude workers of the "wrong" sex, or to get back at their employers. However, in bringing gender into the workplace, the actions of male and female workers sometimes differ.

Many observers have commented on how all-male work groups affirm members' masculinity by discussing such "male" concerns as sports and by sexualizing women. All-male work groups may also engage in gender displays, which are language or rituals so characteristic of one sex that they mark the workplace as belonging to that sex. Male gender displays include sexual language and conversations about sex, as in the chants that sergeants use to drill new recruits in boot camp. In another example, described in the best-seller *Liar's Poker* (Lewis 1989), top securities traders at Salomon Brothers, a leading Wall Street firm, were nicknamed "big swinging dicks." A characteristic type of male gender display in blue-collar settings is macho behavior. Workers who use brute force ("hammer mechanics") rather than standard procedure to accomplish a task or who flaunt safety regulations signal the importance of muscle or bravado on the job and hence imply that women don't belong (Weston 1990:146).

Workers often import gender to the job in order to create solidarity among themselves. In one instance, an almost exclusively male work crew singled out an unmarried man whose sexual orientation was unclear. The group tried to use its only female member to confirm the man's heterosexuality. At the end of the shift one day, crew members locked the couple in a room so the suspect male worker could initiate sex with the female worker (although they had no reason to believe she would cooperate). The male victim's coworkers taunted him for failing to take advantage of this and other "opportunities." This group invoked gender both in trying to pressure a male member to display stereotypically masculine, sexually aggressive behavior and in casting its female member in the role of sex object (Padavic 1991).

When workers use gender to create solidarity among themselves, they simultaneously define the job site as out of bounds for persons of the other sex. For example, men often use sexual language when women are not present; at the same time, most men recognize that sexual language may make female coworkers uncomfortable. Through social interaction, "men constantly remind women where their 'place' is and [through interaction, women] are put back in their place should they venture out" (Henley and Freeman 1975:391). A woman coal miner concluded that her coworkers wanted her off the job when obscene antifemale bathroom graffiti mentioned her by name. The only woman in a power-plant crew felt unwelcome when a list headed "Twenty Reasons Why Beer Is Better Than Women" appeared on the bulletin board. Every item on the list disparaged and sexualized women ("you always know you're the first one to pop a beer"; "when a beer goes flat, you can throw it out"). The list reminded the woman that she was in male territory, where her coworkers saw women as sex objects (Padavic 1991).

Women also bring gender to the workplace. Like men, women may try to force coworkers to affirm their heterosexuality, femininity, or masculinity. Sometimes women do this by swapping stories about their male partners and children or by celebrating marriages and births. Women can also enact gender by defying conventional gender roles. A sociologist observed this phenomenon in Mexico among female factory workers riding the bus home from work. When a man boarded the bus, the women subjected him to the kinds of verbal abuse that they often suffered from men. "They chided and teased him. . . . They offered kisses and asked for a smile. They exchanged laughing comments about his physical attributes and suggested a raffle to see who would keep him" (Fernandez-Kelly 1983:131–2).

Women workers also use gender to resist their employers. In Malaysia, some female factory workers displayed hysteria, alleging they were "possessed by evil spirits" (Ong 1986). In one incident, a woman sobbed, laughed, shrieked, and flailed at her machine before her supervisor sent her home. These outbursts allowed women to stop work and even attack their male bosses (Ong 1986:207).

In sum, employers and workers engage in gender differentiation at work by making sex salient when it is irrelevant and by acting on sex-stereotyped assumptions. Employers also gender work by sex segregating jobs, by setting pay based on workers' sex, and by accommodating a whole set of subtle and not-so-subtle practices. In other words, gender is constructed within institutions through interaction and is a result of organizational practices (Acker 1992; Steinberg and Jacobs 1993). Chapter 7 will discuss employers' and workers' construction of gender on a day-to-day basis.

Diversity in Gendered Work

The ways in which work is gendered depend on the work site and the characteristics of workers. In some situations (such as one-sex work settings), workers' race has a greater effect than their sex on jobs, pay, and day-to-day experiences. More commonly, sex, race, and other characteristics interact to shape workers' outcomes. At colleges and universities, for example, most female workers do clerical work, but white women are more likely to hold such jobs than women of color, who disproportionately hold custodial jobs. Meanwhile, being a white male increases a worker's chance of being an administrator or professor; minority men more often have a blue-collar job. You will see in the chapters that follow that work experiences differ not only by sex but also by other factors. However, without losing sight of this diversity, we will focus on the importance of people's sex on their lives as workers.

Summary

Sex and gender differentiation are fundamental features of work. First and foremost, they operate through the sexual division of labor, which assigns tasks to people partly on the basis of their sex and labels certain tasks as belonging to one sex or the other. Sex and gender differentiation are also expressed in the undervaluation of women's work. These processes occur in the day-to-day interactions among workers and their bosses, as well as in the policies and practices of employers, governments, and families. Their result is to make work a gendered institution, in which employers and workers often place undue emphasis on people's sex.

2

A History of Gendered Work

Although every society assigns some tasks on the basis of people's sex, the kinds of tasks that go to women and men have varied over time and around the world. This chapter traces the evolution of the Western sexual division of labor over the past 400 years. After describing how Western preindustrial societies divided work between the sexes, we show how industrialization, by commercializing work, created a new basis for distinguishing between men's and women's work: whether or not one worked for pay. We then describe the sexual division of labor across nations around the world.

The Sexual Division of Labor in Preindustrial Europe

In preindustrial Western societies, almost everyone worked. Most people devoted their lives to feeding themselves; the rest—except for royalty and the nobility, who lived off the fruits of others' labor—worked at making products or serving others.

Agricultural Work

Prior to industrialization (which began in the eighteenth century), most people in Europe farmed, either as serfs who farmed land held by members of the nobility or, later, as peasants who owned small parcels of land. Among peasants and serfs, men usually plowed, women weeded, and both sexes harvested. Girls and women took charge of raising pigs, sheep, cows, and chickens. Thus they milked, churned butter, made cheese, and butchered animals. Women also made bread, beer, cloth, and clothing.

Consider the division of labor of a seventeenth-century Basque farm couple. The wife rose at dawn and lit the fire. Her husband and the hired men remained in bed while she made breakfast. After the men left for the fields, the wife cleaned the house and prepared the noon meal, which she served standing behind her husband's chair so she could wait on him. In the afternoon, the wife joined her husband and the hired men in the fields until it was time for her to fix the night's meal. In the evening, the husband might repair tools or go to the village tavern. The wife spun by lamplight until around 11 P.M. when she would follow her husband to bed (Shorter 1975:67–72).

Servants' work resembled that of peasants. Both sexes worked as servants, often for just their keep. An English woman who began an apprenticeship when she was 9 years old described

> driving bullocks to [field] and fetching them in again; cleaning out their houses, and bedding them up; washing potatoes and boiling them for pigs; milking; in the field leading horses or bullocks to plough . . . , digging potatoes, digging and pulling turnips . . . like a boy. I got up at five or six except on market mornings twice a week, and then at three. (Pinchbeck 1930:17–8)

Notice that in preindustrial agriculture, women's and men's tasks overlapped, although a sexual division of labor defined cooking, cleaning, and spinning as women's work. Importantly, people did not see the jobs that women usually did as less valuable than those that men usually did. However, we should not conclude that preindustrial agriculture was a paradise of sex equality. In 1823, an observer wrote of the Scottist Highlands that women were regarded as men's "drudges" rather than their companions:

> The husband turns up the land and sows it—the wife conveys the manure to it in a creel, tends the corn, reaps it, hoes the potatoes, digs them up, carries the whole home on her back, [and] when bearing the creel she also is engaged with spinning. (Quoted in Berg 1985:142)

Manufacturing Work

Even in the preindustrial era, some people worked in manufacturing—in workhouses, in workshops, or in their own cottages as craftworkers. However, men's and women's manufacturing work was organized in different systems of production. And as a rule, although the sexes had similar levels of skills, men involved in manufacturing earned substantially more than women and enjoyed more autonomy.

Women's workshops. In medieval Europe, all-female workhouses existed in which women lived and worked at manufacturing textiles.[1] These

---

[1] When Japan was industrializing at the end of the nineteenth century, it had similar all-female workshops (Kondo 1990:269–70).

highly skilled workers dyed, wove, and embroidered fabric that they sewed into clothing for monks and nobles. In exchange for their labor, the women received their board and room. Many were slaves of the nobility or the monasteries or the wives and children of slaves. Others were serfs or imprisoned in the workhouses for crimes like prostitution.[2]

These women's workshops died out before industrialization, but their legacy lives on. The textile factories that sprang up in the early years of industrialization relied almost exclusively on female workers, and in most of the contemporary world, textile manufacturing continues to be women's work.

Artisans. A more enduring preindustrial system of production was the guild system, in which **artisans** (craftworkers) produced a variety of products from scratch. **Guilds**—associations of tradespeople or craftworkers organized to protect their members' interests—oversaw most production that occurred outside the home: from silverware, iron tools, and wheels to fabric, bread, and beer. Like the textile workers in the women's workshops, artisans were highly skilled workers who produced fine products. Unlike the workshop workers, artisans were almost always males, and they earned an income from the products they made.

The guilds controlled the apprenticeship systems that taught artisans their craft. Their goal was to reduce competition, and one way they did this was by closing apprenticeships to young women. The wives of master craftworkers worked alongside their husbands, and in the early Middle Ages, guilds sometimes allowed widows to continue their late husbands' work. Gradually, however, guilds restricted wives' and widows' rights to carry on their husbands' trade, and eventually the status of master craftworker was virtually off-limits to women (Howell 1986). This monopoly of artisan work in the preindustrial period gave men a head start in the skilled trades, the benefits of which they continue to enjoy at the end of the twentieth century.

Cottage industry. Before industrialization shifted production to factories, peasants—mostly women and children—manufactured some goods at home through a system of **cottage industry.** Cottage workers might spin wool, make lace, weave cloth, or attach shirt collars, for which they were paid on a **piecework** basis (by the amount of work they completed).

Peasant women, whose first priority was work for their own families, made time for cottage industry by laboring late into the night. Their

---

[2]In fact, some historians believe that the owners treated the women's workshops as brothels (Herlihy 1990:85).

earnings were often the household's only cash income. Cottage industry was not simply a source of supplemental income. A historian described seventeenth-century British women whose work spilled out of their cottages: They "knitted as they walked the village streets, they knitted in the dark because they were too poor to have a light; they knitted for dear life" (Berg 1985:103). As cottage workers, then, women and children were well represented in the earliest labor force.

The Industrial Revolution

For many centuries, people met their needs through agricultural and preindustrial manufacturing work. Then, in the eighteenth century, capitalism transformed the ways that Western Europeans produced and distributed goods and services. Family production was replaced by market production, in which capitalists paid workers wages to produce goods in factories and mines. As paid workers, people manufactured products that they bought with their wages. This **Industrial Revolution,** which took over 200 years in the Western world, is still under way as countries around the globe industrialize.

The Emergence of the Labor Force

In moving the production of commodities from home to factory, industrialization created the **labor force,** or the pool of people who work for pay, as a major institution. In England, industrialization's major changes occurred in the last half of the eighteenth century and the early nineteenth century. Armies of peasants who were forced off the land made their way into the cities to search for jobs. These peasants were the first recruits into the modern industrial labor force.

The emergence of wage workers created a new social distinction: people who work for pay versus those who do not (the **nonemployed**). Of course, a class of nonemployed was not new; throughout history, privileged classes have been exempt from productive work. But the new category of nonemployed did not distinguish nonworkers (students, the retired, the "idle rich") from unpaid workers (those who cook, clean, and shop for family members; raise children; care for sick relatives; and provide social and emotional support to family, friends, and community). What set the new labor force apart from the nonemployed was not the kinds of work they did, but the fact that they were paid for their work.

This distinction has had important consequences for gendering work, because for the last 200 years, men have been more likely than women to belong to the labor force.

Industrialization and the Sexual Division of Labor

Prior to industrialization, each sex produced goods for their household, although they specialized in different tasks. Industrialization created two new distinctions between men's and women's work roles. The first assigned men to paid work and women to unpaid work. Although women predominated in some sectors of the early industrial labor force, once industrialization was well under way, men became the majority in the labor force. Running the household became women's responsibility. As a result, employers organized work and systems of pay on the assumptions that workers are men and that male incomes support women. This division of paid and unpaid work according to sex is the subject of the rest of this chapter. The second new division of labor was among women and men who worked in the labor force. This division segregated women and men into different jobs. It is the subject of Chapter 4.

The Division of Paid and Unpaid Work by Sex

Although early **labor force participation** was just as likely for women as for men, with advancing industrialization throughout the nineteenth century, the labor force became more male. In the eighteenth century, as cottage industries gave way to small textile factories, many employers continued to hire women and children. Not only were women and children more likely than men to be available in some areas, but they worked for lower wages than men did. However, as displaced peasants flocked to urban labor markets seeking jobs, women's representation in the labor force declined. The entry of large numbers of men into the labor force unleashed new forces that led to the **masculinization** of the labor force, making it progressively more male.

The number of people seeking jobs often exceeded the number of jobs. The result was hordes of **unemployed** people desperate for work. Employers took advantage of the situation by cutting pay. Furthermore, eighteenth- and nineteenth-century British mine and factory owners openly exploited workers. Girls as young as 6 and women in their 60s worked in coal pits and in copper and lead mines. According to a mining supervisor, they worked "up to their knees in water." A commissioner described girls and women as "chained, belted, harnessed like dogs . . . crawling on hands and knees . . . dragging their heavy loads over soft slushy floors" (Pinchbeck 1930:248–9). Factory and mining work were dangerous for men too. For example, men who ran "spinning mules" in textile factories had to lift 160-pound frames every three seconds for 12 hours a day (Cohen 1985).

Early unions, viewing women and children as a threat to men's jobs and wages, mounted campaigns to drive children and women out of factory and mining jobs (Pinchbeck 1930). Unions found allies in middle-class reformers, who fought for laws to protect children and women from dangerous or immoral working conditions. Pressure from both unions and reformers led nineteenth-century lawmakers in Europe and the United States to pass **protective labor laws** banning many employment practices. These laws prohibited firms from employing children and women to work more than a fixed number of hours a day, to lift more than specified weights, to work at night, or to hold certain jobs. Although these laws may have protected some women, they denied many other women high-paying factory jobs. Gendered assumptions gave women but not men protection from hazardous work and gave men but not women the right to weigh risks against rewards in deciding for themselves how to earn a living. In putting many lines of work off-limits to women, protective labor laws thereby contributed to the masculinization of the labor force.

Despite protective labor laws, many women continued to work for pay. Fortunately for women, the movement to bar women from all factory jobs failed. Employers still hired women for low-paid factory jobs, which offered better pay than the alternative: becoming a servant (Pinchbeck 1930). Because women could be paid less than men, textile-mill owners actively sought unmarried female workers, promising fathers to keep their daughters from the "vices and crimes" of idleness (Lerner 1979:189). Families welcomed their daughters' income (Pleck 1976:181).

Nonetheless, the labor force became increasingly male throughout the nineteenth century. In 1840 women and children made up about 40 percent of the industrial workforce in the United States; by 1870 three out of four nonfarm workers were male (Baxandall et al. 1976:83); by 1890 only 17 percent of women were employed outside the home (Goldin 1990). Women's labor force participation did not drop uniformly across all groups, however. For instance, at the beginning of the twentieth century, only 6 percent of married women were in the labor force, compared to 40 percent of single women over age 10 (Folbre 1991:465).

The Doctrine of Separate Spheres

Why was married women's labor force participation so low? A major factor was the doctrine of separate spheres. This doctrine, which was born among the English upper-middle classes, called for the separation of work and family life. It held that a woman's proper place was in the home and not in the workplace; a man's natural sphere was in the world of commerce—or, at any rate, at his job—and not at home (Davidoff and Hall 1987:364–7; Skolnick 1991:30–1). These ideas encouraged male workers who had some voice in the matter to work away from home. Reinforcing these beliefs were stereotypes of men as strong, aggressive, and competitive and of women as frail, virtuous, and nurturing, images that depicted men as naturally suited to the highly competitive nineteenth-century workplace and women as too delicate for the world of commerce.

To earn respect, married women had two responsibilities: creating a haven to which their husbands could retreat from the world of work and demonstrating their husbands' ability to support their families. An employed wife was a sign of her husband's failure (Westover 1986). As one British woman who worked as a tailor recalled,

> I never went out to work after I was married. There wasn't many who did. They used to cry shame on them in them days when they were married if they went to work. They used to say your husband should keep you.

The doctrine of separate spheres led to extremes. The tiny waists that women achieved through tightly laced corsets both ensured and symbolized their incapacity to do any work. Middle- and upper-class families hid the parts of the house devoted to productive work (cooking, bathing, laundry) out of sight from the areas of relaxation (parlor, dining room), furthering the illusion that the home was not a place of work (Davidoff and Hall 1987:359).

In reserving paid jobs for men, the doctrine of separate spheres especially victimized working-class wives whose families needed their earnings. Many employers refused to hire married women for "respectable" jobs; indeed, some firms enforced rules against employing married women until World War II (Goldin 1990). As a result, working-class women had to find ways to earn money at home, such as taking in laundry, sewing, or boarders. Conforming to the social standard meant doing piecework at home, which paid less for more hours of work (Westover 1986).

Around the turn of the twentieth century, the movement of people into and within the United States significantly affected patterns of paid labor. One such population shift was the migration to northern cities of 2 million African Americans from the rural South. After Emancipation, most former slaves in the South became sharecroppers, with entire families working in the fields. But in the late nineteenth century and early twentieth century, many sharecroppers sought to move North, where both the women and the men hoped to get paid jobs.[3] Another population shift occurred in the early decades of the twentieth century, when the United States recruited families from Mexico for temporary agricultural jobs. Mexican women worked alongside their husbands at back-breaking work on huge "factory farms" in the Southwest (Amott and Matthaei 1991:75).

As these examples indicate, even during the heyday of the doctrine of separate spheres, thousands of women worked for pay: minority women, young single women, widows, and married women whose husbands had deserted their families or could not earn enough to support them. Employers in the market for cheap female labor did not care whether the women were married. Married immigrant women and former slaves were particularly likely to be employed. They labored in sweatshops, factories, offices, schools, and other families' homes, and some did paid work in their own homes. For sharecropping women who plowed the fields and for many immigrant and African-American women who worked 14-hour days as servants, staying out of the labor force would have meant starvation.

Nevertheless, the doctrine of separate spheres helped to drive all but the poorest married women out of the labor force. By 1890, fewer than one in 20 married American women worked for pay (U.S. Bureau of the Census 1961:72). But racial and ethnic background made a difference. In 1920, for example, only 7 percent of married European-American women were in the labor force, compared to one-third of married African-American women and 18 percent of married Asian-American women. The la-

---

[3]Leaving the South could be dangerous. The Reverend D. W. Johnson, who helped fellow African Americans come North by providing railroad passes, recounted his narrow escape from southern officials:

> There was . . . three great big red-faced guys. . . . [T]hey had a bullwhip on they shoulder and a rope and a gun in each of their hands. They gonna kill every so-and-so Negro that they found had a pass. Well, so they search us one by one and they searched me. Had they pulled off my shoe, that'd been it for me. Because they swo' they was gonna kill the ones who had it. Yeah, it was in the toe of my shoe. (Crew 1987:7–8)

bor force participation rate for unmarried European-American women was 45 percent; for African-American women, 59 percent; and for Asian-American women, 39 percent (Amott and Matthei 1991:table 9.2). Even the Great Depression (1929–1937), which brought record unemployment among American men, did not draw large numbers of married women into the labor force. Families sent their children to work before mothers took jobs outside the home.

The doctrine of separate spheres contributed to the gendering of work in the twentieth century in several ways. First, men gained social approval as workers, but women's work became invisible because it was done at home. Second, social values that encouraged employers to ban women from many jobs made sex discrimination commonplace. Third, employers could justify low pay for women because men presumably supported them. Indeed, people came to define pay as what one earned for going to work; women's relegation to the home put them outside the system of pay for labor.

Finally, the sexual division of labor that assigned men to the labor force and women to the home encouraged employers to structure jobs on the assumptions that all permanent workers were men and that all men had stay-at-home wives. These assumptions freed workers (that is, male workers) from domestic responsibilities so they could work 12- to 14-hour days. These assumptions also bolstered the belief that domestic work was women's responsibility, even for women who were employed outside the home. The chapters that follow will trace the consequences of these gendered assumptions and employment practices throughout the twentieth century, long after economic forces began to erode nineteenth-century sex differences in labor force participation.

The Convergence in Women's and Men's Labor Force Participation

The legacy of the doctrine that married women should not work outside the home has haunted us throughout the twentieth century. Not until the 1970s did married women's likelihood of paid employment catch up with that of single and divorced women. Moreover, the doctrine of separate spheres has not entirely disappeared. You will see in Chapter 8 that although society now expects married women to participate in the labor force, it continues to define domestic work as women's sphere.

As public support for the doctrine of separate spheres has waned, the gap between men's and women's labor force participation rates has narrowed, as Figure 2.1 shows. In 1890, 84.3 percent of males over the age of

FIGURE 2.1

Trends in U.S. Labor Force Participation Rates by Sex,
1890 to 1992

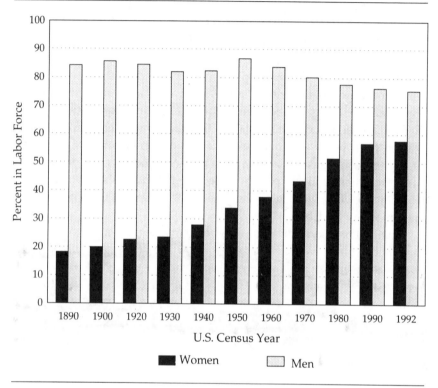

Source: Data from U.S. Bureau of the Census 1975:131–2; U.S. Bureau of the Census
1992d:table 609; U.S. Women's Bureau 1993:1.

14 were in the labor force, compared to only 18.2 percent of similar females.[4] Over the next hundred years, women's participation in the labor
force climbed steadily. In contrast, men's labor force participation fell
slightly. By 1992, 76 percent of men and 58 percent of women were in the
labor force. More than three-quarters of women between the ages of 35
and 44 were in the labor force. Experts project that women's and men's
labor force participation will continue to converge.

___

[4]If the Census Bureau had counted farm wives on the same basis as it counted
farmers, and if it had counted women who ran boardinghouses, women's labor
force participation rate for 1890 would have been about 28 percent (Goldin
1990:44–5).

FIGURE 2.2

Composition by Sex of the U.S. Labor Force, 1870 to 1992

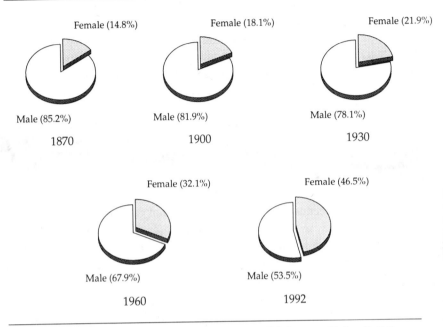

Female (14.8%)   Female (18.1%)   Female (21.9%)

Male (85.2%)   Male (81.9%)   Male (78.1%)

1870   1900   1930

Female (32.1%)   Female (46.5%)

Male (67.9%)   Male (53.5%)

1960   1992

Source: Data from U.S. Bureau of the Census 1975:131–2; U.S. Bureau of Labor Statistics 1993d:table 1.

Although a substantial sex gap remains between men's and women's labor force participation, it has declined sharply, as Figure 2.2 shows. In 1870, during the heyday of the doctrine of separate spheres, fewer than 15 workers out of every 100 were female. In 1992, out of every 100 persons in the U.S. labor force, over 46 were women.

The Devaluation of Women's Work

The shift of production from homes to shops and factories during the Industrial Revolution transformed men into wage laborers who left home each day for jobs in factories, shops, and offices. These jobs expanded men's contribution to their families: They became both the producers of the products their families needed and the earners who could pay for these products. The decline of domestic production, in turn, left women with the invisible and socially devalued tasks of housekeeping and child rearing. Thus, in the wake of industrialization, women found themselves in a no-win situation. Social norms and discrimination by employers reduced their participation in the labor force. As a result, women's path to economic security and respectability was through a husband, and women who worked at home were denied the esteem that society grants those who are economically productive. In sum, the definition of "real" work as paid activities performed away from home and the idealization of the home as a refuge from work rendered unpaid domestic work economically insignificant.

The devaluation of unpaid work in industrialized countries was exported by colonialists to Africa and Asia (Schrijvers 1983). Nowadays, no country counts as "employed" those people who do unpaid work in their own homes. Women who work in subsistence agriculture or who work without pay in a family business are also usually counted as nonemployed. Because laws often stipulate that only men can own farms or other property, in households engaged in farming, census takers tend to list the husband as a farmer and the wife as nonemployed. These practices underestimate women's economic contributions in developing countries, where most people work on family farms. Thus, as an indirect consequence of the Western doctrine of separate spheres, a twentieth-century Iranian peasant woman—who may harvest grain every day for her family's meals, tend animals, and haul water and wood for cooking and laundry—would officially be counted as nonemployed.

Women's and Men's Labor Force Participation Around the World

Today, countries differ widely in the degree to which they enforce a sexual division of labor. Figure 2.3 shows the proportions of women and men who were "economically active" in 1990.[5] The economically active, like the employed, exclude people engaged in unpaid family work that is important in developing countries, such as gathering fuel or water, processing crops, raising animals, keeping a kitchen garden, and laboring in cottage industry (United Nations 1991:85). In Figure 2.3, the large

---

[5]Some societies and organizations, like the United Nations, use the terms *economically active* and *nonactive* instead of *employed* and *nonemployed*.

sex differences in some countries thus stem from the undercounting of women's economic activities and a sexual division of labor that limits women's access to paid work and confines them to unpaid domestic work.

From the data depicted in Figure 2.3, we can draw some conclusions about the global sexual division of labor. Women's formal labor force participation is lowest in Muslim societies that strictly segregate the sexes (such as Saudi Arabia and Algeria). In developing countries that are not Muslim (such as Egypt and Brazil), men also greatly outnumber women in the labor force, because men tend to monopolize the paid jobs in developing labor markets, just as they did in earlier times in Western Europe and the United States. In fully developed capitalist societies (such as the United States, South Africa, Japan, and Canada,) women's rates of labor force participation are somewhat closer to men's. They are even closer in Scandinavian countries (such as Sweden and Iceland), which provide paid leave for new parents and childcare for those who are employed. Finally, the gap between women's and men's labor participation rates is smallest in communist, formerly communist, and socialist societies (China, East Germany, the Soviet Union, Mozambique, Poland, and Vietnam), reflecting the Marxist ideology that all able-bodied adults have both a right and an obligation to work. We see in these patterns the influence of economic development, social policies, and cultural norms.

Women's labor force participation in industrializing countries has been on the rise in the latter half of the twentieth century, at least until the economic recession of the 1980s.[6] In developing countries, transnational corporations have drawn women into the labor force as a source of cheap labor; transnational corporations pay these women between 5 and 25 percent of what Western workers earn for similar jobs (Safa 1990:77). Moreover, developing countries have few if any laws against exploitative conditions for workers. But women work for transnational corporations for the same reasons they left agricultural work and cottage industries in Western societies: These women want jobs that pay more than domestic work, farming, or jobs in the service sector.

------

[6]Women are generally the last to benefit from job expansion and the first to suffer from job contraction, so the recent recession has slowed the growth in women's labor force participation in developing countries (United Nations 1991:chart 6.7).

28

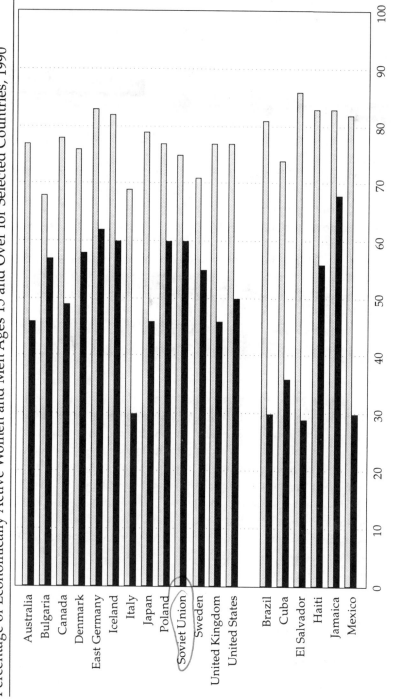

FIGURE 2.3
Percentage of Economically Active Women and Men Ages 15 and Over for Selected Countries, 1990

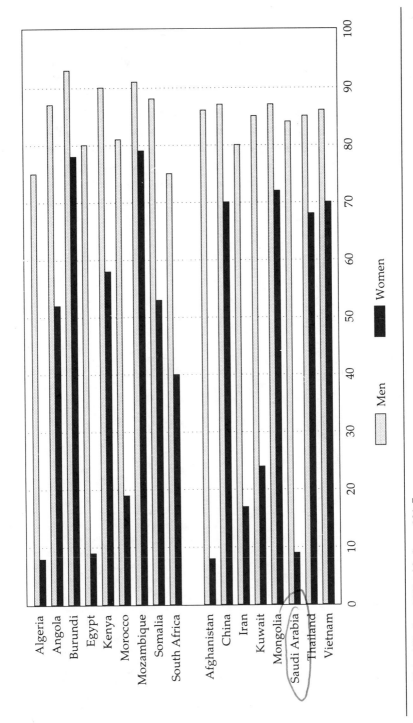

Source: United Nations 1991:table 8, pp. 104–7.

Summary

This chapter has examined one way that industrialization changed the sexual division of labor: It concentrated men in paid work away from home and women in nonpaid domestic work. In the Western world, this division of labor was most extreme during the nineteenth century. Its consequences persist today in gendered assumptions about men's and women's work and in the devaluation of women's work in both Western and non-Western societies. Chapter 4 will examine a second form that sexual division of labor took under industrialization: the segregation of employed women and men in different kinds of work.

3

An Overview of Sex Inequality at v.

This chapter summarizes women's and men's unequal status in the contemporary American workplace and introduces several general explanations that may account for sex inequality at work.

Sex Inequality in the Contemporary American Workplace

The workplace is an important arena for sex inequality in our society. First, the workplace maintains sex differentiation by concentrating women and men in different settings and assigning them different duties. Second, sex differentiation in jobs leads to unequal earnings, authority, and social status for women and men, because jobs are the main way through which most adults acquire income and social standing. Finally, interactions at work subject women to subtle and not-so-subtle expressions of inequality—from paternalism to sexual harassment, from invisibility to ostracism.

Sex inequality at work takes four forms:

- *Sex segregation.* In Chapter 1 you saw that throughout history and around the world, societies have imposed a sexual division of labor in which women and men perform different tasks. Another term for this sexual division of labor is **sex segregation.** (The concentration of men and women in different kinds of work will be the topic of Chapter 4.) Like those in the rest of the world, America's workplaces are sex segregated. Fewer than 10 percent of Americans have a coworker of the other sex who does the same job, for the same employer, in the same location, and on the same shift (Bielby and Baron 1986). Of course other characteristics of workers besides their sex affect what jobs they get. Workplaces are segregated by race and ethnicity as well. African-American women are concentrated in

ent jobs than Mexican-American women, for example, who in
n are underrepresented in jobs in which European-American
omen predominate. The jobs in which women and men are segregated are not only different but also unequal.

Sex differences in promotions. Women are concentrated at low levels in the organizations that employ them and in the lower ranks in their occupations and professions. Even in predominantly female lines of work, such as nursing, the higher the position, the more likely the job holder is to be male (Williams 1992). Women are also more likely than men to work in dead-end jobs and, as a result, are less likely to be promoted. Even women who win jobs in middle management find top-level positions beyond their reach.

- *Sex differences in authority.* Employers tend to reserve powerful positions for men; women are less likely than men to exercise authority in the workplace. Women supervise fewer subordinates than men and are less likely to control financial resources. Even women managers—whose numbers have grown dramatically—are less likely than men to make decisions, especially decisions that are vital for their employer (Jacobs 1992; Reskin and Ross 1992).

- *Sex differences in earnings.* Around the world, men outearn women. In 1992, for example, U.S. women who worked full time, year-round, earned just under 70 percent of what similar men earned. Put differently, for every dollar paid to a woman who worked full time, year-round, a man earned $1.43. What's more, men are more likely than women to have health insurance and other benefits. The consequences of this disparity in earnings and benefits follow workers into old age: Among retired persons, women's resources average about 60 percent of men's.

The three chapters that follow document women's disadvantaged position in the workforce.

Explanations for Sex Inequality in the Workplace

How can we explain systematic sex inequality in the workplace? Social scientists have proposed a variety of explanations, including cultural beliefs, men's actions, employers' actions, and workers' own preferences and abilities.

Cultural Beliefs About Gender and Work

A major category of explanations for sex inequality at work relates to culture. Indeed, gender is the paramount organizing principle in most societies. As we argued in Chapter 1, societies go to great lengths to produce differences between the sexes in appearance, talents, hobbies, and so forth.

Contemporary cultures are so riddled with **sex stereotypes,** or assumptions about individuals based on sex, that we all engage in stereotyped thinking. If a newscaster reports a complaint that a police officer used excessive force, most of us imagine a policeman wielding the nightstick. Some of us may not even think a policewoman is capable of such aggressiveness. In 1993 an elevator operator at the House of Representatives repeatedly told a newly elected African-American woman that she could not use an elevator reserved for members of the House. Finally it dawned on the elevator operator that the woman was a Representative. Note that cultural beliefs about men, women, and work affect everyone in a society: workers, customers, and clients, as well as the people who hire workers, assign them to jobs, and set their pay.

Unless someone directly challenges our assumptions about sex, race, and work, like the congressional elevator operator, we rarely question our stereotypes. This invisibility makes these assumptions especially powerful in shaping our behavior. If it never occurs to a branch manager that a female clerk might accept a promotion to night manager, he will not offer it to her. His assumptions about sex differences in workers' desire for promotion, need for a raise, willingness to work nights, or family responsibilities prevent him from considering whether he should offer the promotion to a woman.

The discussion that follows focuses on Western cultural beliefs about gender and work, although Western beliefs are by no means universal. As you saw in Chapter 1, men's work in one culture may be women's work in another. Cultural values can also change, especially in response to outside influence. Anthropologists, geographers, and historians have documented how the introduction of Western notions about the sexual division of labor into non-Western societies has undermined women's economic roles. For example, in Sri Lanka, British colonialists encouraged the peasants to devote less land to growing millet (which women grew) and more to rice (which men grew) so the country could export rice. The result was local food shortages, the deterioration of women's economic contributions to their families, and hence the deterioration of women's social, economic, and legal status (Schrijvers 1983).

Sex stereotypes. A poem by Alfred Lord Tennyson, although written in the mid 1800s, illustrates several contemporary sex stereotypes about work:

> Man for the field and women for the hearth:
> Man for the sword and for the needle she:
> Man with the head and woman with the heart:
> Man to command and woman to obey;
> All else confusion.

The first stereotype expressed in the poem is that women and men are naturally suited for different tasks. Second, the sexes supposedly differ innately, with men being governed by reason ("the head") and women by emotion ("the heart"). Third, men are assumed to be naturally suited to exercising authority over women. Finally, deviations from these natural patterns will allegedly lead to chaos.

Sex stereotypes like these, along with stereotypes about the characteristics that various jobs require, lead jobs to be labeled male or female (Oppenheimer 1968). For example, Western culture stereotypes men as assertive and competitive. These notions, along with the assumptions that assertive salespeople sell more cars and that combative lawyers win more trials, imply that men will naturally outdo women at selling cars or arguing cases in court. Both sex stereotypes and job stereotypes are often off the mark. Insurance companies, for example, have learned that, although women can sell as aggressively as men, a soft sell is often more effective than a hard sell. Nonetheless, you will see in the following chapters that sex and job stereotypes contribute to various forms of sex inequality at work.

Relations between the sexes. Cultural beliefs about relationships between the sexes also contribute to sex inequality at work. The beliefs of fundamentalist Muslims, for example, which require the physical segregation of the sexes, give rise to employment patterns quite different from those in the Western world. In rural Muslim societies, this segregation has kept women out of the paid labor force and close to home, where they prepare food, do housework, deliver babies, and sew clothing (Sharma 1979).

Western and Eastern cultures share some beliefs that legitimate sex inequality. One of these is that men are inherently superior to women. This view supports greater job authority and higher pay for men. A corollary of the ideology of male superiority is **paternalism,** the notion that women, like children, are inferior creatures whom men must take care of (Jackman 1994). As you will see in Chapter 6, the belief that men support women has helped to justify women's lower pay. The idea that women require protection has also helped exclude women from many jobs. Past actions of the battery manufacturer Johnson Controls illustrate how paternalism can reduce women's job options and pay. Johnson Controls barred women from all jobs that either exposed them to lead (which can cause birth defects) or led to jobs that could expose them to lead, unless they were surgically sterilized. In 1991 the Supreme Court ruled that Johnson's policy violated the Pregnancy Discrimination Act, but this decision was too late for the women who had already been sterilized or transferred to lower-paid work.

In the chapters that follow, you will see that cultural concerns with preserving men's superiority over women and maintaining women's dependency on men support several specific beliefs that contribute to sex inequality in jobs, promotions, authority, and pay.

A woman's place. The doctrine of separate spheres, discussed in Chapter 2, is another cultural belief that restricts women in the labor market. In many developing countries, this doctrine still limits women's chances for employment. In the contemporary Western world, although women have won a place in the paid workforce, the ideology of separate spheres contributes to the unequal division of housework, as Chapter 8 will show.

Men's Efforts to Preserve Their Advantages in the Workplace

A different explanation for sex inequality rests on the idea that privileged or **dominant groups** try to preserve their advantaged position (R. Collins 1974; Goode 1982). Monarchs rarely give up their kingdoms, and millionaires are not known for ridding themselves of their fortunes; on the contrary, the rich and powerful are bent on retaining and even expanding their wealth and power. They do so in a variety of ways, from segregating **subordinate groups** to denying them the opportunity to acquire the skills needed to advance.

Men and women do not differ when it comes to the impulse to retain their advantages. Although women lack the power and the incentive to exclude men from "women's" jobs, history offers examples of white women resisting the entry of women of color into their domain (Anderson 1982; Milkman 1987). However, as a group, working men are indisputably better off than working women, even though many men—particularly men of color—hold low-paying, undesirable jobs, enjoy no authority at work, and have little chance of a promotion.

Why do men see women as threats to their advantaged position? Many men believe that women might take jobs away from men, outperform men in the same job, or lead employers to cut a job's pay. Furthermore, if women can perform "macho" jobs like coal mining, police work, or military combat, these jobs lose their capacity to confirm male workers' masculinity. Some men also fear that having female coworkers will lower the prestige of their work. A male law professor reportedly rejected a female applicant for a faculty position with this explanation: "This is a law school, not a god damn nursing school!" Finally, men may worry that women's equality at work will undermine men's privileges in other realms: If women earned as much as men and had as much authority at work, women could insist on greater equality in the family, the community, and national political life. In view of all the benefits that men, especially white men, enjoy because of their sex and race, it is not surprising that men sometimes take action to preserve their advantaged status.

Like other groups concerned about competition from lower-paid workers, male workers' first line of defense has been to try to exclude women. One strategy is to prevent women from acquiring the necessary qualifications for customarily male jobs. Some unions, for example, have barred women from apprenticeship programs, and before 1970 professional schools admitted few women.

When entry barriers begin to give way and it is harder to exclude outsiders, some workers try to drive out newcomers by making them miserable on the job. For example, when the U.S. Department of the Treasury hired its first women in 1870, men blew smoke and spat tobacco juice at them and made catcalls (Baker 1977:86). A hundred years later, women entering customarily male blue-collar jobs got similar treatment. An African-American woman who took a job as a sheet-metal worker recalled, "When I first starting working there, they gave me a hard time. . . . They would make wisecracks about what they would like to do. I just kept on walking . . . but it made me feel trampy" (Schroedel 1985:134). Another strategy to drive out female pioneers is to prevent their doing the job properly by denying them information, giving them the wrong tools, or sabotaging their work (Bergmann and Darity 1981). Even if most men are neutral or welcoming, a few men can create a hostile environment.

Employers' Actions

It is employers who hire workers, assign them to jobs, decide whom to promote, and set pay. Most sex inequality at work results from these actions. Until recently, employers' main contribution to sex inequality was simply hiring few or no women for certain kinds of jobs. To understand how employers' hiring practices produce sex inequality, consider the three ways that employers locate most workers. Some employers choose from a pool of applicants, some use formal intermediaries such as employment agencies, and still others rely on referrals by employees. This third method—workers' referrals—is most common because it is free and effective (current workers screen out unacceptable job candidates). However, recruiting new employees through workers' referrals tends to perpetuate inequality. First, people's social networks tend to include others of the same sex, ethnicity, and race (Braddock and McPartland 1987). Second, sex stereotypes, fears of competition, and concern with coworkers' and bosses' reactions prevent workers from recommending someone of the "wrong" sex or race. For example, a worker whose sister-in-law is looking for work may hesitate to nominate her for a job in his all-male department because his coworkers may be mad, his boss will hold him responsible if she doesn't measure up, and she may blame him if the boss or workers give her a hard time.

Employers also contribute to sex inequality through job assignments. Who ends up in what job is largely up to employers and managers, whose biases or stereotypes can lead them to assign women and men to different jobs. A recent lawsuit charging Lucky Stores, a West Coast grocery chain, with sex discrimination illustrates both the role of stereotypes and the impact of managerial discretion. At the trial, a Lucky's executive testified that his experience managing a store 30 years earlier had convinced him that "men preferred working on the floor to working at the cash register . . . and that women preferred working at the cash register" (*Stender et al. v. Lucky* 1992). The qualifications that employers require also influence whom they assign to what jobs. Some organizations require qualifications that are more common among men and unnecessary to do the job. Requiring production experience or an MBA for a management job, for example, may unnecessarily restrict the number of women in the pool of job candidates.

Why might employers treat female and male workers differently? They may do so because of biases toward women or because they believe it will be more profitable in the long run.

Discrimination. **Discrimination** is treating people unequally because of personal characteristics that are not related to their performance.[1] Few would claim that a local park is discriminating by refusing to hire a

---

[1]Sociologist Robert Merton (1972:20) proposed a similar definition: Discrimination consists of treating functionally irrelevant characteristics as if they were relevant.

9-year-old girl as lifeguard. Presumably, age is relevant to ensuring the safety of a pool full of swimmers (and the park wouldn't hire a 9-year-old boy either). In contrast, refusing to hire a 19-year-old because she is female is sex discrimination, because her sex is irrelevant to her ability to perform the job.

Around the world and for most of the history of the United States, employers have openly discriminated on the basis of sex, as well as on the basis of race, ethnicity, national origin, age, appearance, and sexual orientation. Employers have refused to hire women and other social minorities, segregated them into jobs different from those held by white men, denied them promotions, and paid them lower wages. Until quite recently, employers discriminated without a second thought. In the mid-nineteenth century, the publisher of the New York *Herald*, for example, stormed into the newspaper's office one day and bellowed, "Who are these females? Fire them all!" (N. Robertson 1992:46). Although such discrimination seems outrageous today, until 30 years ago, it was both legal and commonplace. It took the civil rights movement of the early 1960s to persuade Americans that race discrimination is unfair and to spur Congress and state legislatures to outlaw employment discrimination based on sex and race.

Although antidiscrimination laws have prompted employers to change some of their practices, employers continue to discriminate illegally on the basis of people's sex, race, national origin, and age. (They also discriminate on the basis of people's appearance and sexual orientation, which is legal in most of the United States and the world.) In the last half of the 1980s, the Equal Employment Opportunities Commission received more than 30,000 complaints of sex discrimination per year, and nearly 80 percent of 803 Americans surveyed in 1990 believed that most if not all employers practice some form of job discrimination (National Opinion Research Corporation 1990).

Statistical discrimination. Another reason for employers to discriminate against women is the fear that employing women will reduce profits because women are less productive or more costly to employ. The idea that women may be more expensive employees stems from the assumption that motherhood will cause women to miss more work than men or lead to higher turnover rates. The practice of treating individuals on the basis of beliefs about groups is called **statistical discrimination.** Although employers may legally refuse to hire or promote an individual who cannot do the job, it is illegal to treat an individual differently solely because she or he belongs to a group that is, on average, less productive or more costly to employ. Moreover, because employers are often wrong about which workers are productive, statistical discrimination is not necessarily good business.

Customers' and male workers' opposition to women. Some employers treat men and women differently in deference to the prejudices of their customers or workers. Until the early 1970s, for example, airlines refused to hire male flight attendants because they claimed their passengers preferred stewardesses. Then the Supreme Court let stand a lower court ruling that customers' preferences do not justify sex discrimination (*Diaz v. Pan American* 1971), opening the occupation of flight attendant to men (and eventually to older people). Nonetheless, employers still defer to customers' preferences. For example, a recent lawsuit charged that a white male professor vetoed hiring a female to direct a Pacific-Asian studies program because he claimed that scholars and students from Japan would object to a female director.

Employers may also avoid hiring women out of fear that male workers will take offense. Male workers might sabotage the women's productivity (Bergmann and Darity 1981), insist on higher pay to work with women (Bielby and Baron 1986), or even go on strike.

Sex Differences in Workers' Preferences and Productivity

Up to now, we have focused on the ways that employers' and male workers' actions contribute to sex inequality in the workplace. Now we turn to explanations that emphasize differences between female and male workers. Some social scientists and employers argue that women choose customarily female jobs, do not want promotions, and willingly accept lower wages because, unlike men, they are not primarily oriented to paid work. An employer that was sued for discrimination in promotions, for example, argued that its female employees were just working for extra money and were not interested in moving into management (Hoffman and Reed 1981).

Why should women willingly settle for fewer opportunities and rewards than men? Two explanations that social scientists have proposed boil down to the claim that women's primary orientation is to their families, not their jobs. The first of these is human-capital theory; the second is gender-role socialization theory.

Human-capital theory. Mainstream economic theory assumes that labor markets operate in a nondiscriminatory fashion, rewarding workers for their productivity. Thus, if women are worse off than men, it is because they are less productive workers. This assumption cannot be tested, however, because measuring productivity is impossible for many jobs. So researchers examine characteristics that they assume increase productivity: the skills, experience, and commitment that workers bring to their jobs. Workers' skills and experience, according to economists, constitute their **human capital.** Theoretically, through education, training, and experience, workers invest in their human capital, and these investments make some workers more productive than others. Human-capital theorists assume that women's orientation to their families inhibits their investment in education, training, and experience and thus makes women less productive than men (Becker 1964).

The amount of schooling people have is indeed important. It affects whether they are in the labor force, the jobs they hold, their authority, and their earnings. But differences in education are not very important for explaining most forms of sex inequality in the workplace. Although male and female workers both average a little over 12 years of education, men are less likely than women to finish high school and more likely to go beyond the master's degree. Also, although male and female college students tend to major in different subjects, this difference has been shrinking (Jacobs 1989b).

Training is a different story. Women and men tend to receive different kinds of training, sometimes because of cultural values and sometimes because of employers' actions. In the past, much of the job training that public schools provided was sex stereotyped and sex segregated, channeling males and females into different courses. In fact, the federal law establishing vocational education specified job training for males and home economics for females. A second source of training is apprenticeships, most of which unions run under the auspices of the U.S. Department of Labor. Like their ancestors, the medieval guilds, these training programs often exclude women. The third and most important source of training occurs on the job. Female jobs are less likely than male jobs to provide on-the-job training, however (Carey and Eck 1984:12). For example, employers train 44 percent of construction workers compared to 5 percent of typists (Carey and Eck 1984:5, 18). Employers often expect workers in traditionally female occupations, such as nursing, to obtain and pay for their own training before they start work. These kinds of differences contribute to women's lower workplace status.

Experience, the third element of human capital, presents a more complicated picture. Women average less work experience than men, although the difference is narrowing. In the late 1980s, experts predicted that the average 18-year-old woman would be in the labor force about 29 years, 9.4 years less than the average 18-year-old male (S. Smith 1985). Women are also less likely than men to work continuously (Wilson and Wu 1993:table 5). The chapters that follow will address the effects of experience on the assignment of women and men to different jobs and on women's and men's chances of promotion and earnings.

Before leaving this subject, we should note that more educated or experienced workers are not necessarily more productive and that female workers are as committed to their jobs as males. However, productivity is strongly influenced by the resources that employers make available to workers and the commitment that workers bring to their job. Employers are more likely to give male rather than female workers the kinds of tools that enhance their productivity. International studies of agricultural modernization, for example, revealed that male workers monopolize the most efficient equipment and methods, leaving manual tasks to women (Boserup 1970). Also, recent research has indicated that women's job commitment equals men's (Bielby and Bielby 1988; Marsden et al. 1993). The kind of job a worker has affects commitment more than the worker's sex does (Marsden et al. 1993). The same factors—working conditions, autonomy on the job, and promotional opportunities—increase men's and women's commitment. In fact, researchers found that women devote more effort to their jobs than men do in jobs with similar amounts of autonomy (Bielby and Bielby 1988).

In sum, the human-capital claim that sex inequality at work arises from women's family obligations was more plausible 20 years ago, when it was first proposed, than it is today. Two incomes are now needed to purchase the goods and services that one income bought a generation ago. Thus in most families both men and women must now work for pay. Nonetheless, you will see in Chapters 4 through 7 that human-capital differences between the sexes explain some of the sex inequality in today's workplace.

Gender-role socialization theory. Human-capital theory does not try to explain its assumption that women are oriented primarily to their families rather than their careers. Gender-role socialization theories address that issue. **Gender-role socialization** is the process by which families, peers, schools, and the media teach a society's expectations of "appropriate" dress, speech, personality, leisure activities, and aspirations for each sex (Weitzman 1979).

Gender-role socialization might contribute to unequal workplace outcomes in several ways. First, it might lead women to be oriented more to their families and men more to their jobs. Traditionally, girls have been socialized to want to have babies, bake cookies, and so forth, whereas boys have allegedly been socialized to compete for fame and fortune in the wider world. The different socialization of females and males may incline them to seek only those jobs that society has deemed acceptable for their sex. Also, socialization may contribute to a tendency for men and women to hold different values that affect their work lives, such as how important it is to have authority on the job or make lots of money. Finally, men's gender-role socialization may encourage them to expect a sexual division of labor at work that reserves for them certain jobs, an inside track on promotions, a position of authority, and higher pay for their work, as well as a sexual division of labor at home that relieves them of most day-to-day domestic work. Because men are usually the workplace decision makers, they are in a position to enforce these expectations.

Can the concept of gender-role socialization help explain workplace inequality? Some sociologists and economists argue that socialization orients women (but not men) to home and family, so women choose jobs that are easy to combine with their duties to their families. A different path to the same result is the idea that family demands hamper women's ability to compete with men for jobs and promotions. Women's responsibility for most of the domestic work and child rearing and men's avoidance of these tasks are consistent with this explanation for men's advantaged position at work. However, research showing that women work as hard as similar men and are as committed to their jobs indicates limitations in this explanation.

Most people assume that childhood socialization permanently shapes adult outlook. But childhood gender-role socialization is actually not very important for explaining women's and men's concentration in different jobs, their different rates of promotion, and their different average earnings. What is important are the ongoing rewards and punishments people experience in response to their behavior. Imagine a couple with two children. When the wife's employer sends her to a week-long workshop on management training, her husband enjoys the excuse for spending more time with the kids. But when he tells his buddies he can't have a beer after work because his wife is gone and he has to take care of the children, they kid him about it. The next year, when his wife proposes another trip, he balks. We cannot explain his reaction as a result of the subtle messages he may have absorbed as a child; rather, it is more closely related to present-day rewards (enjoying his kids, pleasing his wife) and punishments (being ribbed by his coworkers). His wife's case illustrates the same point. When she was 17 years old, she may have thought that she would work for a few years after marriage and then quit to raise her children. But the reward of being selected for management training and the potential punishment of scraping by on one income may orient her toward pursuing a highly paid, prestigious career.

Summary

Sex inequality in the workplace is manifested in several ways: The sexes are concentrated in different occupations; women are often confined to lower-ranking positions than men and are less likely than men to exercise authority; women earn less than men. Social scientists have advanced several explanations for these disparities: cultural factors, sex stereotypes, the preservation of male advantage, and discrimination by employers. Also contributing to unequal outcomes, however, are men's greater training and experience. In the next three chapters, we will use the concepts presented in this chapter to explain sex differences in workplace opportunities and rewards.

diff occupations
women - low rank
men - authority
women ear less

cultural factors
sex - stereotype
male advantage
discrimination by employe
mens' greater training
→ experience

4

Sex Segregation in the Workplace

When the British Foreign Office hired its first female employees in the last half of the nineteenth century, it hid them in an attic to prevent any contact with male workers. On payday the hallways were cleared of men before the women were sent running downstairs to pick up their wages on the first floor (Cohn 1985:129). However incredible such rigid separation of the sexes seems today, some countries still are similarly strict. So wealthy Saudi Arabian women can conduct financial transactions while physically separate from men, in accordance with Muslim law, banks have built women's annexes. Behind the National Commercial Bank in Riyadh, for example, is a women's branch that employs only women, except for male guards who stand inside the foyer. These guards, who are married to the branch's female employees, pass documents and money back and forth between their wives inside the bank and the men who dominate commerce in the outside world (Mackey 1987:135).

Contrasting these examples with the United States in the 1990s, where women and men often work side by side, you might conclude that Western societies have eliminated sex segregation from workplaces. In this chapter we show that although the forms of segregation have changed, most American women and men are concentrated in different kinds of work. Americans' color further affects the jobs they do. We use the theories introduced in Chapter 3 to explain why segregation persists and to identify the factors that undermine it.

Sex segregation in the workplace refers to the concentration of men and women in different occupations, jobs, and places of work. Sometimes sex segregation physically separates the sexes: Women and men do different tasks or the same tasks in different settings or at different times. For instance, a bank may employ female managers at its suburban branches and employ male managers downtown, or a security firm may hire female guards for day shifts and hire men for night shifts. The concept of sex segregation also applies to situations in which the sexes share the same place of work but do different jobs, as in a research laboratory where female technicians work alongside male scientists or in an office filled with female clerks and male managers. Notice that this second meaning of segregation is identical to the concept of the sexual division of labor, which we discussed in Chapter 1.

Consequences of Sex Segregation

What difference does it make that women and men do different jobs? Sex segregation matters for the same reason that the U.S. Supreme Court outlawed school segregation in 1964: Among socially unequal groups, separate is not equal. Separating groups into different places and different roles makes it easier to treat them unequally, and it implies that treating them differently is acceptable. In contemporary societies, which use people's jobs to place them in the status system and distribute income and prestige, segregating the sexes into different jobs contributes to women's lower pay and lesser social power—at work, in their families, and in the larger society.

The best-documented consequence of sex segregation in the workplace is its effect on the pay gap between the sexes (the focus of Chapter 6). The higher the proportion of female workers in an occupation, the less that both male and female workers earn. Pursuing a disproportionately female line of work also costs workers prestige. In fact, people assign less prestige to an occupation if researchers describe it as predominantly female than if researchers describe it as predominantly male (Jacobs and Powell 1985). Finally, workers in heavily female occupations have less authority and less chance of promotion to more lucrative, powerful, and prestigious jobs. Thus, women's concentration in predominantly female occupations means that, as a group, they earn less and enjoy less power and prestige than men. The consequences of these differences reverberate throughout society. For example, the most common path into Congress is through the practice of law. The mechanisms that consign women to jobs as legal secretaries, legal assistants, or even legal-aid lawyers and that keep them from becoming partners in major law firms limit the number of women lawmakers. In this way and many others, sex segregation in the workplace plays a fundamental role in maintaining sex inequality in modern societies.

Society as a whole pays a price when employers use workers' sex— or other irrelevant characteristics, such as race, age, or sexual orientation—to segregate them into jobs that fail to exploit their abilities. As long as the United States was the only economic superpower, it could get by with wasting the talents of most of its female and minority citizens. Those days are over. Our nation faces keen international competition, we buy more products from other countries than we sell to them, we are trillions of dollars in debt, and our infrastructure (for example, highways, bridges, and the public transportation system) is falling apart. Today, no country can afford to bury intelligent, energetic, talented workers of any color or sex in jobs typing insurance claims, emptying wastebaskets, or serving french fries.

If sex segregation is so harmful, why does it persist? It benefits men. Clearly, not all men—or even all white, Anglo, native-born men—end up in prestigious, high-paying jobs. However, sex, race, and ethnic segregation favor many men by reducing the competition for their jobs. As Chapter 3 suggested, the beneficiaries of inequality have an incentive to preserve it, even if they are unaware that they enjoy advantages because of their sex.

A History of Sex Segregation in the United States

The chronicle of sex segregation in the United States is a story of progress and setbacks. In this section we review historical trends in sex segregation. We then examine sex segregation today, looking separately at four broad racial and ethnic groups.

Sex Segregation in the Seventeenth and Eighteenth Centuries

Segregation among female and male paid workers in the United States had its roots in the unpaid work of the first European and African immigrants. Among the colonists, nine out of 10 people worked at agriculture (Ryan 1983:27), growing food and producing goods mostly for their own families. The sexual division of labor resembled that of European peasants and farmers. Most men did agricultural work, and women managed the household and manufactured most of the items the household consumed. Women also sold or bartered homemade products like soap and lace and earned income by providing such services as spinning or caring for the sick. However, the work of the sexes overlapped, depending on what needed to be done and who was available to do it.

The growth of the United States during the eighteenth century permitted commerce to thrive. Many families ran small businesses (Ryan 1983), but for women, widowhood was the only path to independent entrepreneurship (Ryan 1983:24). Widows ran businesses as shopkeepers, butchers, shoemakers, apothecaries, printers, coopers, silversmiths, inn-keepers, and jailers. At the same time, thousands of women and men worked without pay as slaves or indentured servants. Male slaves usually did field work, and females did both field and indoor work. But the precise sexual division of labor among enslaved people depended on slave owners. During the seventeenth and eighteenth centuries, then, a line divided women's work from men's work among both slaves and free people. This line, however, was not strictly drawn.

Sex Segregation in the Nineteenth Century

During the nineteenth century, the United States began to industrialize. Although most Americans still worked as farmers, industrialization altered what jobs each sex did. Some of the tasks that women had done at home moved to the market and into men's hands—for example, preparing the dead for burial. And the doctrine of separate spheres pushed women out of small businesses.

As a rule, men and women who participated in the labor force held different jobs. But the fact that men heavily outnumbered women in the labor force made men a majority in most occupations. Because men dominated almost all lines of work, most jobs were defined as men's work, including several that we think of as women's work today. For example, the few clerical workers that most small businesses employed were male. In 1870, only 3 percent of office clerks, stenographers, typists, bookkeepers, cashiers, and accountants were women (Davies 1982:table 1).

Women dominated a few occupations, especially those whose low pay and poor working conditions did not attract men. The Civil War expanded women's access to factory jobs and such jobs as nurse and teacher (Hooks 1947:10). But most employed women worked in domestic service, farming, and textiles (Hooks 1947:52).

By the end of the nineteenth century and the early twentieth century, immigrants were providing a continuous supply of cheap workers to most industries. Employers chose workers by their ethnicity as well as their sex. Native-born men worked in factories or as craftworkers, clerks, or managers; others were self-employed or professionals. The most common work for single female immigrants—especially Irish, Scandinavian, and German women—was **domestic service.** Women who had come from Ireland were also frequently employed in the textile mills, where they replaced the New England farm girls who had left in rebellion against increased hours and pay cuts. The garment industry drew heavily on immigrant women. Bohemian women who had made cigars by hand before immigrating could not get jobs practicing their trade in the United States because employers reserved those skilled jobs for men. Women had to settle for the hardest part of the process: stripping tobacco (Amott and Matthaei 1991:111). A few women worked as nurses or teachers, but most employed women toiled 12 hours a day for subsistence wages in sweatshops or as domestic servants.

By the beginning of the twentieth century, the sexes were sharply segregated into different kinds of work. Some occupations that women had pursued fifty years earlier at home for their families (for example, manufacturing soap) or in commerce as small-scale entrepreneurs (for example, printing) had become men's work. Sex segregation in the workplace was firmly established by the end of the nineteenth century. However, the twentieth century would bring new opportunities for women.

Sex Segregation in the Twentieth Century

World War I (1914–1917), like the Civil War and World War II, drew men out of the labor force and into the military. The war also halted the flow of immigrants, and the resulting labor shortage gave all women and African-American men access to jobs that had customarily gone to white men. However, when the soldiers returned home, employers rehired them, forcing African-Americans and women back into menial jobs as laborers and domestic servants. Despite the optimism of a 1919 Women's Bureau poster titled "New Jobs for Women"—which featured female machinists, streetcar conductors, elevator operators, "traffic cops," and mail carriers[1]—women retained few customarily male jobs after the war.

Two institutional changes in the early twentieth century—the bureaucratization of economic organizations and the development of new clerical jobs—altered the sexual division of labor by feminizing clerical work. In the early years of this century, larger, more bureaucratized firms needed armies of clerks. Employers were drawn to women because of their low wages. In addition, public schools had begun to teach women to run the new office machines, such as the typewriter, and women preferred clerical to factory jobs.

Employers segregated female and male office workers, reserving positions of responsibility for men. As late as 1930, men were still two-thirds of all office clerks and almost half of all bookkeepers, cashiers, and

---

[1] A photograph of an office filled with typists was captioned "Clerical work—quite a new job for Negro Girls," and the caption for a photograph of women at sewing machines explained, "Laundry and domestic work didn't pay so they entered the garment trade" (Callahan 1992:37).

accountants; in contrast, 95 percent of all typists and stenographers were female. To keep women's wages low, employers encouraged high turnover among women by insisting that they quit when they married. By 1940, however, employers had feminized clerical work. In 1870, 930 women held clerical jobs; 70 years later, the number was over 1.8 million (Hooks 1947:75). However, these female clerical workers were almost all white. Another 40 years passed before most office jobs were open to women of color.

While women gained a foothold in office work, they lost out to men in semiskilled and service jobs in public places, such as hotels, restaurants, and hospitals (Hooks 1947:50). These and other changes helped to segregate women and men into different occupations. In 1940, in almost 80 percent of 451 occupations, men outnumbered women by at least three to one; in more than half the occupations, men outnumbered women by more than nine to one. In contrast, women outnumbered men nine to one in only ten occupations: housekeeper; dressmaker; laundress; trained nurse; practical nurse; attendant to physicians or dentists; telephone operator; stenographer, typist, and secretary; servant; and boardinghouse keeper (Hooks 1947:30).

The growth in jobs and opportunities for women and racial and ethnic minorities ground to a halt in the 1930s. The Great Depression brought historic levels of unemployment among both male and female wage earners. Men reclaimed some jobs that had begun employing women during World War I, such as bank teller, but most men preferred unemployment to work in predominantly female clerical jobs. By 1940 the top 10 occupations for women included four that were among the top 10 in 1870: servant, teacher, nurse, and "apparel operative" (the twentieth-century descendant of the 1870s occupations of seamstress and dressmaker). The remaining occupations that employed the most women in 1940 included office worker, salesclerk, cashier, and waitress (Hooks 1947:52, 56). All but one of these occupations—waiter/waitress—still remained predominantly female half a century later.

World War II (1941–1945) again brought labor shortages that disrupted sex and race segregation. During the war, industries turned to women and minority men to maintain production. African-American men who were not eligible for military service won access to unionized craft jobs, and unfilled factory and clerical jobs gave African-American women a popular alternative to domestic work. The U.S. government used the labor shortages to justify a program that brought Mexican nationals to the United States on temporary work permits but confined them to farm labor in a program that a Department of Labor employee later called "legalized slavery" (Amott and Matthaei 1991:79).

The war years gave women access to jobs that custom had closed to them: from practicing medicine to working as streetcar conductors, from building cargo planes to flying them. Employers tried to attract women to skilled blue-collar jobs by comparing them to women's homemaking activities. Slogans assured women that "if you can run a sewing machine, you can operate a rivet gun."

When the war ended, employers predictably laid off women from customarily male jobs. The Air Force grounded its female pilots without providing any veterans' benefits, and civilian employers laid off female welders, machinists, and electricians or transferred them into low-paying jobs as assemblers and clerk-typists. Thus, World War II had little long-run effect on how paid work was divided between the sexes. Despite steady growth in the proportion of women who worked for pay, not until the 1970s did customarily male occupations admit large numbers of women.

Sex Segregation in the Contemporary United States

A casual look at the world around us—especially the world that magazines, movies, and television programs depict—suggests that women and men are finally integrated at work. Certainly they are less segregated in the United States today than at any time in the country's history. But integration has been an uphill battle, and the biggest hills are invisible because the terrain is still overwhelmingly sex segregated. For example, although in 1990 women made up almost half the country's bus drivers and bartenders, they held fewer than 3 percent of the nation's construction jobs and just 4 percent of repair jobs. In Washington, D.C., women were one-fifth of the police officers in 1990, a proportion that was unimaginable twenty years ago; but among firefighters, men still outnumber women 20 to one.

Job-level sex segregation. To get a true picture of how much sex segregation exists, we must distinguish between **job-level segregation** and **occupational-level segregation**. The difference relates to the difference between jobs and occupations. **Jobs** are specific positions in specific establishments in which workers perform specific activities. Here are some examples of jobs: produce clerk at the Big Bear Grocery in Columbus, Ohio; health-insurance claims adjuster at the Prudential Insurance Company in Topeka, Kansas; custodian at the Bryn Mawr elementary school in Seattle, Washington.

To measure the full extent to which women and men are segregated at work, we would need to know what job every man and woman holds.

Knowing people's jobs tells us about both the sexes' physical separation into different work settings and the sexual division of labor that assigns them to different tasks. Unfortunately, collecting information on the exact tasks and place of work of every worker in America would be impossible. We know that 71 million men and 62 million women were employed at some time during 1992 (U.S. Bureau of Labor Statistics 1993d), but we cannot tell the extent to which they were segregated into different jobs.

We can list every worker's job within an "establishment" (a firm or a branch of a larger company), however, and a few studies have assessed job segregation within establishments. The most comprehensive of these used data for California establishments between 1959 and 1979 (Bielby and Baron 1984). Of 393 establishments, 30 employed only one sex, and 199 more were totally segregated: No men and women shared the same job title. Only 41 percent had any jobs filled by both female and male workers. Among the few firms in which both sexes held the same job title were a dance studio that needed to provide partners for male and female customers and a company that hired women for day shifts and men for night shifts.

Occupational-level sex segregation. **Occupations** are collections of jobs that involve similar activities in different establishments. The U.S. Census Bureau distinguishes over 500 different occupations. For example, a produce clerk belongs to the occupational category of "stock handlers and baggers"; a health-insurance claims adjuster belongs to the category "insurance examiners, adjusters, and investigators"; a school custodian belongs to the category "janitors and cleaners." Every 10 years, America's census provides information about workers' occupations that lets us estimate women's and men's segregation into different occupations.

There is a drawback, however, to using people's occupations to estimate sex segregation: Considerable sex segregation exists within occupations. In other words, men and women within the same occupational category perform different jobs for different employers. Male bakers, for instance, are concentrated in unionized, high-paying establishments that mass-produce baked goods; most female bakers work in retail bakeries, where pay is low (Steiger and Reskin 1990). Multiply this difference within one occupation by 500 occupations, and you can see that data on people's occupations will underestimate the amount of sex segregation in the workplace.

In 1990 many women still worked in primarily female occupations. Of the 56 million women in the labor force when the 1990 census was conducted, one-third worked in just 10 of the 503 detailed occupations

TABLE 4.1

Top 10 Occupations for Each Sex, 1990

Women

Total labor force	56,487,249
Secretary	3,966,179
Elementary school teacher	2,372,174
Cashier	2,259,316
Registered nurse	1,777,885
Bookkeeper, accounting clerk	1,721,202
Nurse's aide	1,621,981
Salaried manager, administrator, nec*	1,585,636
Sales representative, other commodities	1,231,579
Waitress	1,197,485
Salaried sales supervisor, proprietor	1,050,658

Men

Total labor force	66,986,201
Salaried manager, administrator, nec*	3,355,970
Truck driver	2,733,620
Salaried sales supervisor, proprietor	1,964,716
Janitor, cleaner	1,700,984
Carpenter, except apprentice	1,337,544
Sales representative, mining, mfg., wholesale	1,179,380
Construction laborer	1,103,482
Cook	1,085,895
Supervisor, production occupation	1,069,504
Automobile mechanic	936,977

*The Census Bureau uses the abbreviation *nec* for miscellaneous occupations that are "not elsewhere classified."

Source: Data from U.S. Bureau of the Census 1992a:table 1.

(see Table 4.1). Of these occupations, secretary tops the list. If we add the related occupations of typist, stenographer, and office clerk, these occupations employ about one woman in 10. Other traditionally female lines of work that employ millions of women include retail sales, including sales of personal services (4.5 million women); food preparation (3.4 million); school teaching (3.4 million); nursing (3.4 million); and cashiering

and bookkeeping (4 million).[2] Despite World War II, the women's libera-
tion movement, and affirmative action, the most common occupations
for women in 1990 were almost identical to those that employed the most
women in 1940. The only recent addition to women's top 10 occupations
is the category "miscellaneous salaried managers."

Men's distribution across occupations in 1990 differed from women's
in two ways. First, men were more evenly distributed across the 503 detailed occupations. Of the 67 million men in the labor force when the
1990 census was conducted, one-quarter worked in the 10 occupations
that employed the largest numbers of men (compared to one-third of
women in the top 10 female occupations). Second, only two of the 10
occupations that employed the most men also employed the largest
numbers of women: "salaried manager, administrator, nec" and "salaried
sales supervisor, proprietor." These two occupations include many diverse jobs, however, so the women and men in them may do very different kinds of work.

The corollary of women's heavy concentration in a few occupations
is that only 11 percent of working women worked in occupations that
were at least 75 percent male (Kraut and Luna 1992:3). Indeed, in most
occupations, men substantially outnumbered women. For example,
1,829,964 men and 35,714 women repaired vehicles; 1,337,544 men and
23,163 women worked as carpenters; and 314,915 men and 37,364
women sold motor vehicles and boats (U.S. Bureau of the Census
1992a:table 1). Still, hundreds of thousands of women worked in some of
the occupations that employ the most men. In 1990, more than 987,000
women were cooks and more than 780,000 were janitors and cleaners.

Comparing the numbers of women and men across specific occupations indicates sex segregation in the workplace but does not indicate
how much segregation exists. For a single summary measure of the extent of sex segregation, however, we can use the **index of segregation,**
which represents the proportion of all female (or male) workers that
would have to change to an occupation in which their sex is underrepresented for the sexes to be completely integrated across occupations.
The index would equal 0 if men and women were perfectly integrated
across all occupations; it would equal 100 if every occupation employed
either only men or only women. In 1990 the index of occupational segregation was 53, meaning that 53 percent of the female labor force, or more

---

[2]This list omits the most female-dominated occupation in the United States:
homemaker. In 1990, about 25 million women worked full time at unpaid
domestic work in their own homes.

than 32 million American women, would have to shift to mostly male occupations to achieve occupational-level integration.

Of course, job-level segregation considerably exceeds occupational segregation. In 1989 the job segregation index for North Carolina workers was 77 (Tomaskovic-Devey 1993a:63). To integrate American men and women in all jobs would require shifting tens of millions of workers. In short, the American workplace remains overwhelmingly sex segregated.

Race and sex segregation. In the United States, employers are more likely to consider workers' sex than any other personal characteristic in assigning them to jobs. However, employers also take into account workers' race, ethnicity, age, appearance, and other irrelevant characteristics. Black women's work history illustrates the combined effects of sex and **race segregation** (Jones 1985). When the hope of better jobs and schools drew African-American men and women to the North in the late nineteenth century and early twentieth century, employment discrimination kept them out of all but the worst jobs. Employers refused to hire African-American women for clerical and sales jobs, and most had to settle for jobs as domestic servants, at their employers' beck and call 24 hours a day (Jones 1985). The available factory jobs—often in the steel, automobile, garment, and meat-processing industries—were physically punishing and mentally deadening, and they paid rock-bottom wages. Not until the civil rights movement of the 1960s did employers assign large numbers of African-American women to clerical jobs, and today's employers still tend to segregate women of color from white women. In clerical work, for instance, minority women are overrepresented in low-paid occupations, such as file clerk, keypunch operator, social welfare assistant, and insurance examiner (Glenn and Tolbert 1987; King 1993:18).

Like black women, black men were also confined primarily to service jobs in the past, but they were more likely to work in public places rather than private homes—for example, as doormen, elevator operators, railroad porters, waiters, and janitors. An employer that hired both whites and African Americans often segregated them from each other as well as from workers of the other sex (Jones 1985:182). For example, during the 1930s, Philco employed a few black men but so thoroughly segregated them as laborers in the shipping room that many white employees did not realize that Philco employed any African Americans (Cooper 1991:326). Only in the late 1930s and the 1940s did employers place African-American men in skilled jobs.

Employers have also historically segregated Asian and Hispanic women into different lines of work from men of their own ethnic background and from white Anglo women. In the canning factories of 50 years ago, for example, employers put Mexican-American women to work chopping vegetables and gave Anglo women the easier job of packing cans (Amott and Matthaei 1991:77).

Today, we still have a substantial amount of occupational sex segregation and a moderate amount of occupational race segregation among workers of the same sex. As Table 4.2 shows, in 1990, of the eight occupations that employed the most men from the four racial-ethnic groups, only two also employed large numbers of women. The occupation of cook—which employs significant proportions of African-American, Asian-American, and Hispanic men (and which fell just short of the top eight occupations for white men)—was the fourth largest occupation for African-American women. A miscellaneous category of managers and administrators, not elsewhere classified, was among the top eight occupations for each group of men but appeared among the top eight occupations only for white women. Secretary was one of the top three occupations among African-, Hispanic-, and European-American women. Elementary school teacher, registered nurse, office clerk, and cashier were also among the biggest employers for at least three of these groups of women. The most opportunities for Hispanic- and African-American women lay in clerical and service occupations, as well as semi-skilled blue-collar jobs (assembler for black women, sewing machine operator for Hispanic women). White women stood out from the other three groups of women because a managerial occupation was among their top eight occupations, and their list included no blue-collar operative or service occupations, such as cleaning, cooking, or operating sewing machines.

Race and sex are bases for segregation among **professionals** as well. Professional occupations are medium- to high-prestige occupations whose workers usually earn high pay and enjoy considerable autonomy, such as physician, professor, architect, and librarian. Their high status permits them to limit access to training; as a result, practitioners enjoy a monopoly on the service they provide. In general, people of color are underrepresented among the professions. For instance, only one professional occupation employed large numbers of Hispanic women: elementary school teacher. Only two professional occupations—elementary school teaching and registered nursing—were among the top eight occupations for European- and African-American women. The only professional occupation on Asian-American women's top eight list was accountant.

The United States had so many managerial occupations and janitorial occupations in 1990 that both appear on the top eight list for every group of men. Among men, the occupations that employed the highest proportions of at least three of the four racial groups were truck driver, janitor and cleaner, construction laborer, cook, and assembler. The list for white men, however, includes the most desirable jobs and the fewest undesirable jobs. White and Asian-American men worked disproportionately in sales, and white men also worked disproportionately in blue-collar jobs as supervisors. Asian men were concentrated in several other high-status, well-paying occupations (physician, accountant, and technician) but also in several occupations lower in the occupational hierarchy (cook, assembler, janitor/cleaner). The top eight occupations for African-American and Hispanic men, in contrast, included only one managerial occupation and no sales occupations. Instead, African-American and Hispanic men were concentrated in relatively low-paid service and laborer jobs, such as groundskeeper and gardener, assembler, construction laborer, farm worker, and guard.

This examination of occupational segregation by race and sex yields two important generalizations. First, almost twice as much segregation is based on sex as on race. Men and women of the same race are more segregated from each other than are African Americans and whites of the same sex. Second, within each sex, people of color and Hispanics, regardless of color, tend to work in less desirable occupations than whites and non-Hispanics do. Indeed, the occupations with the greatest concentrations of men and women of color pay the lowest average earnings of all occupations (Sorensen 1989).

Cross-National Differences in Sex Segregation

Countries differ in the particular occupations that usually employ women, men, or both sexes. In Japan, for example, women sell insurance door to door; in the United States, most door-to-door insurance sales agents are men (Leidner 1993:196). Women do unskilled construction work in India, where men predominate in clerical occupations. According to the United Nations (1991), in almost every country, women hold a narrower range of jobs than men, and some jobs are defined as women's work. In Uganda, selling charcoal is a female job "ghetto"; in Hungary, assembling electronics; in Turkey, processing tobacco; in Egypt, harvesting cotton; in Nepal, building roads; in Nicaragua, picking coffee (Seager

TABLE 4.2

Top Occupations for Blacks, Hispanics, Asians, and Whites by Sex, 1990

Black Women		Black Men	
Total labor force	6,847,642	*Total labor force*	6,247,539
Cashier	346,359	Truck driver	342,492
Secretary	294,437	Janitor, cleaner	337,996
Elementary school teacher	257,434	Cook	194,282
Cook	192,660	Construction laborer	148,861
Janitor, cleaner	179,734	Guard	138,304
General office clerk	169,735	Assembler	136,189
Maid, "houseman"	162,870	Salaried manager, administrator, nec*	111,904
Registered nurse	157,515	Stock handler, bagger	92,378

Hispanic Women		Hispanic Men	
Total labor force	4,133,543	*Total labor force*	5,888,180
Secretary	219,115	Janitor, cleaner	255,573
Cashier	199,779	Truck driver	240,989
Janitor, cleaner	124,696	Farm worker	207,238
Sewing machine operator	123,539	Cook	191,390
Nurse's aide, orderly	123,131	Construction laborer	188,082
Elementary school teacher	104,645	Gardener, groundskeeper	151,017
Maid, "houseman"	103,022	Salaried manager, administrator, nec*	125,977
General office clerk	95,836	Assembler	123,232

Note: Blacks, Asians, and whites include people of Hispanic origin.

*The Census Bureau uses the abbreviation *nec* for miscellaneous occupations that are "not elsewhere classified."

Asian Women		Asian Men	
Total labor force	1,684,082	*Total labor force*	1,918,998
Registered nurse	80,494	Salaried manager, administrator, nec*	85,999
Cashier	77,490	Cook	80,976
Secretary	62,929	Salaried sales supervisor, proprietor	56,068
Sewing machine operator	57,602	Physician	45,483
Accountant, auditor	49,971	Janitor, cleaner	39,322
Bookkeeper	43,741	Food service, lodging	38,685
Waitress	40,722	Accountant	37,734
General office clerk	38,392	Cashier	36,479

White Women		White Men	
Total labor force	45,826,627	*Total labor force*	55,699,109
Secretary	3,504,652	Salaried manager, administrator, nec*	3,107,913
Elementary school teacher	2,038,535	Truck driver	2,231,097
Cashier	1,725,368	Salaried sales, supervisor, proprietor	1,779,842
Bookkeeper	1,548,980	Carpenter	1,187,316
Registered nurse	1,517,912	Janitor, cleaner	1,182,001
Salaried manager, administrator, nec*	1,428,336	Sales representative, mining, manufacturing, wholesale	1,109,573
Sales, other commodities	1,066,418	Supervisor, precision, production	930,804
Waitress	1,065,475	Construction laborer	832,692

Note: Blacks, Asians, and whites include people of Hispanic origin.

*The Census Bureau uses the abbreviation *nec* for miscellaneous occupations that are "not elsewhere classified."

Source: Data from U.S. Bureau of the Census 1992a:tables 1 and 2.

and Olson 1986:table 18). Overall, however, the extent of sex segregation in other industrialized countries is similar to that in the United States (Rosenfeld and Kalleberg 1991). Differences in the degree to which the sexes are segregated are due to differences in ideology and public policy. For example, workers in Norway and Sweden are somewhat more sex segregated than are workers in the United States. Public policies in the two Scandinavian countries advocate equality for women and men but also encourage mothers to work part time, and employers are likely to channel part-time workers into predominantly female occupations.

Trends in Sex Segregation

As we showed earlier, in its most fundamental form, the preindustrial sexual division of labor has persisted throughout the twentieth century, reflecting the importance that societies attach to gender. However, the sexual division of labor has varied over time. Families, employers, and societies are flexible in allocating tasks by sex. When not enough male workers are available or male workers are too costly, women do customarily male tasks. In this section, we first consider how types of work have shifted between the sexes over the centuries. Then we examine trends in the degree to which American women and men have been segregated in different occupations.

Shifts in Sex-Typed Jobs

Although paid work has always been segregated by sex, over time some tasks have switched back and forth between the sexes. Consider the production of cloth. Textiles were produced in women's workshops during the Middle Ages; these workshops were disappearing by the thirteenth century, although in some parts of Europe women continued to weave silk. By the sixteenth century, men had begun to take over the production of cloth. Women spun thread and wove cloth for their families, but through their guilds, men gained control of commercial weaving. Then, in cottage industry and later in factory industry, employers returned to women. By the 1840s, factory needlework and cottage industry—usually involving textiles—were among the most common kinds of employment for English women (Pinchbeck 1930:315). Textile production has also been one of the top occupations for American women for over a century.

A few other occupations have shifted from men to women. For example, AT&T recruited the first telephone operators from the boys who delivered telegrams. AT&T replaced them with young women, however, after customers complained about the boys' rudeness and pranks. Only after the Equal Employment Opportunity Commission charged AT&T with sex discrimination in 1970 did AT&T once again hire male operators. In 1990, however, 87 percent of telephone operators were still female.

Through the first several decades of this century, most bank tellers were men, but during both world wars, banks hired women to replace the young men who enlisted in the military. After World War II, men found more promising jobs elsewhere, and so women's share of bank teller jobs grew from 45 percent five years after the war's end to almost 90 percent by 1990.

A more recent shift occurred in typesetting, a male craft for centuries. When typesetting was computerized in the 1970s and 1980s, the workforce flipped from 17 percent female in 1970 to 70 percent female in 1990.

These examples are definitely not typical. In the first place, shifts in which sex does a job are unusual. When they do occur, occupational **feminization,** with women replacing men as the majority, is far more likely than masculinization. Men almost never take over predominantly female work. This fact should not be surprising. As you saw earlier, predominantly female jobs pay less than male jobs and are generally less desirable. Because men have more choices, few have to settle for customarily female jobs.

Twentieth-Century Trends in Sex Segregation

Between 1900 and 1970, the index of occupational sex segregation hovered between 65 and 69. During these 70 years, women's share of the labor force grew dramatically, and employers reorganized work and introduced new technologies, causing some occupations to die out and others to emerge. However, employers continued to assign men and women to different occupations. Then the 1970s brought a seven-point drop in the index of occupational sex segregation.

This decline in occupational segregation had several causes. Both the growth of already integrated occupations and the decline of heavily segregated occupations helped. But the 1970s also witnessed a historic movement by women into traditionally male jobs. Thousands of women became bank managers, bartenders, public relations specialists, book editors, pharmacists, insurance adjusters, bus drivers, and typesetters. Employers turned to women because these occupations (or certain specialties within them) had become less attractive to men, leading to a shortage of male workers.

Although women in these feminizing occupations earned more than the women who remained in customarily female occupations, many still worked in low-paying specialties, some of which became female ghettos. For example, female real estate sales agents were concentrated in residential sales while men continued to dominate in commercial sales; female bank managers were often assigned to personal banking while men held on to commercial banking. Thus, declines in occupational-level segregation left job-level segregation intact.

During the 1980s, America's occupations continued to become more integrated, although a few male occupations have resegregated as female occupations. Also, some integration may be short lived. For example, although women are now as likely as men to work as writers, fewer than one-quarter of the writers for prime-time television are female (Bielby and Bielby 1992a). Producers are more likely to hire women to write for programs with a largely female audience, such as situation comedies, than for crime or action programs. The popularity of sitcoms in recent years has created more TV writing jobs for women, but when the industry returns to action programming oriented to male audiences, women writers risk losing ground (Bielby and Bielby 1992a).

Looking at the entire occupational structure, however, we can see some real progress. By 1990 the segregation index had declined to about 53 (Reskin 1994). Figure 4.1 tracks this change in occupational sex segregation during the twentieth century. For the post-1940 period, Figure 4.1 also presents separate estimates of sex segregation for African Americans and whites. Levels of sex segregation in these two groups are similar, but race segregation still confines African Americans of both sexes to different and less desirable occupations than those that white men and women hold.

Figure 4.1 shows three other important trends. First, until 1960 black and white women were more segregated from each other than were black and white men—largely because of African-American women's heavy concentration in domestic service. Second, by 1980 racial segregation had declined sharply, especially among women. It is now virtually the same for men and women. Third, throughout the twentieth century, sex has been more important than race in allocating workers to occupations. Notice that the two lines in Figure 4.1 that denote sex segregation lie above the two lines that denote racial segregation.[3]

In sum, Figure 4.1 shows that during the last 50 years the United

[3]When we speak of "occupational race segregation," we refer to the segregation of African Americans and whites into different occupations. Information is not available to trace longer-run segregation trends for other racial and ethnic groups.

FIGURE 4.1

Indexes of Occupational Sex and Race Segregation, 1900 to 1988

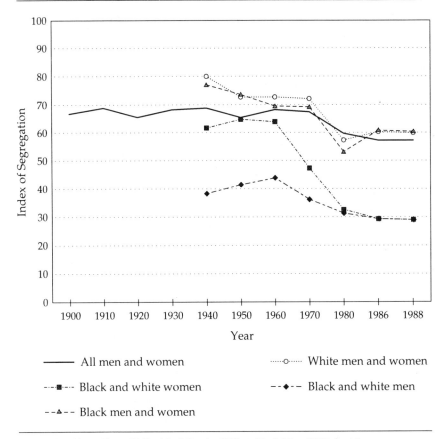

———— All men and women   ⋯⋯o⋯⋯ White men and women

–⋯■⋯– Black and white women   – – ◆ – – Black and white men

– – ▲ – – Black men and women

Source: Data from Gross 1968:table 2; Jacobs 1989a:table 2; King 1992:chart 1.

States has reduced African Americans' occupational segregation from whites more than it has reduced women's segregation from men. Between 1940 and 1988, the index of race segregation among women dropped from 65.4 to 29.2; the race segregation index for men declined from 44.4 to 31.8 (King 1992). Because African Americans compose a much smaller share of the labor force than women, integrating blacks into occupations dominated by same-sex whites is easier than integrating tens of millions of women into mostly male occupations. The social processes described in the next section have made occupational sex integration an uphill battle.

Explanations for Sex Segregation

The universality of the sexual division of labor has led people to conclude that each sex is naturally better suited to different kinds of work. For virtually every job, however, it is social factors rather than biological sex differences that dictate what tasks societies (and often employers) assign to each sex. What causes sex segregation? Why has it declined so slowly? The answers to these questions lie in the actions of the three groups that influence the sex composition of occupations: employers (most of whom are male), male workers, and female workers.

Experts disagree about which of these groups are most important for preserving sex segregation in the workplace. Some stress the actions of employers, because it is employers who assign women and men to jobs. Others place most of the responsibility for sex segregation on women, who (they claim) prefer predominantly female occupations. Still others emphasize the actions of male workers that exclude women from customarily male jobs. Others see a more complex interplay: "Employers do not simply erect 'barriers' [in response] to already-formed preferences: they create the workplace structures and relations out of which those preferences arise in the first place (Schultz 1991:141). The rest of this chapter examines the actions of each group that have maintained or reduced segregation and considers remedies appropriate to each group.

Employers' Actions

A few workers can pick and choose among prospective employers. Film studios compete for actors who are a sure bet at the box office, sports superstars can write their own ticket, and lucrative consulting jobs are open to former presidential aides. But most of us are in a different position. We hear about only a small fraction of the jobs for which we are qualified. And even when we learn of and apply for a job, the employer chooses whether to hire us and for what job.

Employers play a central role in concentrating women and men in different jobs. They, or their agents, may intentionally separate the sexes or do so simply by adhering to past recruitment practices, requiring unnecessary qualifications, or indulging the preference of some male workers. Their pivotal role in job assignment makes employers the most effective avenue for integration. Employers under pressure from regulatory agencies or shortages of male workers have demonstrated that they can reduce segregation on the job.

Intentional discrimination. Prospective workers' sex, race, and ethnicity often influence the personnel decisions of gatekeepers—bosses, managers, and supervisors who have the authority to restrict access to jobs. Discrimination occurs when gatekeepers use irrelevant characteristics in hiring workers and assigning jobs, whether they do so out of hostility or ignorance. Discrimination on the basis of sex, race, age, and certain other characteristics is illegal: nonetheless, the records of enforcement agencies and the courts contain thousands of legitimate complaints of employment discrimination.

To see how discrimination can segregate the sexes, consider some of the questions Sears Roebuck asked of applicants for commission-sales jobs in the 1970s: "Do you have a low-pitched voice?" "Have you ever done any hunting?" "Have you played on a football team?" (Schultz 1991:129). Few women could answer yes to any of these questions, much less to all three of them. The U.S. Steel Corporation turned down hundreds of female applicants who sought jobs as coal miners between 1976 and 1978; a court decree eventually insisted that it make restitution. In 1990, a federal agency established that Dart, Inc., gave male applicants mechanical-aptitude tests and placed successful applicants in well-paying, semiskilled jobs, while giving female applicants manual-dexterity tests and placing them in heavily female, low-paid jobs. In 1992—13 years after three women sued State Farm for sex discrimination—State Farm Insurance paid $157 million in back pay to 814 women to whom it had refused jobs as insurance agents because of their sex.

Gatekeepers' stereotypes about the sexes or about jobs can prompt them to discriminate. For example, until early in this century, restaurants hired only male food servers, allegedly because women lacked the strength to carry trays of food. Stereotypes are quite flexible, however, and open to various interpretations. Jobs often involve both stereotypically male and female tasks. Police officers must be honest, reliable, and authoritative; have good communication skills; and be physically fit. Is this configuration of traits male or female?

Furthermore, beliefs and stereotypes change in concert with changes in the real world. When shortages of male workers have led employers to turn to women for customarily male jobs, for example, employers have come up with new stereotypes to justify women's presence. In 1917, war-time shortages of male workers prompted banks to define women as well suited to low-level managerial jobs, because of their "neatness, deft handling of money and papers, tact, and a certain intuitive judgment" (Kessler-Harris 1986:770). Fifteen years later, during the Great Depression, banks justified not hiring women by claiming that the public would refuse to entrust its money to women. When World War II created another shortage of male workers, banks justified hiring women by citing women's expertise in interpersonal relations (Strober and Arnold

1987). Although cultural values, sex stereotypes, and traditional practices may encourage employers and workers to act in ways that perpetuate segregation, what creates segregation is not people's beliefs but their actions. When actions change, stereotypes give way.

Even when an employer is committed to equal employment opportunity, supervisors' actions can help maintain segregation. For example, a company that temporarily transferred white-collar employees to power-plant jobs during a strike had in effect assigned women to traditionally male jobs. However, plant supervisors reassigned most of the women to jobs cleaning the plants, so experience in a blue-collar setting failed to expose the women to a range of traditionally male skilled jobs (Reskin and Padavic 1988). In another case, an African-American woman who had been struggling for 10 years to become a journeyman sheet-metal worker (in other words, a full-fledged member of her craft) reported that her supervisor would not teach the black apprentices how to do any paperwork, a skill they had to learn in order to become journeymen (Schroedel 1985:137). A woman who had recently joined an all-male road crew spoke of her supervisor's antipathy. When she asked him to stop at a restroom, he refused, telling her, "You wanted a man's job; you learn to pee like a man" (Faludi 1991:390).

Sometimes women find ways to elude gatekeepers' stereotypes. For example, a training program for women who were seeking customarily male blue-collar jobs advised the women to show up for job interviews with a banged-up toolbox and scuffed work boots. The goal was to rebut employers' stereotypes that women lack experience and know-how (Weston 1990).

Discriminatory employment practices. Sex discrimination—whether based on employers' and supervisors' overt hostility or their stereotypes—makes a significant contribution to sex segregation. However, even employers that are not intentionally discriminating may have employment practices—in recruitment, training, and other areas—that segregate the sexes into different jobs.

As Chapter 3 indicated, the methods that employers often use to recruit workers affect the likelihood of hiring nontraditional workers. In filling job openings, many employers depend on referrals from current workers. More often than not, however, workers' friends are their same sex and race. Therefore, as long as white men monopolize the most desirable jobs and recruiting occurs through informal networks, employers will hire white men for these jobs (Corcoran et al. 1980:60). At the same time, the informal networks of minority men and women and white women concentrate them in jobs that are already filled by women and minorities.

In contrast, **open recruitment** techniques publicly announce job openings and thus let outsiders learn about sex-atypical jobs. Effective methods include advertising in places that are accessible to different groups of people, posting job openings where people from different groups can see them (in other words, not in the men's locker room), and using employment services that do not cater primarily to whites. Employers that are subject to affirmative action regulations must use open recruitment methods.

Open recruiting does not ensure that everyone has equal access to jobs, however. Other barriers exclude women from typically male jobs. One such barrier is job qualifications that women are less likely than men to have—such as a particular educational degree or the ability to lift a specified weight—and that are not essential for the job. Consider the female shipyard worker whose union's apprenticeship program barred her because she had not taken shop in high school. Her high school did not let girls take shop, and the apprenticeship program taught all the necessary skills (Schroedel 1985:169).

By reexamining requirements that tend to segregate the sexes, employers can open sex-atypical jobs to women. Until the 1970s, large banks required that managers have MBA degrees, although bright clerical workers could easily learn through job experience most of what they needed to know to be managers. After the federal government warned banks to eliminate discriminatory practices, some let women substitute experience for an MBA degree. This change opened bank management positions to thousands of women (Reskin and Hartmann 1986).

Often, of course, women lack the skills that are necessary to do a job. Men do too. But employers are more likely to provide on-the-job training for male employees than female employees. Consider the modern Japanese confectionery factory that employed men as skilled artisans and women as semiskilled workers. Anthropologist Dorinne Kondo (1990:251) observed young male artisans being taught to make delicate flower decorations. Although the female workers watched, nobody offered them a chance to try making the decorations, and none of the female workers asked to try, because they had too much work to do. As Kondo pointed out, teaching these skills to only the male artisans ensured women's exclusion from the skilled jobs.

The ways that employers organize work can also either hinder or expedite women's entry into and performance in customarily male jobs. A telephone company told a female office worker who asked to be transferred to installation that she was too short to get the ladder down from the top of the truck. When she showed the supervisor that she could get it by climbing on the bumper, he told her that climbing on the bumper was against the rules (Schroedel 1985:217).

Other personnel practices can deter women from seeking customarily male jobs as well. For example, white female clerical workers at a utility company were reluctant to transfer to better-paying plant jobs because the jobs involved rotating shifts: two weeks on the day shift, two weeks on the evening shift, and two weeks on the "graveyard" shift. This schedule made childcare arrangements impossible for most women (Padavic 1991). The company had designed the plant jobs with male workers in mind, assuming that male workers did not have to worry about childcare arrangements.[4]

In sum, by formulating job requirements and workplace rules on the assumption that men will hold some jobs and women will hold others, employers often make integration difficult to achieve. These employers do not necessarily intend to exclude women, but they have built gender into jobs. We will discuss this issue further in Chapter 7.

Regulation of employer behavior. Over the past 150 years, government actions often increased sex segregation. The so-called protective laws, which regulated how employers treated their workers (see Chapter 2), were meant to protect women and children (and less often men) from exploitative or dangerous working conditions. But they had the effect of reducing women's access to many jobs. By the middle of the nineteenth century, the British Parliament had barred employers from requiring women to work more than a fixed number of hours. These laws, common also in the United States, contributed to segregation. Other laws actually required employers to segregate specific lines of work by denying some jobs to women—such as practicing law, tending bar, delivering telegrams, and working as a streetcar conductors.

When employers challenged protective laws early in this century, the U.S. Supreme Court forbade states from restricting men's hours or working conditions, on the grounds that such laws interfered with employers' and workers' right to enter into contracts (*Lochner v. New York* 1905). But the Supreme Court allowed states to pass protective labor laws that ap-

---

[4]Although mothers are usually responsible for arranging childcare, thousands of couples manage childcare by working different shifts (Chira 1993). Fathers in such families could not have held plant jobs in this company either.

plied only to women. In the late nineteenth century, Myra Bradwell challenged an Illinois law that denied women the right to practice law. The Supreme Court upheld the Illinois law, writing,

> The natural and proper timidity and delicacy which belongs to the female sex evidently unfits it for many of the occupations of civil life. The constitution of the family organization which is founded in the divine ordinance, as well as in the nature of things, indicates the domestic sphere as that which properly belongs to the domain and functions of womanhood. The harmony of interests . . . which belong . . . to the family institution is repugnant to the idea of a woman adopting a distinct and independent career from that of her husband. (*Bradwell v. Illinois* 1873)

Laws that limited women's hours or working conditions restricted women's access to many factory jobs and other customarily male lines of work. Given a choice between male workers who could work 12-hour days and women who could work only 10 hours, employers chose men. Thus, the effect of early government's regulation of employer behavior was to encourage or even require women's segregation into different jobs from those men held.

Except during the two world wars, the U.S. government followed this protectionist—and hence segregationist—policy until 1964. That year Congress passed the Civil Rights Act, which includes a section (Title VII) outlawing job discrimination. Although the Civil Rights Act focuses on racial discrimination, Title VII explicitly forbids employers with more than 15 employees from discriminating on the basis of sex (as well as other characteristics) in hiring, promotion, job assignment, and other conditions of employment.

The Civil Rights Act created the Equal Employment Opportunities Commission (EEOC) to administer Title VII. Over the years, the EEOC has made important contributions to reducing segregation. Its cases against a few large employers have expanded all workers' legal right to jobs, irrespective of their sex or race. With some of these firms, it negotiated consent decrees that led the employers to restructure their personnel practices. However, the EEOC is part of the executive branch of the federal government, and so the enthusiasm with which the EEOC enforces the law has varied with presidential administrations. During the 1980s, the agency played a limited role in enforcing Title VII.

The Civil Rights Act is not the only weapon against discrimination that the federal government has provided. Between 1961 and 1973, Presidents Kennedy, Johnson, and Nixon issued a set of executive orders whose goal was to ban discrimination and eliminate the effects of past discrimination. These regulations required federal contractors (firms that did business with the federal government) to engage in **affirmative action**. Affirmative action means modifying employment practices to ensure that minorities and women (the "protected groups" to whom the regulations apply) have equal job access with white men. The executive orders direct contractors to set goals for integrating minorities and women into their workforce and to develop "results-oriented" mechanisms to achieve those goals. Such mechanisms include announcing job openings in places that will bring them to the attention of minorities and women. The federal code noted that

> procedures without efforts to make them work are meaningless; and efforts, undirected by specific and meaningful procedures, [are] inadequate. An effective affirmative action program must include an analysis of areas within which the contractor is deficient in the utilization of minority groups and women . . . at all levels and in all segments of its workforce where deficiencies exist. (U.S. General Services Administration 1990:121–2)

In singling out federal contractors, these presidents reasoned that since taxpayers are footing the bill for federal contracts, all taxpayers should have access to the jobs that result. Concrete procedures recommended to achieve this goal include replacing customary recruitment methods, such as referrals by current employees, with methods that can locate qualified persons from "protected groups" (for example, one utility company went to health clubs to recruit women for jobs as overhead lineworkers); training and promoting members of protected groups; and giving preference to qualified members of protected groups until they are fairly represented across all jobs. This last provision has been the most controversial. Among white men, support for affirmative action is low. Although some people recognize that affirmative action attempts to redress the effects of past discrimination, others view it as "reverse discrimination."

Whether or not employers obey a law depends on whether it is enforced. The enforcement of discrimination and affirmative action regulations has been hit or miss. When the administration has opposed affirmative action, enforcement agencies have lacked adequate staff and budgets. President Reagan's and President Bush's opposition to affirmative action brought enforcement activity to almost a standstill between 1980 and 1992. An example of the way that federal disinterest can impede women's progress occurred in California during this period. Despite an affirmative action plan that had been in effect for years, Diane Joyce was the first woman that the Santa Clara County Transportation

Department assigned to one of its 238 skilled crafts jobs; seven years later, only 13 women worked in one of the 412 skilled crafts jobs, and only 158 women held one of the 1,216 service and maintenance jobs. It took a court order to get the agency to set up a mechanics training program that would include women, and a year later only three women had been admitted to the program (Faludi 1988:26).

Other federal actions can rapidly reduce sex segregation when the need arises. The military offers an excellent example. As the number of male recruits has shrunk, the military has eliminated various exclusionary policies and looked with increasing favor on women. As a result, the number of women in the military service more than quadrupled between 1972 and 1992—from less than 45,000 to over 211,000 (U.S. Women's Bureau 1993:3).

Despite the government's ambivalence about enforcing discrimination and affirmative action laws, many employers have implemented affirmative action plans and modified their personnel practices on their own. In fact, the National Association of Manufacturers opposed a change proposed by President Reagan that would have gutted affirmative action rules. Many employers have discovered that an affirmative action plan is good business. It not only is a defense against discrimination suits, but it also helps employers recruit talented employees. Most employers who have incorporated affirmative action into their personnel practices see no reason to return to the old system.

It is impossible to determine exactly how much federal regulations have reduced segregation, but without doubt, federal regulations have expanded women's access to nontraditional jobs. Title VII of the 1964 Civil Rights Act required states to either get rid of laws that discriminated against women or extend the laws to men as well. The law also gave the victims of discrimination a legal remedy. Although some cases languish for years in court, the effects of a lawsuit against one firm often reverberate through an entire industry, putting other firms on notice. The existence of these laws and regulations also encourages women to apply for jobs that they might otherwise have thought were off limits. One beneficiary of the law recalled that in 1974, when employers had begun to talk about equal rights, she knew that people with federal contracts had to start hiring minorities. So she went to a sand and gravel company that had two federal contracts, and announced that she wanted to learn to drive a truck. The company hired and trained her. Other women who have mentioned the role of government pressure in their getting nontraditional jobs include a graduate of truck-driving school, who found a firm that "needed a woman on their list for their minority quota," and a painter, who said, "I got the job because I'm a woman. [My employer] had to meet their quota" (Schroedel 1985:145, 154). A third woman recalled that "to get a jump on the government, [the telephone] company went around and asked all the women if they wanted to do nontraditional jobs" (Schroedel 1985:217). In these cases and others, government regulation effectively changed employers' behavior.

Male Workers' Actions

Employers are not solely responsible for the sexual division of labor at work; male workers' actions also influence the amount of sex segregation in the workplace. As Chapter 3 explained, men have often resisted women's entry into customarily male jobs, just as white workers have resisted workers of color, American citizens have resisted immigrants, and insiders everywhere have resisted outsiders. In each case, workers believe that it is in their interest to curtail competition from other groups—especially groups that might work for lower pay. Observers speculate that men oppose women's entry into traditionally male jobs for other reasons as well: They fear that women's performance may make men look bad, that women may not do their share, that women may use their sex to get out of work, that men may have to clean up their language or change their behavior, and that women's very presence may diminish the prestige of their jobs or undermine the status men derive from doing "real men's" work (Astrachan 1986).

Interviews with people who worked at Philco in the 1930s illuminate men's hostility to women entering customarily male jobs. To save money, Philco assigned women to some all-male jobs and lowered the pay. A man who remained in one such job did everything he could to drive out a woman who had been transferred into it. As historian Patricia Cooper observed,

> Having a woman do his job challenged one of the implicit meanings of his being a man in the plant—having a different and better-paying job than a woman could hold. His own definition of masculinity in the context of work had been until now clarified by contrast to the definition of femininity and the associated jobs for women. The sudden disjuncture between his sex and job title created confusion and anger because he stood to lose what he saw as respectable male work. (1991:346)

Substantial evidence shows that male workers have resisted women's entry into traditionally male jobs through heckling, sabotage, and worse. In the past, many male unions and professional associations refused to admit women, but nowadays most resistance, which may be subtle and even unintentional, comes from informal work groups or just a few individuals. For instance, talk about sex in a predominantly male work setting can make women feel unwelcome, even though its goal may not be to drive women out. Gary Fine's study (1987) of restaurant workers illustrated the sexual joking that women encounter in mostly male settings. Fine concluded that women who wanted to join male-dominated groups had to "accept [these] patterns of male bonding" and learn to "decode" male behavior, including coarse joking and sex talk. In short, he said that women had to "become one of the boys" (p. 145).

Others disagree with Fine. A double standard permits sexual remarks from men but not from women. As researcher Cynthia Cockburn (1991:156) recognized, what is funny when it comes from a man may be viewed as obscene when it comes from a woman. A female sales trainee referred to this problem in deciding whether to accompany her mostly male sales team when they went out drinking: "You can't tell dirty jokes. Clean jokes would go over like a lead balloon. So I sit there like a dummy and don't tell jokes" (Kanter 1977:226).

Other aspects of men's work culture as well can make women uncomfortable. When a female rapid-transit conductor went to the crew room for a meal break during an 11-hour shift, she encountered several men she didn't know watching a rape scene in a *Death Wish* movie:

> I was so beside myself that I just walked over and changed the channel. One changed it back and someone said, "That's the best part. . . ." I went towards the television again, and someone . . . physically pushed me away from [it].
> I left my food, I couldn't keep eating. I started crying and walked out of the crew room. (Swerdlow 1989:379)

Some men do intentionally try to drive women out of male jobs. On a female maintenance worker's first day in a customarily male job, a male coworker told her that "he knew someone who would break your arm or leg for a price" (Faludi 1991:91). Fortunately, such men are the minority, except perhaps in occupations with a strong male subculture, such as police work, construction work, and mining. In fact, many men are neutral, and some are supportive. The rapid-transit worker whose crew mates watched *Death Wish* had coworkers who taught her the ropes (Swerdlow 1989:384). She was lucky, however. Female newcomers in heavily male jobs often run into problems with on-the-job training, because it requires their male coworkers' cooperation. Failing to help train female coworkers is a key way that men resist women's entry into customarily male jobs.

Too much help can also hinder women's success in predominantly male jobs. One way that dominant groups can control and exclude outsiders is through paternalism. An overly protective attitude toward women sets them apart and prevents them from learning their jobs and establishing their ability to succeed. As Mary Jackman (1994:11) argued, in practice, paternalism combines positive feelings toward a subordinate group with discriminatory intentions toward them. The paternalism of a union representative's opposition to female rapid-transit workers, because "it's just a matter of time before one of those animals out there takes advantage" of them (Swerdlow 1989:376), is identical in its effect to outright sex discrimination.

In sum, some male workers think they have a stake in excluding women from traditionally male jobs, and a few act on this belief. Others help to create an environment that feels uncomfortable to some women simply by behaving in ways that are normal in all-male settings. However, we suspect that a hostile environment is much less to blame for maintaining segregation than are the actions of employers and other gatekeepers. Still, male workers do play a role. A male worker passed along this warning to a woman whom Philco had transferred to a formerly all-male job: "Do you know that can explode and hit you in the face? That'll mutilate your face." The woman was alarmed, but she stayed in the job because she needed the money (Cooper 1991:347). Like men, women need well-paying jobs. Sometimes male colleagues make those jobs harder and actually drive some women out. But other women are likely to come along who want those jobs too (Jacobs 1989b).

Female Workers' Actions

The third group whose actions contribute to sex segregation is women. As Chapter 3 indicated, some theorists imply that sex segregation results from women's and men's choices of different occupations. It is easy to see why men might choose male-dominated lines of work and reject mostly female occupations: Predominantly male occupations provide higher pay and more opportunities than predominantly female occupations do. But why should women choose "female" jobs? The opinion of the judge who decided a discrimination case filed against Sears, Roebuck provides one answer. When the Equal Employment Opportunities Commission sued Sears for excluding women from high-paid commission-sales jobs, the judge concluded that women did not want to sell items on commission:

Women tend to be more interested than men in the social and cooperative aspects of the workplace. Women tend to see themselves as less competitive. They often view noncommission sales as more attractive than commission sales, because they can enter and leave the job more easily, and because there is more social contact and friendship, and less stress in noncommission selling. (*EEOC v. Sears, Roebuck, & Co.* 1988)

Chapter 3 summarized the two theories that underlie the judge's opinion: human-capital theory and gender-role socialization theory. We now examine each theory's ability to explain sex segregation.

Human-capital theory of sex segregation. Human-capital theorists assume that women's top priority is raising a family, which implies that they will limit their time in the labor force (see, for example, Polachek 1981). Starting from this premise, human-capital theorists conclude that women prefer occupations that are easy to reenter, because these occupations involve general skills that do not get rusty while women are at home raising their children; that women "invest" in less education, training, and experience than men do because they are less attached to the labor force, and therefore women are less qualified for customarily male jobs; and that women prefer jobs that do not demand much effort, so they can save their energy for their families. In short, the human-capital approach to segregation concludes that millions of women have chosen to be secretaries, cashiers, teachers, nurses, and waitresses because doing so is rational, given their family demands. Investing in the education, training, and experience they need for better-paying jobs as sales supervisors, truck drivers, managers, carpenters, and many other male-dominated occupations would be economically irrational.[5]

Given the sexual division of labor that makes women responsible for the domestic sphere, the idea that women give their family roles priority over their jobs is plausible. You saw in Chapter 2, however, that during this century married women have increasingly participated in the labor force. Their participation has increased both because employers need female workers and because paid employment offers economic security and the psychological satisfaction that family work cannot always provide. With the growing number of women who are the primary support

---

[5]Karen Nussbaum, founder of the clerical workers' union 9to5 and director of the U.S. Department of Labor's Women's Bureau, called this idea the "lemming theory" of sex segregation, in reference to the mouselike animals in Scandinavia that periodically march to the sea, where they inexplicably drown themselves.

of their families (see Chapter 8) and the unpredictable economy, economic security is indeed increasingly important to women. Even before these social and economic changes, however, a variety of studies cast doubt on the human-capital explanation for sex segregation. First, researchers have found that single women are as likely as married women to work in predominantly female occupations (Reskin and Hartmann 1986:71-2). In any event, even women who plan to leave the labor force to have children would earn more in customarily male jobs. Second, researchers have found that predominantly male and female occupations require similar levels of education and skills (England et al. 1982) and that most workers acquire the necessary skills on the job. Thus it is hard to argue that women's concentration in certain occupations represents their rational decision to maximize short-run earnings or minimize their investment in training.

In one respect, the human-capital explanation of sex segregation has strong support. Women's family responsibilities, which we will discuss in Chapter 8, can make it hard to pursue a full-time job. Some women have responded by seeking part-time jobs, and employers are more likely to provide part-time work in customarily female occupations—thereby contributing to women's and men's segregation into different jobs. Of course, many women who work part time actually would prefer full-time jobs. Furthermore, employers could structure both mostly female and mostly male jobs to be part time. Indeed, economic trends in the early 1990s led many employers to rely more on part-time workers of both sexes.

Human-capital theory remains vulnerable on a couple of other counts as well. As Chapter 3 showed, women exert as much effort on the job as men and, on average, are as committed as men to their jobs (Bielby and Bielby 1988; Marsden et al. 1993). Finally, the job characteristics of even female jobs are not especially compatible with women's family roles: Jobs in mostly female occupations are, on average, no more flexible, easy, or clean than heavily male occupations (Glass 1990:791; Jacobs and Steinberg 1990).

Socialization theory of sex segregation. Chapter 3 indicated that differences in the socialization of females and males could contribute to job segregation by encouraging them to pursue different occupations. Socialization could create a preference in each sex for different kinds of work or for working with members of one's own sex or could teach each sex only the skills needed in sex-typical occupations. Such socialization is ubiquitous. In the 1990 Christmas season, for example, Parker Brothers marketed a "career" game for 8- to 12-year-old girls that featured six career options: "supermom," school teacher, rock star, fashion designer, veterinarian, and college graduate. The media regale us with starkly different images of men and women, so it is easy to imagine how girls and boys might come to prefer different occupations.

Although gender-role socialization leads some young people to aspire to jobs that society labels as "appropriate" for their sex (Subich et al. 1989), such aspirations are highly unstable; in fact, young people's occupational aspirations are virtually unrelated to the occupations they actually hold as adults (Jacobs 1989b). Moreover, adults—especially women—move back and forth between mostly female and mostly male occupations (Jacobs 1989b). These results make us question how much gender-role socialization contributes to sex segregation in jobs. Far more influential than the messages we picked up 20 years earlier as children are the opportunities, rewards, and punishments we encounter as adults. The young women who began moving into traditionally male jobs in the 1970s and 1980s demonstrate this point. Most of these women were raised by parents who subscribed to traditional gender roles (dad at work, mom at home), and the messages these women received from the media—*Ozzie and Harriet, Leave It to Beaver,* and *The Flintstones*—reinforced this traditional socialization.

Opportunities and choices. Explanations of sex segregation that claim women freely choose traditionally female occupations are inconsistent with our knowledge of how workers get into jobs. No one would dream of suggesting that men or women of color choose the poorly paid jobs in which they are overrepresented or that poorly educated white men choose unskilled, dead-end jobs as laborers. We recognize that these people settle for the only jobs they can get. If traditionally female jobs do not enable women to easily combine work and family (and most do not) and if, as we have argued, gender-role socialization is not responsible for women's concentration in customarily female jobs, then why should women choose them? The answer, we contend, is that women—like men—choose among the best opportunities open to them. Women do make choices, but employers and society limit their choices to a narrower range of options than men have.

Several studies have suggested that women like the same job rewards as men: good pay, autonomy, and prestige (Jencks et al. 1988). According to a 1984 survey of Santa Clara County (California) employees, for example, 85 percent of the female clerical workers wanted skilled crafts jobs, which paid two to three times as much secretaries earned, but 90 percent said those jobs were closed to women (Faludi 1988:64). To the extent that women's and men's jobs reflect their preferences, these are preferences they formed in response to the opportunities that employers provide (Schultz 1991:141). When employers make customarily male jobs available to women, women usually flock to them. During World War I, for example, African-American women seized the chance to leave jobs as domestic workers to work in industry, where they helped to manufacture everything from munitions, gas masks, and airplane wings to tires and shoes. As railroad employees, they cleaned cars, repaired tracks, sorted salvage, and flagged trains (Jones 1985:166–7).

Most people do not apply for jobs unless they have reason to hope they will be hired. In 1972, no women applied to work in the mines of Kentucky's Peabody Coal Company, the nation's largest producer of coal. But in 1978 the word was out that Peabody was hiring women, and 1,131 women applied for mining jobs (Working Women 1981). Coal mining was just one of the customarily male occupations that hundreds of thousands of women entered in the 1980s. Given the opportunity, women took jobs as bartenders rather than cocktail waitresses, as pharmacists rather than drugstore clerks, as bank managers rather than bank tellers, and as insurance sales agents rather than receptionists (Reskin and Roos 1990). Why did African-American women take jobs in railroad yards and Kentucky women seek jobs mining coal? Because these jobs paid more and offered more freedom and self-respect than domestic work did. Most job seekers have only one or two job offers, and most take the first offer that meets their minimum acceptable pay level. In other words, both sexes settle for the best options that are open to them. But the best jobs that employers offer men are usually superior to the best jobs that employers offer women.

The point is that choice-based explanations for sex segregation are inadequate. Because the most privileged members of our society (white men from economically comfortable backgrounds) are able to choose their life's work, many are tempted to extrapolate to women's occupational outcomes. However, women's socialization-induced preferences or orientation to the family cannot explain their concentration in predominantly female occupations. Past research largely fails to support these theories' assumptions, and their logic seems less plausible as women spend more of their adult lives in the labor force and as women's earnings become increasingly essential for their families. We contend that women, like men, accept the best jobs that are open to them. When employers open traditionally male occupations to women, neither custom nor occupational **sex labels** deter women from accepting them.

Summary

The segregation of workers of different sexes and races into different and unequal jobs is, at the same time, both invisible because we are used to it and one of the most striking features of the workplace. Employers and workers tend to take for granted jobs' labels as male or female work. When we see that almost all auto mechanics are male and almost all kindergarten teachers are female, it is easy to conclude that there is something natural about this state of affairs—that some occupations are female because women are better at them than men are, and vice versa. However, the sex label of a job has little to do with the tasks it involves.

Although sex and other forms of segregation are an inefficient use of human resources and costly for women, people of color, and other groups, segregation persists both because it benefits those people for whom the better jobs are reserved and because employers' personnel practices tend to perpetuate the status quo. Nevertheless, during the 1970s and 1980s, social, legal, and economic forces led occupational sex segregation to decline for the first time in this century. Women whose mothers were teachers, typists, waitresses, and homemakers now work as veterinarians, sales managers, bus drivers, and physicians. Twenty years ago a popular riddle told of a boy who was badly injured in a car crash. His father rushed him to the hospital, where he was taken directly into the operating room. There the surgeon took one look at the boy and said, "I can't operate on him; he's my son." The riddle—who was the surgeon?—baffled people in the early 1970s, but no one tells this riddle in the 1990s. Its demise signals the entry of large numbers of women into medicine and other formerly all-male occupations.

Yet most women and men remain segregated into different occupations and jobs. For every female lawyer in 1990, 101 women still did clerical work, 33 women operated factory machines, 30 were sales clerks, 9 worked as nurses' aides, and 8 worked as waitresses. As the twentieth century draws to a close, segregation continues to separate working women and men into different and unequal jobs.

5

Sex Differences in Moving Up and Taking Charge

Men who enter traditionally female occupations often rise to the top, despite being outsiders in a mostly female environment. Women, on the other hand, typically remain in the lower echelons, whether their occupation is mostly female or mostly male. This hierarchical segregation is part of the larger pattern of sex segregation discussed in Chapter 4. Besides facing barriers in moving up, women workers also face difficulties that prevent them from exercising authority on the job. Problems in moving up and taking charge plague women in many kinds of occupations, from manager to secretary to warehouse worker.

Until 20 years ago, few employers even considered women for promotions that would take them outside the female clerical or assembly-line ghetto. Although more women have been promoted in recent years, women still have a long way to go. Now they may get some help from the legal system, however. For instance, the Supreme Court ruled in 1990 that Ann Hopkins should be promoted to partner status at the Big Six accounting firm of Price Waterhouse. The decision put other companies on notice that discriminating in promotions could be costly. Then in 1991 a jury awarded $6.3 million to a woman whom Texaco had twice passed over for promotion. On the legislative front, the Civil Rights Act of 1991 now allows employees to sue not merely for lost wages and litigation expenses but also for punitive damages. Similarly, the Glass Ceiling Act of 1991—designed to encourage employers to remove barriers to the progress of women and minorities—reflects increasing public concern with barriers to job mobility. But how effective this legislation will be remains to be seen.

As for access to authority, women have also made some strides. In 1940 many firms explicitly prohibited women from occupying managerial positions (Goldin 1990). By the 1970s, with women flooding the labor market and the number of managerial jobs expanding dramatically, unprecedented numbers of women were entering the ranks of management. Since then, American women have increased their representation in management ranks from 18 percent of all managers in 1970 to 30 percent in 1980 and 40 percent in 1990. These figures indisputably show that thousands of women are gaining access to jobs that usually confer organizational power. Whether women in these positions actually are able to act on the authority typical of managerial positions is a question we address in this chapter.

Women, Men, and Promotions

Television shows and movies offer a distorted image of women who have done well in the business and professional world. The successful woman is depicted as beautiful, white, and heterosexual. She has a spectacular wardrobe and plenty of money, and the people she works with take her seriously. She is sometimes ruthless in exerting her power. Few real women match this glamorous image.

The Promotion Gap

In the real world of work, just a handful of women reach the top of the corporate hierarchy. In 1990, only 19—or fewer than 0.5 percent—of the 4,012 highest-paid officers and directors in top companies were women (Fierman 1990). Within Fortune 500 companies, women and minorities held fewer than 5 percent of senior management posts (Fierman 1990), indicating snail-like progress from the early 1970s, when 1 to 3 percent of senior managers were women (Segal 1992).

A **glass ceiling** blocks the on-the-job mobility of women of all classes, as well as minorities of both sexes. Indeed, in some organizations the glass ceiling may be quite low; for many women of all races, the problem is the **sticky floor,** which keeps them trapped in low-wage, low-mobility jobs (Berheide 1992). Data from a study conducted in the early 1980s in Illinois found that the average man had 0.83 promotions and the average woman, 0.47 promotions (Spaeth 1989). National data for 1991 show a smaller but still significant promotion gap: 48 percent of men had been promoted by their current employer but only 34 percent of women (Reskin and Kalleberg 1993). Both these studies underestimate the promotion gap by failing to distinguish between small-step promotions (for example, clerk-typist 1 to clerk-typist 2) and larger ones (for example, sales representative to sales manager).

Historically, African-American women and men have fared worse in promotions than other groups have (Jones 1985).[1] In 1988, 72 percent of managers in companies employing more than 100 people were white men, 23 percent were white women, 3 percent were African-American men, and 2 percent were African-American women (Alexander 1993). Although some people believe that affirmative action programs give women of color an undue advantage over other groups, this is not the case (McGuire and Reskin 1993; Sokoloff 1992). Being a "twofer" (a term that personnel directors sometimes use for people who fill two Equal Employment Opportunity categories) may help some minority women get jobs, but it hurts them in promotions because it undermines their credibility. Many people assume that minorities—and especially minority women—are hired or promoted only to fill quotas. According to Ella Bell, an Organizational Behavior professor and consultant, "Being a twofer doesn't give you legitimization, doesn't give you a voice or power and doesn't move you up" (Alexander 1993).

Several studies have indicated that men do not confront blocked opportunities because of their sex; in fact, as one sociologist noted, men tend to "rise to the top like bubbles in wine bottles" (Grimm 1978). Christine Williams (1992) found that employers singled out male workers in traditionally female jobs—nurse, librarian, elementary school teacher, social worker, and the like—for an express ride to the top on a "glass escalator." Some of the men in Williams's study faced pressure to accept promotions, like the male children's librarian who received negative evaluations for not "shooting high enough."

The country's largest employer, the U.S. government, has a better record in promoting women and African Americans than private industry does. Historically, the government has been the only place outside the black community where African-American female managers, administrators, and professionals could find jobs in their fields (Higginbotham 1987). Even now, African-American women do better in government jobs than in private industry. In 1992 both black and white women were better represented in governor-appointed cabinet-level positions than in top jobs in private industry (Harlan 1992). In other nations as well, women

---

[1]A study in the late 1920s of a northern meat-packing plant found that African-American women were assigned to the worst departments—hog killing and beef casing—and had no access to the better jobs. They were denied promotion to jobs in the bacon room supposedly because the public did not want black hands to touch meat in the last stages of processing (Jones 1985:177)

tend to do better in the public sector than in the private sector (Antal and Izraeli 1993).

Even inside government, however, men have a substantial edge in access to top jobs. In this country, women accounted for 43.5 percent of the workforce in state and local governments but only 31.3 percent of high-level state and local government jobs (Harlan 1991). Minority women were 9.8 percent of jobholders but only 5.1 percent of top-level jobholders. Although women held half of all federal government jobs in 1992 and made up 86 percent of the government's clerical workers, they were only a quarter of supervisors and only a tenth of senior executives (U.S. Merit Systems Protection Board 1992). Minority women were fewer than 2 percent of senior executives and were promoted less often than white women with equivalent experience (U.S. Merit Systems Protection Board 1992).

What is striking about these disparities among government workers is that they exist 15 years after the 1978 Civil Service Reform Act. In fact, a government report declared that the 1980s had brought "a resurgence of discrimination" (U.S. Merit Systems Protection Board 1992). Ironically, senior-level women and minorities employed in the Department of Labor division that is charged with enforcing discrimination regulations recently filed a grievance, claiming that sex discrimination has prevented their advancement. Alluding to the glass ceiling, one worker told *The Wall Street Journal* (1992), "We need Windex and paper towels because we can't even see [it]!"

Although American women lag behind men in promotions, compared to women in most other countries, American women are doing relatively well. American women were four times more likely than French women to hold administrative and managerial jobs and six and a half times more likely to do so than British women (Crompton and Sanderson 1990:176). In no country, however, were women represented in top-level jobs on a par with their numbers in administrative and managerial positions (Farley 1993). In Denmark, women were 14.5 percent of administrators and managers in 1987 but only between 1 and 5 percent of top management; in Japan, women were 7.5 percent of administrators and managers but only 0.3 of a percent of top management in the private sector (Antal and Izraeli 1993:58; Steinhoff and Kazuko 1988). In all the countries for which information was available, women were vastly underrepresented in top-level jobs (Antal and Izraeli 1993).

Consequences of the Promotion Gap

Does it matter that women are locked out of the higher-level jobs? Yes. First of all, the practice is unfair. Americans of both sexes value promotions as a path to greater pay, authority, autonomy, and job satisfaction (Markham et al. 1987:227). And both sexes are ready to work hard for a promotion. In a recent survey of federal employees, 78 percent of the women and 74 percent of the men agreed that they were willing to devote whatever time was necessary in order to advance in their career (U.S. Merit Systems Protection Board 1992). Among minority women, 86 percent were willing to devote as much time as it takes (minority men's responses were not reported separately). Upward mobility is the heart of the American dream, and its denial to women reflects poorly on our society. A second reason to be concerned about the promotion gap is that it depresses women's wages. At a time when women's wages average only 70 percent of men's, this is a serious consideration. Third, promotion barriers reduce women's opportunities to exercise authority on the job (as we discuss later) and to have autonomy from close supervision. **Autonomy**—the freedom to design aspects of one's work, to decide the pace and hours of work, and to not have others exercising authority over oneself (M. Adler 1993)—enhances job satisfaction. A fourth consequence of women's blocked mobility is that it often leads women to quit in frustration.

Some women try to get around blocked mobility by starting their own business. In 1990 women owned 30 percent of all small businesses, and the Small Business Administration expects the number to rise to 40 percent by the year 2000 (Shellenbarger 1993). Yet women are less successful than men in these ventures; in 1982 the average business run by a woman grossed only 35 percent of what the average man-run businesses grossed (U.S. Small Business Administration 1988). A partial explanation is that women-run businesses are usually economically marginal. Many women business owners have the legal status of entrepreneur but are **independent contractors**: workers hired on a freelance basis to do work that regular employees otherwise would do in-house (Christensen 1989). Far fewer women own a business that employs others. The median hourly wage for a full-time, self-employed woman was $3.75 in 1987, compared to $8.08 for a full-time female employee (N. Collins 1993b). Often self-employed women provide services that help other employed women cope with domestic work, such as catering, housecleaning, caring for children, and being a "mother's helper."

Explanations for the Promotion Gap

Many factors impede women's mobility. Although women are as committed to their careers as men are, women have less of the education, experience, and training that employers desire. Women also tend to be located in jobs that do not offer the same diversity of experience or the same opportunities for upward mobility as men's jobs. Finally, in making promotion decisions, employers discriminate against women. These are the three basic explanations of why companies still promote more white men than women and minorities.

Human-capital inequities and promotion. Human-capital theorists claim that sex differences in promotion rates are due to sex differences in commitment, education, and experience. These differences are presumed to make women less productive than men.

The claim that men are more committed than women to their jobs is based on the idea that women place family responsibilities ahead of career commitment. According to this reasoning, family demands do not allow women to devote as much time to their careers as men, and therefore women are unable to do all the things necessary to get promoted rapidly. Although employers act on this stereotype of women's lesser commitment, it is not founded on reality. As we showed in Chapter 3, women's career commitment does not differ from men's.

The second human-capital claim is that educational differences account for the promotion gap. Indeed, in 1992, women earned 47 percent of the bachelor's degrees in business administration but only 34 percent of the master's degrees. Thus educational differences do contribute to the sex disparity in promotion rates. However, they do not account for all of the disparity. Women with the same educational credentials as men are not attaining top-management jobs at the same rate. When told that women will slowly make their way to the top as more get advanced degrees, one woman manager countered, "My generation came out of graduate school 15 or 20 years ago. The men are now in line to run major corporations. The women are not. Period" (Fierman 1990).

As for the third human-capital claim, women do receive less training and have less experience both within a firm and within the labor force. It is implausible, however, that women voluntarily acquire less experience. In many settings, employers prevent women from acquiring the essential experiences needed for advancement. For example, military promotion to the rank of commissioned officer is usually reserved for people with combat experience, but Congress and the military have banned women from combat positions. In banking, managers who hope for a top spot need extensive experience in commercial lending. But until recently, most women bank managers were not given the chance to work in commercial lending, so few women could acquire the expertise needed to rise beyond middle management. In the same way, the sex segregation of blue-collar production jobs denies women the experience they need to rise to management positions in manufacturing firms.

Similarly, in an increasingly global economy, some corporations are requiring international experience for future executives. However, women are far less likely than men to receive international assignments. According to *The Wall Street Journal*, international experience is increasingly crucial for advancement, and researchers agree (N. Adler 1984; Antal and Izraeli 1993). A human-resources vice president admitted, "No one will be in general management [in this company] by the end of the decade who didn't have international exposure and experience" (A. Bennett 1993). This trend will benefit white men more than women and minorities (Antal and Izraeli 1993). Many companies think twice before posting a woman or an African American to a foreign assignment, partly because they fear that sexist or racist attitudes will hinder their employee's ability to get the job done. Among industrial and service companies that regularly post employees to international assignments, 36 percent post men exclusively (Moran, Stahl & Boyer, Inc. 1988). Employers' fears are often unfounded, however: Most women posted to foreign assignments have succeeded in them, and their employers subsequently have made women a large proportion of the employees sent on international missions (N. Adler 1988). Those women will be in a better position than many others to advance in their careers.

Segregation and promotion. The segregation explanation of the promotion gap focuses on differences between men and women's organizational locations. A key concept in this explanation is the **internal labor market** or a firm's system for filling jobs by promoting experienced employees. Internal labor markets are composed of related jobs (or job families) connected by **job ladders**, which are promotion or transfer paths that connect lower- and higher-level jobs. These ladders may have only two rungs (as in a take-out restaurant that promotes counter workers to delivery persons), or they may span an entire organization. Job ladders also differ in shape. Some are shaped like a ladder—for example, a company's sales division whose job ladder includes one stock clerk, one sales trainee, one sales representative, one assistant sales manager, and one sales manager. When the vice president in this division retires, everyone moves up one step. In contrast, other job ladders are shaped like a pyramid, with many entry-level jobs feeding into smaller and smaller numbers of jobs at progressively higher levels of the organization, so many workers compete for relatively few jobs. The broader the base of the pyramid, the smaller a worker's odds of being promoted.

The basic idea behind the segregation explanation is that women are promoted less often than men partly because access to internal labor markets is gendered. Women workers are more likely than men to be in jobs with short job ladders or to be in dead-end jobs. This sort of sex segregation begins with entry-level jobs. Men, but not women, are more often placed in jobs with long job ladders and chances at top jobs.

Many traditionally female jobs, such as switchboard operator or teacher, do not have job ladders (Tomaskovic-Devey 1993b). Employers have often designed these sorts of jobs without job ladders because they were not interested in reducing turnover and in fact wanted to encourage turnover in order to keep wages low. (Job ladders discourage turnover by giving workers an incentive to stay.) Women in traditionally male occupations are also more likely than men to have dead-end jobs. Women faculty in law schools, for example, disproportionately work as clinical instructors or instructors of research and writing, where they teach professional skills; these jobs usually are not on the tenure ladder (Reskin and Merritt 1993).

For workers who are on job ladders, men tend to be found on longer ladders that reach higher in the organization. In contrast, women and minorities are concentrated on short ladders, with just one or two rungs above the entry level. Clerical work, for example, is usually part of a two-rung system. A typical word-processing office, for instance, consists of many word-processing workers and one supervisor; a travel agency employs many reservation agents and one supervisor (Gutek 1988:231).

An illustration of how internal labor markets can affect promotion comes from a grocery chain whose female employees sued for discrimination because it had promoted almost no women or minorities to store manager. A diagram of this chain's internal labor market (Figure 5.1) shows that women's underrepresentation in the top jobs stemmed largely from sex segregation of lower-level jobs. Job ladders in the predominantly male produce departments led to top management. In contrast, the most heavily female departments—bakery/deli and general merchandise—were on short job ladders not directly connected to the ladder to top management.

FIGURE 5.1

Internal Labor Market for Grocery Store Chain, 1981 to 1984

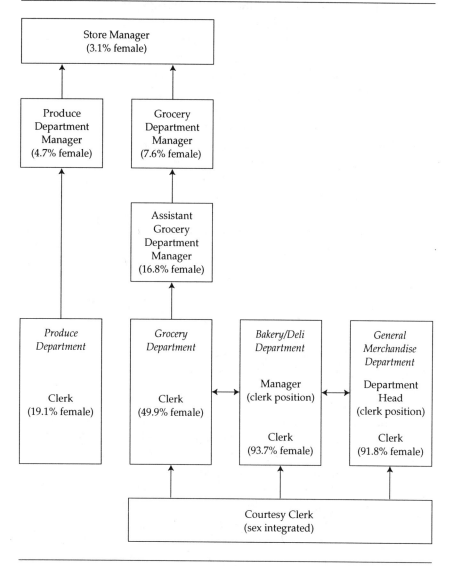

Source: Unpublished data from *Marshall et al. v. Alpha Beta.*

The different kinds of establishments that employ women and men explain much of the promotion gap. Large organizations are more likely to have the resources that allow them to create promotion ladders. Moreover, their sheer size lets them create more opportunities to promote deserving workers (Spaeth 1989). Therefore, women's greater concentration in small, entrepreneurial firms and nonprofit organizations and men's concentration in large corporations and for-profit companies also reduce women's odds of promotion relative to men. In one survey, corporations employed 47 percent of a random sample of men, compared to 34 percent of women (Reskin and Kalleberg 1993).

Segregation also contributes to the promotion gap by making women's accomplishments invisible. In prestigious Wall Street law firms, for example, senior partners have tended to assign women lawyers to research rather than litigation. Appearing in the courtroom less often than their male peers made women less visible, thus hampering their promotion to partner (Epstein 1993). In corporations, women mangers are concentrated in staff positions, such as personnel or public relations, and men are concentrated in the more visible and important line positions, such as sales or production. Staff positions involve little risk and therefore provide few opportunities for workers to show senior management their full capabilities. When top executives are looking for people to promote to senior management, they seldom pick vice presidents of personnel management or public relations. They usually pick vice presidents in product management or sales, who more often than not are male.

Discrimination and promotion. Sex discrimination by employers is a third explanation for the promotion gap. In brief, it recognizes that employers reward men's qualifications more than women's. The case of Ann Hopkins, mentioned earlier, illustrates blatant discrimination. Despite having brought more money into Price Waterhouse than any other contender for promotion had done, Hopkins was denied promotion to partner. According to the court that ruled in her favor, the senior partners based their evaluation on her personality and appearance and ignored her accomplishments. Her male mentor had advised Hopkins that her chances of promotion would improve if she would "walk more femininely, talk more femininely, wear makeup, have [her] hair styled, and wear jewelry" (White 1992:192).

Actually, appearing feminine does not help a woman get a promotion. In fact, the mere fact of being a woman may be an insurmountable barrier. A male personnel officer told a female bank manager that her career had stalled because what the chairman and presidents want are people that they are comfortable with, and they are not . . . comfortable with women. It doesn't even get to the . . . level of you as an individual and [your] personality; *it is the skirt that's the problem.* (Reskin and Roos 1990:156)

Top-level management is a male environment, and some men feel uncomfortable with women. The result is discrimination. The Federal Bureau of Investigation (FBI), for example, refused to even hire women as agents until the death of Director J. Edgar Hoover in 1972 (Johnston 1993). The lingering effect of this discrimination is that the highest-ranking woman is the agent in charge of the FBI's smallest field office, in Anchorage, Alaska.

Statistical discrimination comes into play as well. Employers statistically discriminate against women when they stereotype them as disinterested in advancement or as lacking the attributes needed in higher-level jobs. According to Rosabeth Moss Kanter (1977), when managers are uncertain about the qualifications necessary to do a job, they prefer to promote people who have social characteristics like their own. Kanter called this practice **homosocial reproduction**. Presumably managers believe that similar people are likely to make the same decisions they would. Thus they seek to advance others who are the same sex, race, social class, and religion; who belong to the same clubs; who attended the same colleges; and who enjoy the same leisure activities. Homosocial reproduction is especially likely in risky ventures, like launching a new TV series. Denise Bielby and William Bielby (1992a) argued that, because most studio and network executives are male, they view male writers and producers as "safer" than women with equally strong qualifications and are more likely to give men rather than women long-term deals and commitments for multiple series. The fear that someone who seems different—a woman, perhaps, or a Hispanic—will conform to executives' negative stereotypes results in a cadre of top managers who look alike and think alike.

Women, Men, and Authority

In addition to getting promoted less often than men, women are allowed to exercise less authority. Exercising **authority** means, broadly, having power: the capacity to mobilize people, to get their cooperation, to secure the resources to do the job (Kanter 1983). A person with job authority is someone who sets policy or makes decisions about organizational goals, budgets, production, and subordinates (for example, about hiring, firing, and pay).

Women's lack of authority in the workplace appears in two guises. First, women usually do not occupy the kinds of positions that offer opportunities to exert power. Second, when they are in such positions, they are not usually given as much power as men are. These barriers affect women at all levels, including managers, professionals, and blue-collar workers.

Women's Blocked Access to Jobs with Authority

One of the consequences of employers' failure to promote female workers is women's poor representation in the jobs that usually confer authority—generally, the top-level, decision-making positions. In the field of law, for example, in 1990 slightly more than one in 3 associates in large firms were women, but only one in 11 was a partner (Epstein 1993), and partners make the firm's important decisions. At the pinnacle of the legal profession—and certainly at the height of decision-making power—are federal judges, less than 10 percent of whom were women in 1993 (Administrative Office of the U.S. Courts 1994). Other professions generally show the same pattern. In 1993 women made up only 4 percent of the PhDs in upper management at AT&T/Bell Labs; at Dupont, none of the nine vice presidents of research and development were women, and only three out of 40 to 50 laboratory technology directors were (Benditt 1993).

The pattern is similar in the female-dominated professions that are called the semiprofessions. The majority of nurses, teachers, librarians and social workers are women. However, women are underrepresented as nursing administrators, school principals, head librarians, and social work administrators.

Female blue-collar workers face similar impediments. In a study of 10 utility companies, women craftworkers said that it was unrealistic for them to expect to advance to supervisory positions because it was hard enough for men to accept women as coworkers, much less to tolerate them as supervisors (Meyer and Lee 1978:52). Some of their managers agreed: They refused to promote women because they worried about women supervising men (Meyer and Lee 1978:86).

Some industries are better than others in promoting women to positions that confer authority. In industries that are mostly female—for example, apparel, banking, retail trade, and insurance—women are more likely to be found in higher-level occupations (Shaeffer and Lynton 1979). For example, in 1990 only 2.2 percent of officers in the chemicals industry were women, but 10 percent of officers in the apparel industry were. Although in the late 1980s only 5 percent of the directors in the electronics industry were women, almost 17 percent of the directors in the cosmetics and soap industry were (Von Glinow 1988). In a study of the United States, Canada, Norway, and Sweden, Wallace Clement and John Myles (1994) found that women had far greater access to positions of authority in service industries than in industrial ones.[2] Why do women in female-dominated industries have greater access to jobs that confer authority? Perhaps the companies' greater experience with female workers makes them less likely to stereotype women and better able to spot talented individuals. Furthermore, jobs in female-intensive industries pay less and are thus less desirable to men. Because of the small pool of male competitors, women get more opportunities to exercise authority than they would in male-dominated industries.

Women's Blocked Attempts to Exercise Authority

Women who achieve jobs that typically involve decision-making power cannot always exercise the same level of authority that men can. Women are often denied the use of this power. Employers often give women less authority than they give men with similar qualifications. A national study found that, if employers had rewarded other workers' credentials the same as they rewarded white men's, the authority gap between white men and others would shrink by 62 percent for white women, 71 percent for black women, and 93 percent for black men (McGuire and Reskin 1993).

Government pressure for affirmative action has induced employers to put more women and minority men in jobs with managerial titles, sometimes helping them to break through the glass ceiling. But affirmative action has also led to other kinds of ghettoization: giving women titles without authority. The growing numbers of women who have the title of manager are concentrated lower in chains of command than men are and tend not to supervise men (Reskin and Ross 1992). A study of decision making among a cross section of workers found that women managers participated in decision making by gathering information and making recommendations but that men usually made the final decisions (Reskin and Ross 1992). Men more often had the authority to make decisions

---

[2]Compared to women in United States and Canada, Norwegian and Swedish women were less likely to hold jobs involving authority (Clement and Myles 1994). The high level of part-time employment among the Nordic women explains this difference. Although part-time work helps women to combine paid and domestic work, it reduces their chance to obtain jobs that involve authority.

about bread-and-butter issues like hiring, firing, promoting, and giving raises and were more likely to have had a say in decisions that affected other units. The large number of relatively powerless female managers has led some researchers to question whether women's increasing representation in managerial occupations represents genuine progress or is what Jerry Jacobs (1992) termed the "glorified secretary" phenomenon, in which employers bestow managerial titles on women but not the responsibilities and authority that usually accompany the titles.

Differences between people of color and whites parallel those between women and men. Research based on a 1980 national sample demonstrated that African Americans had little authority because superiors rewarded their credentials at a lower rate than white men's; employers were also more likely to place African Americans in the less important divisions of a company (McGuire and Reskin 1993). Regardless of their area of expertise, African Americans are often relegated to positions that serve African-American customers and employees, such as community relations or affirmative action (Collins 1989:329; Collins 1993). An African-American engineer with years of experience before his "promotion" into a job involving affirmative action noted,

> When they would send me to some of these conferences about affirmative action . . . you'd walk in and there would be a room full of blacks. . . . It was a terrible misuse at that time of some black talent. There were some black people in those jobs that were rather skilled, much like myself. (Collins 1989:329)

Coworkers and customers may also actively deny women the chance to exercise authority. Women in traditionally male blue-collar jobs, for example, encounter problems in exercising authority even when their job explicitly confers it. For example, an African-American woman in a supervisory position at a power plant described her male subordinates' difficulties in adjusting to her telling them what to do:

> They didn't really rebel. If I told them something they would turn around and mumble. Or they would say "you shouldn't be telling us that" or "you should do it this way." It didn't really get out of hand; there was just a lot of animosity. (Padavic 1987)

In the airline industry, a male flight attendant said he would not obey a female superior's orders unless she asked nicely (Hochschild 1983:179). And passengers who do not obey a female flight attendant will often obey a male. One passenger refused to give up his oversize luggage to a female attendant but willingly turned it over to a male flight attendant (Hochschild 1983:178).

The authority gap is hardly unique to the United States. Canadian researchers found that women there are equally likely to report to a male or a female supervisor but that men are almost never directly subordinate to a woman (Boyd et al. 1991). In the whole Canadian economy, only 7 percent of employed men are under the direct authority of a woman. The researchers concluded that an invisible law forbidding women from supervising men exists in the Canadian workforce. This invisible law also operates in cultures around the world.

Consequences of the Authority Gap

Having authority on the job has four main consequences. First, workers value authority in its own right; indeed, having authority increases workers' job satisfaction. Second, authority is essential for managers and many professionals to do their jobs effectively. The kind of boss that workers like and work hard for is the one who has the power to reward them with raises and promotions for doing a good job (Kanter 1977). Third, a position of authority provides visibility and permits jobholders to display their talent to best advantage; exercising authority may raise one's odds of promotion. If the job is to edit the company newsletter or write affirmative action reports, then no matter how smart, hardworking, or carefully dressed a worker is, the work will not be noticed by the people with real clout. Finally, as we will show in Chapter 7, a lack of authority can leave workers vulnerable to sexual harassment.

Explanations for the Authority Gap

As with the promotion gap, the authority gap has three explanations: human-capital inequities, segregation, and cultural bias.

Human-capital inequities and authority. One explanation of why women have less access to authority than men do is the human-capital one. According to this explanation, women have not yet acquired the experience and education that will allow them to rise to positions in which they can exercise authority. Over time, they will gain authority as their numbers expand and as some of the women currently in the pipeline advance to top positions.

Although this reasoning sounds logical, it is flawed. Women have not advanced into authority-conferring jobs in proportion to their presence in the lower ranks. Women were 15 percent of all managers in 1968, so they should be 15 percent of senior managers today (Morrison et al.

1987). Instead, in 1990 they were only 3 percent of senior managers. According to the Women's Research and Education Institute, if women's rate of progress proceeds at the present pace, women will not achieve equitable representation and pay at all management levels for another 75 to 100 years (Beller 1984).

Segregation and authority. Sex segregation produces an authority gap because women are less likely than men to hold positions that confer authority. Women managers, as we noted earlier, tend to be concentrated in such departments as personnel and public relations, which involve little authority. Women may rise to the top of the public relations division but still be unable to make decisions important to their organization.

Cultural bias and authority. Most cultures share the social value, often rooted in religious beliefs, that women should not exercise authority over men. The New Testament of the Bible contains these lines: "Let a woman learn in silence with all subjection. But I suffer not a woman to teach, nor to usurp authority over the man, but to be in silence: (1 Timothy 2:11–2). In 1558 Scottish religious reformer and historian John Knox expressed much the same view: "The same [God] that hath denied power to the hand to speake, to the bely to heare, and to the feet to see, hath denied to women power to commande man" (Starr 1991:186). Nor is Western culture the only one to have a bias against women exercising authority over men. According to a Japanese proverb, "For a woman to rule is as for a hen to crow in the mornings."

The belief that women should not have authority over men is embedded in employers' personnel practices. According to Barbara Bergmann (1986:114–6), many employers adhere to an informal segregation code that keeps women from supervising men and that reserves the training slots leading to higher-level jobs for men. Men rule over women and junior men, women rule over women, but women rarely if ever rule over men. This code applies to minorities as well: Minorities may give orders to one another but not to members of the dominant group.

Bergmann (1986:114–6) dubbed this set of principles the **segregation code**. In many lines of work, coworkers often help enforce the code. Many men resent women who are promoted above them, and they often make their resentment known. According to one male corporate manager. "It's okay for women to have these jobs, as long as they don't go zooming by *me*" (Kanter 1977:218). A woman pipefitter recalled how,

> when I first made [pipe]fitter, the helpers were really pissed and angry that they were going to have to work with me. There was a lot of talk about

having to work for a woman, take orders from a woman. Some of them came right out in saying I didn't know what I was doing. . . . One man [was] marching around telling everybody that he was . . . too important to have to work for a woman. (Schroedel 1985:23)

Similarly, male bus drivers found it difficult to take a female supervisor seriously. According to the female supervisor,

It was a blow to their ego to have a woman tell them what to do. . . . Some would not respond at all, and there was no way you could make them do it. . . . A lot of the drivers tell me now that they're glad I'm not in [supervision] any more. They couldn't handle a woman telling 'em what to do on the road. (Schroedel 1985:209–211)

Waitresses, too, experience limits to their authority on the jobs. Although it is in the nature of the waitress-cook relationship that waitresses give orders to cooks, the fact that most waitresses are women and many cooks are men has led to the use of a spindle and wheel for posting orders. By putting written orders on one of these devices, women are not directly telling men what to do (Whyte 1948).

The sex stereotypes of women as irrational and as primarily sexual rather than intellectual support the norm that women should not supervise men. These stereotypes imply that women are ill suited to positions that require making important decisions. With great irony, a Hispanic woman listed the negative ethnic and gender stereotypes that disqualified her from promotion: "That we like to be pregnant. We don't like to take birth control. We're 'manana' [tomorrow] oriented. We're easy. We're all overweight, and I guess we're hot [she laughed] and submissive" (Segura 1992:173). Stereotypes like these seriously undermine women's authority on the job, as well as their chances for advancement. As one woman said, "Let's face it, how is an employer going to think a woman is manager material if he thinks her maternal instincts have primacy over business priorities?" (Kleiman 1993b). Such deep-seated cultural stereotypes allow the segregation code to remain.

Remedies for the Promotion and Authority Gaps

The social forces that maintain sex differences in opportunities to move up and take charge are resistant to change. Yet employers can help increase women's access to promotion and authority in many ways. To improve advancement opportunities for clerical and service workers, for example, companies could create "bridge" positions that help workers to switch job ladders—for example, move from a clerical ladder to an administrative one—without penalty (Kanter 1976). Some large companies have already made such changes, usually in response to court decrees that they promote more women. USX (formerly U.S. Steel) changed its rules so that women in traditionally female jobs could transfer to more promising steelworker jobs without losing their seniority (Ullman and Deaux 1981). The plan was highly successful: In just four years, the number of women in production and maintenance jobs in two steel mills increased threefold (Reskin and Hartmann 1986:93). AT&T's modifications of its promotion and training policies brought similar results. In the early 1970s, the Equal Employment Opportunities Commission required the company to improve its record of promotions for minorities and women. The nondiscriminatory promotion policies that the company instituted yielded a 300 percent increase in the number of women in middle- and upper-management positions (Northrup and Larson 1979).

Another way that organizations can shrink the promotion and authority gaps is by replacing informal promotion practices with formal ones. In the absence of formal criteria for personnel decisions, managers' biases are more likely to come into play (Roos and Reskin 1984). Lucky Grocery Stores, for example, did not formally post announcements of promotion opportunities because male store managers thought they knew which employees were interested in promotion. The result was that few women were promoted, prompting a successful lawsuit by women who had been passed up (*Stender et al. v. Lucky* 1992). In general, formal recruitment methods and promotion procedures—such as job advertisements, objective hiring criteria, and open transfer policies—help ensure women's access to jobs that bring authority (Szafran 1982; Roos and Reskin 1984).

Raising the price that employers pay to discriminate would help eliminate several of the obstacles described in this chapter. Despite the wastefulness of excluding potentially productive people from top jobs on the basis of their sex and color, employers have done just that. Organizations have multiple goals, and they act on the ones that have the highest priority. Making a profit is usually the highest goal, so higher fines and other financial sanctions could raise equal opportunity on the agenda of priorities.

Another avenue that women and minorities can follow to increase their promotion opportunities is to pursue additional litigation and legislation, as we described in Chapter 4. However, powerful remedies are necessary in the wake of the Reagan and Bush administrations, which severely undermined laws intended to protect women and minorities from discriminatory practices in the workplace. In addition, anti–affirmative action decisions of the Supreme Court have now trickled down into lower courts, slowing the pace of change (White 1992:201). Still, the courts and the legislature have provided some help in recent years. For example, a 1991 court case led Marriott Corporation to pay $3 million to women managers who had been denied promotions. At fault was the company's informal promotion policy and a work culture that "froze women out" (Goozner 1991). A legislative example is the Glass Ceiling Division within the U.S. Department of Labor, established by Congress in 1991, which is supposed to eliminate the barriers to women's and minorities' promotion to top posts. Although the division has little enforcement power, it works with the Office of Federal Contract Compliance, which has the rarely used power to debar discriminating companies from receiving government contracts. It is too soon to tell if enforcement agencies will actively enforce the Glass Ceiling Act. Much depends on the political process that allocates budget resources and penalties. In addition, the 1992 Civil Rights Act, which allows for punitive damages, may also help increase promotion opportunities for excluded groups.

These are potentially powerful weapons because they impose a cost on employers. However, their ability to close the promotion and authority gaps still depends on two things: the willingness of aggrieved parties to press for change and the willingness of enforcement agencies to enforce.

Summary

In the past 20 years, women have made progress in closing the promotion and authority gaps, but they still have a long way to go. Will the outlook be better for the college students of today? We don't know. History shows that women's job options do not improve automatically. They improved during the 1970s through the efforts of federal agencies enforcing new laws, advocacy groups, and companies voluntarily establishing Equal Employment Opportunity programs (Reskin and Hartmann 1986:97). Further progress depends on similar efforts in the 1990s and beyond.

Sex Differences in Earnings

From the earliest records of paid work, which date from the fourteenth century, employers have paid men more than women. Nowadays, this disparity in earnings is accompanied by similar disparities in fringe benefits, pensions, and Social Security payments. Sex differences in earnings occur in virtually every occupation and in every country throughout the world. This chapter examines the trends in earnings disparities, their causes, and ways to reduce these sex differences.

The Cost of Being Female

The disparity in earnings between men and women is called the **pay gap**; it is calculated by dividing women's earnings by men's to yield a percentage, also known as an earnings ratio. Tax records provide the earliest documentation of a disparity between women and men. Paris tax records for the year 1313, for example, show a disparity in the sexes' taxable wealth that is remarkably similar to the pay gap in twentieth-century America: Among 4,495 Parisian taxpayers, women's wealth was 65.6 percent of men's (Herlihy 1990:149).[1] The gap was largest among workers in the most lucrative occupations—goldsmiths and tavern keepers—where men possessed more than three times the wealth of women. Among launderers and dressmakers, women had 90 percent as much wealth as men, because all workers in these occupations had next to nothing.

The pay gap did not disappear with the spread of industrialization. Statistics collected by the British Factory Commission in 1833 on how much textile factories paid male and female workers revealed that, among the youngest workers (under the age of 16), girls slightly outearned boys. Girls below age 11 earned a halfpence a week more than boys, and girls from 11 to 16 received two pence a week more than boys

---

[1]Most of the wealth on which fourteenth-century Parisians were taxed was acquired through the work they did.

did. But after reaching age 16, males had a decided advantage. Employers paid 16- to 20-year-old women 70 percent of what they paid young men. Within six months of turning 16, boys would have made up for all those extra halfpennies and pennies that younger girls had received. The pay gap widened as workers grew older (as is true 260 years later): Among adult workers, employers paid women less than half what men took home. In some cases, women averaged only one-third to one-fourth of what adult men earned (Pinchbeck 1930:193–4). In 1909 Britain passed a minimum-wage law, but the law set a lower minimum wage for women than for men (Westover 1986:60). Thus the historical precedent for paying women less than men is well established.

The Pay Gap in the United States

In the early years of industrialization in the United States, employers exacted a large wage penalty from female workers. According to economic historian Claudia Goldin (1990), early in the nineteenth century, women working full time in agricultural and manufacturing industries earned between 29 and 37 cents for every dollar a man earned. Men's wages were not particularly high, and women could not possibly support themselves on a fraction of men's pay. In the 1860s, one woman came up with an effective but unusual solution:

> I was almost at the end of my rope. I had no money and a woman's wages were not enough to keep me alive. I looked around and saw men getting more money, and more work, and more money for the same kind of work. I decided to become a man. It was simple. I just put on men's clothing and applied for a man's job. I got good money for those times, so I stuck to it. (Matthaei 1982:192)

The pay gap narrowed by mid-century, partly because the increased use of machinery reduced the importance of strength. By 1885 manufacturers paid women about half what they paid men[2] (Goldin 1990:table 3.1). Nonetheless, in 1915 a New York State commission found that most women in certain industries, but only a minority of men, took home poverty-level pay (Tentler 1979:195).

In many clerical and professional occupations, the pay gap narrowed between 1890 and 1930. Contributing to the decline in pay inequality were women's increasing education and the growth of white-collar jobs (Goldin 1990).

---

[2]However, the pay gap in manufacturing has scarcely budged since then (Goldin 1990).

FIGURE 6.1

Women's Median Earnings as a Percentage of Men's Earnings, Among Full-Time Workers, 1955 to 1992

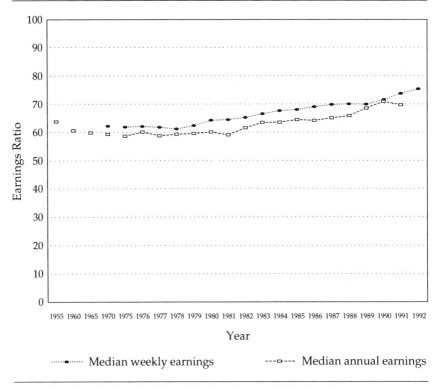

Year

⋯⋯•⋯⋯ Median weekly earnings   ⋯⋯▫⋯⋯ Median annual earnings

Source: Data from Institute for Women's Policy Research 1993b:table 1.

For the 50 years between 1930 and 1980, women's median yearly earnings fluctuated between 55 and 64 percent of men's earnings.[3] As Figure 6.1 shows, not until 1986 did women's annual earnings, as a share of men's, surpass the 1955 level of 63.9 percent. Between 1930 and 1980, jobs were almost always exclusively male or female, so the pay gap was due to higher wages for men's jobs than women's jobs. Over the next 20 years, the pay gap among workers employed full time, year-round widened. In 1965 it was 59.9 percent, and in 1975 the pay gap reached its peak for the previous half century: 58.8 percent.

[3]These statistics exclude the self-employed, among whom the pay gap is substantially larger (N. Collins 1993b:4).

By 1990 the pay gap had narrowed to 71.1 percent. But it widened slightly—to 69.9 percent—in 1991 (Institute for Women's Policy Research 1993b).[4] Thus, for every $10,000 that employers paid the average man in 1991, they paid the average woman only $6,990. To put it another way, for every $10,000 the average woman earned, her male counterpart received $14,306. The narrowing of the pay gap in the 1980s resulted from several factors we discuss later in this chapter. It narrowed partly because women have been catching up with men in their experience and the kinds of jobs they do and partly because men's real earnings have dropped over the last 20 years.[5]

Most women work to support themselves and their families. High divorce rates; low child-support payments, and over 10 million women raising children on their own make the pay gap a significant problem. The pay gap also puts more women than men at risk of poverty.

Race, ethnicity, and the pay gap. So far we have compared all employed women in the United States with all employed men. But people's color, as well as their sex, affects their pay. When employers began paying African Americans for their work in the nineteenth century, they paid them substantially less than they paid whites. Black women, who earned less than half of what white women made, suffered discrimination based on both their race and their sex (Kessler-Harris 1990:16). Significant discrepancies persisted until 1950 (Jones 1985:261), when the gap began to narrow.

A pay gap remains, however, as you can see in Figure 6.2.[6] Hispanic women who worked full time, year-round in 1992 earned only 78 percent of what white women earned, and African-American women earned only 87 percent. Black men who worked full time at least 50 weeks a year in 1991 earned less than three-quarters of what white men averaged, a difference of almost $8,000; Hispanic men earned less than two-thirds as much as white men, a difference of almost $10,000. All women earned less than men of their own race and ethnicity, and all earned less than

---

[4]As we show later, some of this gap stems from men's working slightly more hours per week and more weeks per year than women. In 1991, women's median weekly earnings were 74.0 percent of men's—$368 for women and $497 for men (U.S. Bureau of Labor Statistics 1993c:table 5).

[5]Only men with at least six years of college did not experience losses in hourly pay between 1979 and 1991 (McNeil 1992).

[6]The statistics for whites and African Americans include people of Hispanic origin; the U.S. Census Bureau classifies as "Hispanics" people of any race who report a Hispanic origin.

FIGURE 6.2

Pay Gap in Median Annual Earnings of Full-Time, Year-Round Workers, by Sex, Race, and Ethnic Origin, 1991

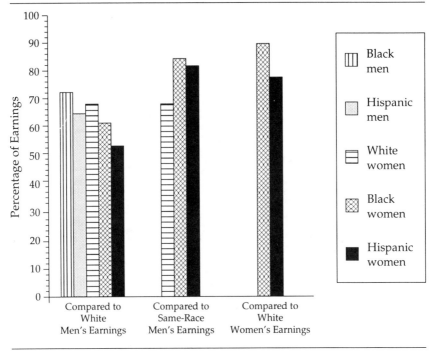

Source: Data from U.S. Bureau of the Census 1992b.

white men.[7] In short, African-American and Hispanic women lost pay because of both their sex and their race or ethnicity. Hispanic women were the biggest losers relative to white men: Employers paid them $15,756 in 1992, compared to white men's $29,936.

Trends since 1975, summarized in Figure 6.3, indicate that women have been slowly closing the pay gap with white men, but that African-American and Hispanic men have been losing ground relative to white men. One cause of both trends is change in the American economy. Since

---

[7]We could not obtain comparable data for Asian Americans. However, among full-time, year-round Asian and Pacific Islander workers who were over 25 years old, women earned 78.2 percent of men's median earnings (Bennett 1992:table 5). We also know that women of Chinese, Japanese, and Filipino origin average higher earnings than women with European roots.

FIGURE 6.3

Median Incomes of Full-Time, Year-Round Workers as a Percentage of White Men's Incomes, by Sex, Race, and Ethnic Origin, 1955 to 1990

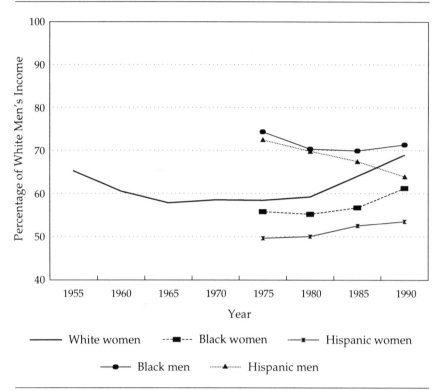

Source: Data from U.S. Bureau of the Census 1981:table 67; U.S. Bureau of the Census 1983:tables 37 and 39; U.S. Bureau of the Census 1988:tables 27 and 29; U.S. Bureau of the Census 1991:table 24.

the early 1970s, the United States has been losing well-paying production jobs, as in the automobile industry, and the lower-paying service sector has been growing. The loss of manufacturing jobs has reduced men's average earnings, and the effect has been most severe for men of color. In contrast, women's segregation in low-paying service jobs has insulated them from the big drops in pay that men experienced when they lost manufacturing jobs. As a result, between 1979 and 1992 women's median hourly wage rose 31 cents, to $8.42 per hour; men's median hourly wage fell by $1.84, to $11.03 per hour (Rigdon 1993:B1). The narrowing of the hourly pay gap resulted 14 percent from women's slowly rising pay and 86 percent from men's dropping earnings.

The pay gap over the life span. The pay pattern for female and male British textile workers in 1833, described earlier, still holds true: The younger workers are, the more equal is women's and men's pay. In 1991 the weekly earnings of 16- to 24-year-old women were over 90 percent of the earnings of 16- to 24-year-old men (U.S. Bureau of Labor Statistics 1992c:table1). Employers paid the average 25- to 34-year-old woman who worked full time only about 80 percent of what they paid her male counterpart (Institute for Women's Policy Research 1993b:table 4). Compared to the overall pay gap of 69.9 percent, 80 percent may sound pretty good. But in dollars, the average young woman employed in 1991 full time, all year lost $5,302 because of her sex. For older workers, the pay gap was much wider. Women between 35 and 44 averaged 68.4 percent of the pay that men their age earned, and those over 44 made about 61.2 percent of the pay that men their age earned (Institute for Women's Policy Research 1993a:table 4).

Two factors explain the bigger pay gap among older workers. First, men's earnings tend to increase as they age, at least until they are into their 50s. Women's earnings rise more slowly and drop off when women reach their late 30s or early 40s (Institute for Women's Policy Research 1993b). Until these long-standing trends disappear, the earnings of young women will fall further below those of men as they age. The second reason the pay gap is smallest among the youngest workers is that workers who are newest to the labor force are least segregated on the job. Young women who remain in sex integrated jobs, instead of customarily female jobs, can look forward to a smaller pay penalty as they grow older.

The pay gap within occupations. Later, this chapter shows that women's and men's segregation into different jobs is the most immediate cause of the pay gap. However, employers also pay women less than men within the same occupations; in most occupations, women's proportion of men's earnings fall between 70 and 85 percent. Figure 6.4 compares women's median weekly earnings to those of men, computed from pooled data for 1990, 1991, and 1992. Women who worked full time selling securities and financial services, for example, earned 61 percent of what men made each week ($534, compared to men's $871), and female financial managers averaged just over 62 percent of men's weekly earnings ($578 and $926).

108

FIGURE 6.4

Women's Median Weekly Earnings as a Percentage of Men's Earnings for Selected Occupations, 1990 to 1992

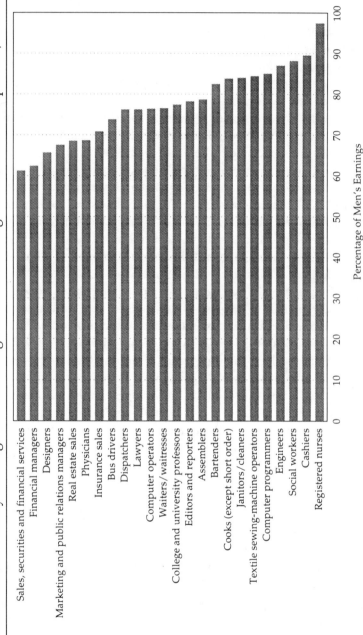

Percentage of Men's Earnings

Sources: Data from U.S. Bureau of Labor Statistics 1991:table 56; U.S. Bureau of Labor Statistics 1992a:table 56; U.S. Bureau of Labor Statistics 1993a:table 56.

Although men's earnings advantage held in predominantly female occupations, the edge was smaller. Among sewing-machine operators, for example, an occupation that is almost 90 percent female, women averaged $213—84.5 percent of men's average of $252; among cashiers, women's average weekly pay was $213—90 percent of men's $238. In many occupations in which women's weekly earnings were closest to men's, both sexes' pay tends to be low.

Women outearn men in very few occupations. For example, out of a total of 481 occupations, California women outearned men in 1990 only as typists, food preparers, waiters' assistants, and repairpersons for some electronic equipment. However, in some occupations, such as household cleaning, California men earned, on average, more than twice what women made (Hubler and Silverstein 1992).

Even the most successful women in America are docked because of their sex. According to a 1993 survey of corporate executives at the vice presidential level and higher, top-level women earned just 70 percent of what their male counterparts earned (Brooks 1993). And reportedly in 1991 the male Wimbledon tennis tournament champion walked away with $408,000, while the women's champion received just $367,000 (Bovee 1991).

The Pay Gap Around the World

In every country in the world, men outearn women. According to United Nations statistics collected between 1983 and 1987, women earned barely half what men made in Japan and the Republic of Korea. Cyprus and Egypt also had larger pay gaps than the United States.

The diffusion of Western practices has not helped women in the developing countries. According to a 1985 study by the International Labor Organization, transnational industrial firms paid women in developing countries as little as half what they paid men (Safa 1990:77).

In most countries, however, women's earnings are closer to men's than they are in the United States. In Kenya, El Salvador, Belgium, Germany, Swaziland, Canada, Great Britain, Czechoslovakia, and Switzerland, women earned between 66 and 76 percent of men's pay; in Denmark, New Zealand, Jordan, and the Netherlands, employers paid women about 80 percent of what they paid men; in Norway, the pay gap was 85 percent, and in Tanzania, Iceland, France, and Australia, women averaged almost 90 percent of men's pay (United Nations 1991:88–9). The small earnings gap in Australia results directly from social policy. Several years ago, the government implemented a policy of pay equity, which substantially raised women's pay relative to men's.

Explanations for the Pay Gap

How can we account for men's almost universal earnings advantage? Economists and sociologists have advanced several theories to explain why American women of all races, as well as black and Hispanic men, earn only 55 to 75 percent of what white men earn.

To understand the causes of the pay gap, you need to understand how employers set workers' pay. The mainstream economic approach holds that capitalists invest their money to produce goods or services whose sale they hope will yield a profit. Let's imagine these capitalists are producing chips. Their profit will be the difference between the costs to produce each chip (raw materials, rent, wages, and so forth) and the price they sell it for. The less they pay for production, the more profit each chip will bring. Acme Chip Company shouldn't care whether its workers are male or female (or whether they are high school dropouts or hold doctoral degrees in chipology); its only concern is getting workers to produce as many chips as possible for the lowest pay. If the sexes do not differ in their productivity or the pay they will accept, Acme Chip should pay them equally.

Sex Differences in Productivity

Mainstream economists would attribute any pay gap at Acme Chip to sex differences in productivity. We can imagine reasons why men might outproduce women. One sex may have a biological or physiological edge in doing various tasks. Men, for example, have more upper-body strength, on average, than women. An employer who is paying workers by how much pig iron they can load in a day will pay the average man more than the average woman. If a worker's job is to sell appliances, however, there is no reason to suspect that either sex enjoys a physiological advantage. More controversial is whether men might outproduce women for social reasons. Proponents of this view argue that men's traditional role as breadwinner pressures them to maximize their earnings, so they are more productive workers than women. However, testing this possibility is no easy matter. Nor can researchers readily discover whether any sex difference contributes to the pay gap. In the first place, few people do the kind of work in which their productivity is easily measured. To complicate matters, one's job strongly influences how productive a worker is, and women and men hold very different jobs.

Only one factor associated with productivity is easy to take into account: how much time workers spend at work. Men who are employed full time work more weeks a year, on average, than similar women, and this difference accounts for about 14 percent of the pay gap in annual earnings. You can see the effects of this difference if you turn back to Figure 6.1. In 1991, although the annual earnings of women employed full time were 70 percent of men's earnings, the ratio for weekly earnings was 74 percent. If women worked as many hours per week and weeks per year as men do, the earnings ratio would approach 77 percent. (Why men average more weeks of work a year than women do is another question.) Even if women put in as much time at work as men do, over three-quarters of the pay gap would remain.

Sex differences in human capital. Lacking direct measures of productivity, researchers have looked for proxies that they can use to compare the sexes' productivity. Mainstream economists argue that we can indirectly gauge the impact of sex differences in productivity in the pay gap if we are willing to assume that better educated, more experienced workers are more productive. Men are more productive than women, they hypothesize, because men make greater investments in their human capital. As Chapter 3 explained, *human capital* refers to the education, training, and experience that economists assume workers invest in to enhance their productivity.

Because human-capital indicators are associated with how much workers earn, they can potentially help to explain the pay gap. Educational differences do indeed play a role, but it is small. A 1976 study found that educational differences explain only 2 percent of the pay gap between white women and white men and 10 percent of the gap between African-American women and white men (Corcoran et al. 1984). Even among people with about the same number of years in school, men substantially outearn women. In 1990, for example, among workers with no more than a high school education, women earned about half what men made. Among people who attended college, the earnings ratio was around 55 percent. Among master's degree holders, the ratio was almost 70 percent, but among people who had earned a doctorate, it was almost 65 percent ("Statistical Portrait" 1993). Some of these sex differences stem from men's and women's concentration in different college majors. Nonetheless, among workers employed full time, year-round, white men who dropped out of high school earned about as much in 1990 as white women who had from one to three years of college; in 1991 white women who had graduated from high school earned almost $3,000 less than white men who had not graduated from high school (U.S. Bureau of the Census 1991). This difference was less striking among Hispanics and

African Americans, but for both those groups, male high school graduates outearned females with one to three years of college (U.S. Bureau of the Census 1991:table 29).

Another indirect indicator of productivity is experience. On average, men have more job experience than women do. The 1976 study mentioned earlier found that several measures of experience explained 30 percent of the pay gap (Corcoran et al. 1984). However, since 1976 women have been catching up to men in work experience, so this factor can explain less of the 1993 pay gap. Moreover, some evidence suggests that employers' actions contribute to sex differences in pay based on experience. For instance, some employers reward job seniority at a lower rate in female jobs than in male jobs. A Pittsburgh firm surveyed early in the century paid "unskilled workmen who have not yet acquired a certain dexterity and familiarity with their tasks" $2.00 a day but paid "unskilled working women who have made themselves valuable by length of service and familiarity with a certain operation" $1.00 a day (Tentler 1979:20). Notice that the men whom the firm classified as "unskilled" were described as unfamiliar with their work, whereas the "unskilled" women were described as experienced and familiar with their work. Some things have not changed. In 1991 the Institute for Women's Policy Research found that a year's experience added 7 cents an hour to women's pay and 24 cents an hour to men's (Bovee 1991).

The human-capital explanation of the pay gap also reasons that men participate in the labor force continuously, whereas women leave temporarily to raise their children. If women's job skills get rusty while they are out of the labor force, their productivity could decline and their pay drop accordingly. In fact, however, employment interruptions explained only 2 percent of the pay gap in 1976 (Corcoran et al 1984). Such interruptions are much less common today.

Sex differences in effort. Might men be more productive than women and thus earn more because they work harder? The few studies that have assessed this possibility indicate that women work as hard as men do and are equally or more committed to their jobs. In laboratory experiments, for example, college women did more work than college men for a preset amount of pay and did it more accurately and more efficiently (Major et al. 1984). In a survey of workers, women reported devoting more effort to their jobs than men reported (Bielby and Bielby 1988).

In studies conducted during the 1970s, measures of human capital (education, training, experience, continuity of workforce participation) were found to explain up to 44 percent of the pay gap between the sexes

(Treiman and Hartmann 1981). However, more recent studies indicate that sex differences in education, continuity of workforce participation, and effort play little role in the pay gap. In fact, human-capital differences could account for only 3 percent of the pay gap between female and male workers in North Carolina in 1989 (Tomaskovic-Devey 1993a).

Sex Discrimination

Sex discrimination creates a pay gap when employers pay women less than men who are doing the same work or when they pay less to women than men who are doing different but equally valuable work. Chapter 3 discussed some reasons that employers might treat women less favorably than men, such as cultural beliefs, sex stereotypes, the tendency to devalue women's work, and men's impulse to preserve their advantaged status or to induce women to perform domestic tasks. A nineteenth-century British inspector expressed this last motive as follows:

> The low price of female labor makes it the most profitable as well as the most agreeable occupation for a female to superintend her own domestic establishment, and her low wages do not tempt her to abandon the care of her own children. (Pinchbeck 1930:194)

As the inspector implicitly recognized, men's higher pay helps them win arguments about whose career should come first, whether the problem is deciding who will stay home with a sick child or deciding whether to move to a different city for a better job. Usually, however, discrimination is cloaked in gender ideology.

Gender ideology and pay discrimination. All societies have **ideologies**— shared sets of beliefs—that justify why some workers should earn more than others. For example, most Americans subscribe to an ideology of meritocracy, which favors higher pay for people who are better workers. This ideology, however, often conflicts with traditional **gender ideology,** which supports women's subordination. Three components of Western gender ideology have contributed to pay discrimination: the assumption that men's needs are greater than women's, the belief in female dependence, and the tendency to devalue women's work.

The belief that men need higher pay and women can get by on less is a long-standing one. A British poor law from the late eighteenth century set the allotment for a single woman at about two-thirds of what it provided for a single man (Pinchbeck 1930:74). Late in the nineteenth century, among the "potent and logical reasons" a social scientist listed for women's low pay was that "woman occupies a lower standard, which is caused to some extent by a lower standard of life, both in physical features and in mental demands" (Wright 1892:634). This was not simply the biased view of a single man. Early in the twentieth century, an official of the International Harvester Company sounded the same theme while testifying against a minimum-wage bill in Illinois. He admitted that his employer paid women low wages, but explained that the "girls" who received the lowest pay were mostly foreign and were not required to dress up for their jobs (Kessler-Harris 1990:16). Perhaps he thought foreign women eat less than native-born women. In 1925, a pay consultant to the state of California argued that workers' cost of living should partly determine their salaries, and he proposed examining the budgets for "the single man, the single woman, and the head of a family" (Kim 1989:42). Although today few would openly justify women's lower pay by claiming that they can survive on less, this assumption is built into many employers' pay policies.

A second justification for paying women less than men is that women do not support themselves. In the words of the nineteenth-century social scientist quoted earlier, woman "is also the victim of the influence of the assistance which she receives from . . . her family and friends" (Wright 1892:634). This assumption implies that it is acceptable for employers to pay women less than men because some man—a father, husband, brother, or "sugar daddy"—is supplementing every woman's pay. This way of thinking has not died. In 1990 representatives for a grocery chain in the Southwest that had been sued for sex discrimination argued in court that women did not want careers but were working only for extra money. The belief that women's economic dependence on men legitimates women's low pay is even stronger where most women live at home until they marry, as is true today in developing countries (Salaff 1990:123).

Taken together, the beliefs that women need less than men to live on and are supported by men led to the stereotype that women work for "pin money" or "pocket money" and, by corollary, that women's earnings are not "real" or essential for their families (Zelizer 1989:366). A British historian asked women who had done tailoring at home around the turn of the century if they had worked "for a bit of pocket money." Women's outrage at the question comes across in one woman's response:

> Pocket money! They was pocket money! To fill the kids tummies. No-one worked on the tailoring at home unless it was to fulfill a need. . . . They had to. If the husband lost his job—no dole—no money coming in. (Westover 1986:72)

In reality, few women can be confident that men will support them and their children. Of course, many men are the sole earner in their household and earn enough to adequately support their family. But millions of men around the world either cannot earn enough to support their family or do not choose to do so. No country has ever provided enough well-paying jobs so every male wage earner could support himself and several dependents. And no country has ever made sure that men support the women with whom they have formed households and the children whom they have helped to bring into the world. Finally, even if societies were to provide enough well-paying jobs and men were never to abandon their families, some women would not be connected to a man from whom they could or would want to claim support.

Although high divorce rates and the growing number of female-headed households make a mockery of the idea that women generally depend on men for economic support, the ideology of female dependency is embedded in pay systems in the United States and in many other countries. During the nineteenth century, unions pressed employers for a **family wage**—a wage sufficient to support a worker's wife and children. This goal emerged during the early years of industrialization, when all employed family members pooled their wages. As competitive pressures and an appetite for profits led employers to cut already-low wages, unions began to lobby for wages that would allow a male worker to support his entire family (Kessler-Harris 1990:8).

Eventually industrial unions won the battle for a family wage for some unionized jobs. In the United States, however, only white men enjoyed the victory. Employers rarely paid a family wage to minority men or women of any color, regardless of whether they were their families' sole support. In fact, employers rationalized paying women low wages because they were paying family wages for men. An employer testifying in 1914 before the New York State Factory Investigating Commission expressed this justification for women's low pay:

> When you say "living wage," of course I will admit that it is very hard for a woman to live on six dollars a week if she had to support herself, but I think you will find that cases of that kind are a great exception. I know in our stores . . . we really only like to employ people who live at home, . . . and I do not think they are at all dependent on the salary they make. (Tentler 1979:13)

The pay scale that the state of California adopted in the 1930s further illustrates the consequence of setting pay based on workers' sex and marital status. A personnel officer who opposed raises for clerical and other workers wrote that clerical and some other jobs "probably should get increases from every standpoint *except of the type of individual employed* [italics added]. That is to say, the clerical workers are generally younger single persons not having the same degree of family responsibility" (Kim 1989:43).

California was not alone in incorporating gender ideology into its pay policies. Many past textbooks on compensation advocated setting pay partly on the basis of workers' sex (Kim 1989:43). After World War II, Westinghouse revised its pay system to ensure that the female production workers it had hired during the war would earn less than male workers whose jobs involved similar responsibilities.

Employers' use of gendered assumptions to set lower pay levels for typically female jobs was rarely challenged. Indeed, workers gradually accepted these discriminatory pay rates as inevitable and even legitimate. Today discriminatory pay can take the form of wage discrimination or comparable-worth discrimination, which occurs in conjunction with job segregation. We discuss each now.

Unequal pay for equal work. Unequal pay for equal work is **pay discrimination**. Pay discrimination occurs when employers pay workers from one group less than members of another group who are doing exactly or substantially the same jobs. For example, the state of California engaged in pay discrimination in the 1930s when it formulated a pay scale that paid "somewhat more for occupations filled predominantly by men than for those occupations filled predominantly by women, *where, aside from sex, the qualifications are substantially the same [and] men and women do the same kind of work* [italics added]" (Kim 1989:42). This policy officially gave men a pay bonus based solely on their sex, creating a difference in the pay of men and women in the same line of work. For example, the weekly salary for the all-male cook classifications ranged from $110 to $150, whereas the all-female cook classifications ranged from $90 to $110. Although California raised state workers' pay over the years, 50 years later it still paid predominantly female jobs less than jobs that employed mostly men (Kim 1989).

In 1963 Congress passed the **Equal Pay Act,** which made pay discrimination illegal. Since then, thousands of women have filed complaints of pay discrimination, and the courts have found scores of employers guilty. In 1986, for example, the steelworkers' union charged Bethlehem Steel with paying 104 female clerical workers $200 a month less than men doing the same work. Four years later, Bethlehem agreed in court to pay each woman $3,000 (National Committee on Pay Equity

1991:3). The state of Rhode Island assigned a pay grade to a female equal-employment officer four steps below the pay grade assigned to the man who held the job before she did. A court awarded her $32,854 (National Committee on Pay Equity 1991:3). In the early 1990s, an assistant metropolitan editor at the *New York Times* earned $6,675 to $12,511 less than her male coworkers on the same job, as well as $2,435 less than the man whom she replaced and $7,126 less than the man who succeeded her (Robertson 1992:181). Pay discrimination based on race and ethnicity has also been an issue. In 1992 a court found a Beaumont, Texas hospital guilty of paying lower salaries to Asian nurses than to non-Asians.

Sex Segregation

The pay gap that results from pay discrimination is small compared to the pay gap that results from devaluing women's jobs. Employers that want to pay women less than men can simply assign them to different jobs. Women's and men's segregation into different jobs is indeed the mainstay of the pay gap.

Two reasons have been proposed for this fact. First, sex segregation may reduce the pay in customarily female jobs by crowding millions of female workers into a small number of occupations. The resulting oversupply of workers allegedly allows employers to lower workers' pay (Bergmann 1986:129–30). As you saw in Chapter 4, women are undeniably crowded into a small number of occupations. But many scholars believe the crowding hypothesis is at best a partial explanation for segregation. Clearly, something besides a mismatch between supply and demand is driving down women's pay (Stichter 1990:60–1).

A second proposed reason that sex segregation reduces women's pay is that employers base workers' pay on their jobs. In other words, the job to which a worker is assigned has a set pay scale. As Chapter 4 showed, employers take into account workers' sex and race in assigning them to jobs, earmarking the best-paying jobs for white men. This practice inevitably leads to pay differences between workers of different sexes and races. A study of pay practices in the British Bakers' Union illustrated the ease with which different jobs give rise to different pay. Commercial bakeries hired men to bake bread, but women baked cakes and cookies for the lowest union pay rates. Moreover, men received bonuses at least twice as large as women's (Beechey and Perkins 1987:64). In addition female and male cloakroom attendants each day issued clean white hats and coats to bakery workers of their own sex. Both male and female attendants cleaned their sex's washroom, but the female attendants also mended the uniforms. The male attendants received more per hour than the female attendants, because supposedly the men could clean walls up to 8 feet whereas the women could clean walls up to only 6 feet, but the women were not compensated extra for mending uniforms (Beechey and Perkins 1987:66). These examples illustrate how employers' segregation of women and men into different jobs or assignment of slightly different tasks becomes the justification for paying women less.

The pervasive sex and race segregation in the United States that we described in Chapter 4 provides a legal justification for employers to pay women and minorities less than men for as many hours of work. In this country, men dominate wholesale baking, and female bakers are concentrated in retail settings. In 1979 this translated into a pay gap in which women earned 61 cents for every dollar a male baker earned (Steiger and Reskin 1990:271). A study of state and local government employees also showed the effect of sex and race segregation on earnings. Women of color usually filled the three lowest-level jobs, which paid less than $20,000 a year even for people with more than 10 years on the job. Slightly over 60 percent of African-American and Hispanic women held such jobs (Berheide 1992).

Job segregation is the most important single cause of the pay gap between sexes and races. Studies in the early 1980s indicated that occupational sex segregation explained 30 to 45 percent of the pay gap between women and men (Treiman and Hartmann 1981). A 1989 survey of North Carolina workers confirmed the influence of job segregation on the gap between women's and men's hourly pay (Tomaskovic-Devey 1993a:60). Employers could therefore eliminate much of the pay gap between groups of workers by assigning workers to jobs without regard to their sex, color, or ethnicity.

Comparable-Worth Discrimination

Why should jobs whose workers are primarily female or minority pay less than jobs that employ mostly white men? In Chapter 1 we indicated that societies undervalue the work women do, regardless of what those tasks are, *because* women do them. This devaluation of women's work is a fundamental aspect of gender ideology. Physical strength, for example, in which men tend to excel over women, commands premium pay in metalworking industries. But manual dexterity, allegedly more common in women than men, does not raise workers' pay in assembly-line jobs (Humphrey 1985:223). Another example is caregiving, which our culture tends to devalue. Hence, childcare workers and nurses—both mostly women—receive low pay (Ames 1993:18). In the United States, where most dentists are male, dentists are near the top of the income hierarchy; in Europe, where most dentists are female, dentists' incomes are much closer to the average income. In general, the more women in an occupation, the lower its average pay (Treiman and Hartmann 1981).

Earlier we mentioned experiments by Brenda Major that showed college students' judgment of what was fair pay for a job depended on whether they thought women or men usually did the job. Both sexes thought that typically male jobs deserved higher pay (Major and Forcey 1985). Why should women devalue women's work? Major (1989:101) proposed that women use other women as their standard in deciding whether their pay is fair. The study of Philco, mentioned earlier, illustrates this point. Women did not object when Philco paid workers in all-female jobs about 80 percent of what it paid workers in all-male jobs. However, when the company transferred women into formerly all-male jobs and lowered the pay, female employees demanded the same pay that men had been getting (Cooper 1991:348). The women contended that the job's content and not the sex of the worker should determine its pay level. However, as long as the women held traditionally female jobs, their own pay did not seem out of line, because employers have almost invariably paid less for women's work than for men's. Because female and male jobs tend to be concentrated in different departments of large companies, in different firms, and in different industries, women can rarely directly compare their tasks, effort, and pay to men's.

This propensity to devalue the work that women do—in conjunction with sex segregation—leads to a second type of pay discrimination: **comparable-worth discrimination,** in which employers underpay workers who are doing jobs that are different from predominantly male jobs but are of equal value (Treiman and Hartmann 1981:9). The concept of comparable-worth discrimination recognizes that pay discrimination can be a two-part process. Employers first segregate the sexes—and races—into different jobs, and then they pay less to workers in jobs that employ mostly women or minorities. As a result of comparable-worth discrimination, the more female an occupation, the lower its average pay for both female and male workers, after taking into account such factors as education and experience (Treiman and Hartmann 1981). Researchers estimate that between 5 and 30 percent of the pay gap between women and men results from comparable-worth discrimination (Sorensen 1989; England 1992:181).

Comparing the pay in predominantly male and female jobs that experts judge to be of comparable worth offers clear evidence of comparable-worth discrimination. Table 6.1, which presents 1988 salaries for employees of a county in New York, illustrates the relationship between the kinds of workers in a job and what the job pays. The table shows that the best-paying jobs were held overwhelmingly by white males. In general, the more women and people of color in a job, the lower its pay. Other data for New York state show that every 5 to 6 percent increase in the representation of Hispanics and African Americans in a job is associated with 5 percent less pay (Kraut and Luna 1992).

TABLE 6.1

Sex and Race Composition and Salary of Jobs in a New York County, 1988

Job Title	Percent Who Are Female	Percent Who Are People of Color	Average Salary
Psychologist II (less than full time)	0	0	$34,914
Patrol lieutenant	0	0	32,445
Head groundskeeper II	0	0	25,140
Respiratory therapy technician	0	0	21,778
Automotive mechanic	0	33	21,778
Security aide (part time)	0	50	17,205
Public health technician II	14	0	25,121
Management analyst/programmer I	33	0	24,405
Assistant office machine operator	50	0	14,378
District supervisor	50	0	38,149
Municipal aide	59	25	12,716
Mental health worker I	67	0	14,365
Community service aide	75	40	14,716
Practical nurse, institution	93	50	18,082
Community service worker II	100	0	15,054
Medical technologist	100	0	24,054
Principal records clerk	100	0	19,001
Senior accounting clerk/typist	100	0	15,054
Telephone operator/typist	100	0	13,100
Accounting clerk/typist	100	16	13,739

Source: Adapted from Ames 1993:table 1.

Paths to Earnings Equality

As you have just seen, three factors help to maintain the disparity be-tween female and male workers' earnings: differences in productivity, which some assume to be reflected by workers' education, experience, and training; pay discrimination by employers, which lowers women's pay; and the segregation of women and men into different jobs, with "fe-male" jobs paying less than "male" jobs. These factors imply the follow-ing strategies to reduce the pay gap: increasing women's education, training, and experience; eliminating pay discrimination; integrating jobs by sex; and eliminating the wage penalty for predominantly female lines of work.

Enhancing Women's Productivity

By some common measures of productivity, the gap between the sexes is shrinking. Over the past 20 years, women have become more similar to men in the college majors they enroll in. Moreover, women have been catching up with men in likelihood of postgraduate education and in years of job experience. Women have been slower to close the training gap, however, because employers and unions control much of the train-ing for customarily male jobs.

Thus more remains to be done. Increasing women's and minorities' access to training for skilled jobs is critical for reducing inequality in their earnings. Ultimately, women cannot demonstrate that they are as produc-tive as men until employers assign women and men to the same jobs.

Eliminating Pay Discrimination

The Equal Pay Act of 1963, which made it illegal for most employers to pay women less than men in the same jobs, is an important statement of national policy and public values. The Equal Pay Act also provides a remedy for individual women who experienced pay discrimination. Along with Title VII of the 1964 Civil Rights Act, it has led to hundreds of lawsuits that have helped to teach employers that pay discrimination can cost them money.

The New York Times is a case in point. After a discrimination suit that cost the paper $233,500 in back pay, it began closing the gap between men's and women's salaries (N. Robertson 1992:207). In 1987 men in the news division outearned women with the same seniority by $13,000, and in the business division men made $25,000 a year more than women with equal experience. By 1990 women's starting salaries equaled men's in the news division, and the gap in the business division had shrunk to $7,000 (Robertson 1992:232–3).

A recent initiative at the U.S. Department of Labor to shatter the glass ceiling has led to a series of "corporate management reviews." As a result, in 1993 a Washington, D.C., hospital agreed to pay a total of $604,000 to 52 female managers who had received less pay than their male counterparts (Davis 1993).

The effectiveness of any antidiscrimination law depends on whether the government enforces it. Enforcement has varied over time. In 1980, for example, the Equal Employment Opportunity Commission filed 79 lawsuits under the Equal Pay Act, whereas it filed only two cases in the fiscal year that ended October 1992 (Rigdon 1993:B1). Regardless of enforcement activity, however, the Equal Pay Act cannot eradicate the pay gap, because it does not apply to the situation in which most women and men work: sex segregated jobs.

Integrating Jobs

Eliminating all the barriers that exclude women from customarily male jobs and channelling them into predominantly female jobs would go far toward reducing the pay gap. Title VII of the 1964 Civil Rights Act and the Presidential executive orders requiring federal contractors to practice affirmative action (see Chapter 4) were not magic wands, but both contained provisions that can reduce sex segregation. During the 1970s, when the federal government was enforcing these provisions, employers made historic progress in integrating jobs, and the pay gap, which had been stuck for decades at about 60 cents on the dollar, began to shrink.

Early in this century, a supervisor in a plant that bound magazines explained that men did the machine work and women folded pages by hand. He commented:

> I could put a girl to work operating the cutting machine if I paid her $18 a week. . . . I could have a woman tend the large folding machine if I paid her the same as the union scale for men. I don't know why I don't, except that I see no good reason why I should. (Tentler 1979:35)

Enforcement of Title VII of the Civil Rights Act and of affirmative action rules can give employers a good reason why they should integrate jobs.

Instituting Pay Equity

It is perfectly legal for private employers in the United States and in most of the world to pay less to all workers in predominantly female occupations than what they pay to all workers in predominantly male occupations. As long as employers segregate women and men into different jobs, the best hope for narrowing the pay gap and bringing women's pay more in line with the value of their work is **pay equity**, which refers to pay policies that remunerate workers on the basis of the worth of their work and not of the sex, race, or other personal characteristics of the majority of workers in a job. The 1963 Equal Pay Act requires employers to provide equal pay to workers in the same jobs. Pay equity would require employers to provide equal pay to workers in different jobs of comparable worth—that is, jobs that involve similar levels of skill, effort, and responsibility.

The premise underlying pay equity is one discussed earlier: that employers undervalue predominantly female occupations precisely because most of the workers are female. It follows that compensating workers in predominantly female jobs on the basis of their skill, effort, and responsibility would raise their pay—by some estimates, cutting the pay gap by one-third (Institute for Women's Policy Research 1993a:1). A standard argument against instituting pay equity has been the difficulty of deciding how much various jobs are worth.

Job evaluation. Developing a method to measure the worth of jobs is not as hard as it might sound. In fact, for decades American employers—including federal, state, and city governments, as well as virtually all large employers—have used a technique called **job evaluation** to devise fair systems of compensation. Job evaluation, which is used in every industrial country in the world (Acker 1990:147), involves three steps: (1) a formal assessment of the content of all jobs (the tasks they involve, the skills they require, and working conditions); (2) a decision as to how much to compensate each dimension of each job (for example, skill may be weighted twice as much as working conditions); and (3) the uniform application of the compensation system for every job in an establishment.

A job evaluation specifies a set of criteria on which pay should be based—usually skill, effort, responsibility, and working conditions. Then an evaluation team scores each job on each of the criteria and computes a score. The employer uses the scores to set nondiscriminatory salary ranges (which allow the employer to reward seniority and performance).

The value of women's work. In the past, comparable-worth discrimination persisted because employers did separate evaluations for mostly female and mostly male jobs. The tendency to devalue women's work therefore continued to have an effect on pay scales. Also, because employers originally used job evaluations to set pay in managerial jobs, scores were often higher for jobs involving administrative responsibilities and lower for jobs involving manual labor or support functions, as in clerical work (Ames 1993:31).

The effects of devaluing women's work have been revealed in many studies. For example, in Oregon's job-evaluation study, evaluators weighted more highly skills that were common in men's but not women's jobs (Acker 1990:150). A job-evaluation system in New York that was supposed to eliminate sex and race bias measured the worth of jobs by point scores. But then the system gave white men almost a third more money for each point ($107) than it gave women ($81), thus defeating the purpose of job evaluation (Ames 1993:45). If job evaluations are to eliminate comparable-worth discrimination, evaluators must guard against devaluing female tasks. Experts can help employers avoid this bias, but job-evaluation systems are fairest when workers participate in evaluations after being educated about the tendency to devalue traditionally female jobs (Blum 1991).

Pay equity is far from universal, but it is gaining ground. Australia's national pay equity law has brought women's pay within 10 percent of men's, and members of the European Community have voted to implement some form of pay equity. Although no law exists today that requires private American employers to implement pay equity, most state governments assess comparable-worth discrimination in their own pay systems. In the 1980s, 20 states adjusted the pay of predominantly female state jobs to reduce comparable-worth discrimination. And a few private employers, including Yale University, have implemented pay equity in response to pressure from unionized workers.

Nonetheless, the idea of pay equity remains controversial. Here we summarize the most common objections and the responses of proponents of pay equity:

- *It is impossible to determine the worth of jobs.* No, it is not impossible. About two-thirds of all Americans work in firms that use some form of job evaluation.

- *Pay equity would interfere with the operation of the labor market, in which the laws of supply and demand set wages.* The idea that the market sets the wages for most jobs is a myth. If the market set wages, pay discrimination would have disappeared long ago (Becker 1957). Wages are set by employers' bureaucratic procedures (including job classification), union-management agreements, and government policies (such as minimum-wage laws).

- *Pay-equity policies would lead the government to set pay in private firms.* Pay equity does not require a national or statewide wage-setting system. Each employer would set its own pay scales, although these scales could not pay jobs less simply because their workers were predominantly female or minority.

- *Pay equity would bankrupt employers and harm the economy.* This objection has surfaced in response to every proposal to treat workers more fairly, including proposals for a minimum wage, equal pay for equal work, and the abolition of slavery and child labor. In an economy that pays its top executives more than any other in the world, it is hard to argue that firms cannot afford to eliminate sex and race discrimination in pay. Actually, raising women's wages would strengthen the economy by raising women's purchasing power and reducing their dependence on government aid.

- *If women or minorities want to earn more, they should switch to higher-paying jobs.* This solution can help a limited number of people, but it is not a wholesale solution to the pay gap. In 1990 there were more than 7 million clerks, typists, and secretaries; 3.4 million school teachers; 3.4 million nurses and nurses' aides; 2.3 million cashiers; and 1.2 million waitresses. Male-dominated occupations could not absorb more than a small fraction of these workers.

Pay equity will not magically eradicate the pay gap. In the first place, the devaluation of traditionally female tasks (for example, those that involve nurturing) leads to low scores in job evaluations. Second, pay equity will not eliminate the part of the gap that results from women's and minorities' segregation into jobs that require relatively little skill, effort, and responsibility. Under pay equity, low-skill jobs will still receive low pay. Finally, when employers do implement pay equity, they tend to dilute it. The pay-equity plan in San Jose, California, for example, left female-dominated jobs with wages about 10 percent below the wages for male-dominated jobs (Steinberg 1990:470). The pay-equity plan in Ontario, Canada, left many female-dominated jobs paying well below male-dominated jobs (Ames 1990).

Pay-equity policies have reduced some of the gaps between the sexes and races. Over four years, Minnesota narrowed the pay gap among female and male state employees from 72 percent to 82 percent (Institute for Women's Policy Research 1993a).[8] But eradicating pay disparities entirely will also require eliminating the effects of sex, race, and ethnicity on workers' chances to acquire skills and to obtain productive and valued jobs.

Summary

For most of this century, American women's pay has fluctuated around 60 percent of men's. In the 30 years since the 1963 Equal Pay Act outlawed unequal pay for equal work, the pay gap has declined by just a dime. In other words, women have been catching up with men in earnings at a rate of one-third of a percent a year. At this rate of progress, the sexes will receive equal pay in the year 2083. Achieving equality more quickly will require women to accumulate work experience more in line with men's and employers to integrate more customarily male jobs. Equality will also require the spread of pay-equity principles that compensate workers for the worth of their job and not for the sex, race, or ethnicity of their coworkers.

---

[8]Women are not the only beneficiaries of pay equity. In Minnesota, pay-equity adjustments increased women's pay overall by 10.7 percent but increased men's pay in female-dominated occupations by 16.5 percent.

Construction of the Gendered Workplace

You have seen in Chapters 4, 5, and 6 how gender enters workplaces through job segregation and promotion and pay practices. Now we examine how gender becomes salient in the daily lives of workers. Workers and their bosses, coworkers, and sometimes customers all have a hand in producing a gendered workplace. Employers' decisions help shape a gendered work environment, as do workers through group and individual actions.

Actions by Employers

Employers help to construct gendered workplaces both unintentionally and intentionally. Their unintentional actions stem from unexamined stereotypes about the sexes and about the nature of sexuality in organizations. Employers intentionally differentiate the sexes in order to control workers and achieve other organizational goals, such as selling their product.

Unintentional Actions

Some of the actions employers take that contribute to the gendered workplace are virtually invisible to workers. Unexamined assumptions about the qualities of a good worker—for example, that they are available on short notice for overtime work—can lead employers to favor men. Designating jobs as part time and hiring only women for them or assigning only men to jobs that require travel are other ways that employers may gender jobs unintentionally. Because of organizational inertia, unexamined assumptions like these give rise to operating procedures and practices that become part of organizational culture. Employers' indifference to the impact of a sexualized work environment also allows sex discrimination and sexual harassment to flourish.

Acting on sex-stereotyped assumptions. Employers frequently act on cultural assumptions when they create jobs and assign people to them. Some of these assumptions are about gender. According to Rosabeth Moss Kanter (1977), people may think of organizations as "sex-neutral machines," but in actuality, organizations' authority structures are dominated by masculine principles. Male managers' assumptions can help define a job as appropriate for one sex or the other.

If the original organizational policies differentiated women and men, then differentiation becomes embedded in the structure of the organization. Once such policies are in place, they are hard to dislodge (Schultz 1991). For example, Philco initially created a gendered production system (Cooper 1991). Women were assigned to jobs that supposedly were "lighter" and required manual dexterity. Classifying jobs into "light" and "heavy" work and assigning the former to women and the latter to men is a common justification for the sexual division of labor. Managers and supervisors perpetuate such policies. For example, Chapter 1 referred to a study that showed how organizational practices can endure for a long time after they no longer make sense or have even been outlawed. Many years after the U.S. Supreme Court struck down the California law barring women from jobs that require lifting 25 pounds or more, many firms still excluded women from jobs requiring heavy lifting (Bielby and Baron 1986). And the gendered pay system that California designed in the 1930s still lowered women's pay half a century later. These inequities did not result from new decisions. Instead, the employers never noticed or examined the gendered assumptions built into personnel practices.

Other organizational assumptions that perpetuate the gendering of jobs are that the best workers have nothing else in their lives—such as a family—that might prevent single-minded attention to the job and that outside obligations disqualify a worker. Joan Acker (1990) noted that employers appear to have designed responsible jobs only for men. According to Acker, the idea of a job assumes a gender-based division of labor at home and a separation between employment and family life. A man whose life centers on his job and who has a wife at home to tend to his personal needs comes closest to matching an employer's notion of an ideal worker. A single man or woman, who is presumed to have few outside obligations, would come next. But Acker argued that the unexamined stereotype of the good worker excludes married women, because most have home responsibilities. Thus, employers' stereotyped assumptions about good workers make women less desirable for many jobs and restrict their mobility.

Stereotyped assumptions about men's noninvolvement in home life do not favor all men, however; in fact, such stereotypes hurt some men. After all, as we will show in Chapter 8, most men no longer have wives who stay at home. Moreover, the assumption that paid work is men's sole responsibility limits their opportunities for nonwork roles, such as fathering. Many men who work long hours seldom see their children. One father said, "The person whom I damaged most by being away when they were growing up was me. . . . I let my nurturing impulse dry up" (Astrachan 1986:258). Some men fear they would be punished if they took paternity leave. According to one man who considered scaling back his hours of paid work,

> It would be viewed rather negatively, [by] the senior managers. . . . For a manager to come forward and say, ". . . I don't want to drive on this fast track any more, I want to spend some time with my family"—that would be like saying, "I don't want to be part of this club anymore." (Andrews and Bailyn 1993:268)

Thus, employers' assumptions about gender and jobs can hurt both sexes. More frequently, however, they hurt women.

Creating an environment that fosters sexual harassment. Sexual harassment is in the news a great deal, where it is usually depicted as something men workers do to women workers. But sexual harassment is not simply what some workers do to other workers. Employers play a critical role by creating environments that foster sexual harassment.

Sexual harassment involves sex differentiation and power, two gendered aspects of work; thus, it is a fundamental form of gendering. It differentiates women and men by bringing into the workplace something that is ordinarily irrelevant to it—sexuality. Power imbalances facilitate harassment; even though women can and do sexually harass subordinates, because men usually hold positions of authority, it is more common for men to harass women. Sexual harassment is endemic in the workplace: In 1992 workers filed over 5,000 complaints of sexual harassment with the Equal Employment Opportunity Commission (Equal Employment Opportunity Commission 1993).

People rarely see organizational power and hierarchy as contributing to sexual harassment; they tend to pin the blame on a few "bad apples" who misbehave. Yet work organizations are highly sexualized environments: Male sexual language and imagery pervade workplaces, from talk about sex to pornography on the walls. If employers condone these

0 Chapter 7

atmospheres, then they are complicit in sexual harassment. The Tailhook
scandal exemplified organizational complicity. Tailhook is a national association of naval aviators; in 1991, as in previous years, its convention
included organized sexual harassment of women. An annual tradition at
Tailhook conventions was the "gauntlet," in which male officers lined
the convention hotel corridor in order to grab and fondle women who
passed by:

> Men in the gauntlet [would] yell out that they needed more women and
> men would go down to the casino area to recruit them. . . . [One observer
> reported that] as women entered he saw hands reach out for their breasts,
> crotch areas, and buttocks. . . . During that same time, he watched a male
> walk up to [unsuspecting] women . . . and put his arm around them, and
> talk nicely to them [as he led them to the gauntlet]. (Office of the Inspector
> General 1993:46)

The events of the Tailhook Convention were not due to a few bad
apples (23 officers were implicated for assault, 23 for indecent exposure,
and 51 for false statements to investigators). The Navy as an organization was implicated in at least three ways. First, the military has long
fostered a masculine environment. Using drill chants that disparage
women or referring to weak male recruits as "women" (or vulgar equiva-
lents) are just two of the ways it has done so. In his autobiography, newscaster Jim Lehrer recalled his Marine boot-camp sergeant asking, "Where
is the little baby shithead candidate who just opened his pussy little candidate mouth?" and shouting, "If I say your name is Cunt Who Jumped
Over the Moon, your name is Cunt Who Jumped Over the Moon"
(1992:49). This kind of language encourages the sexualization and harassment of women. Second, because of the strict chains of command operating in the Navy, for years superior officers had turned a blind eye to
sexual harassment at Tailhook conventions. Indeed, the Navy even paid
for officers to attend. Third, military rules that exclude women from certain jobs contribute to sexual harassment by setting women apart as different and thus emphasizing their sex and advertising their second-class
status. Women are less likely to be targets if employers treat them the
same as men.

The courts have identified two types of illegal sexual harassment.
One is the *quid pro quo,* in which a supervisor demands sexual acts from
a worker as a job condition or promises work-related benefits in exchange for sexual acts. The other is the "hostile work environment," in
which a pattern of sexual language, lewd pinups, or sexual advances
makes a worker so uncomfortable that it is difficult for her or him to do

the job. The courts have held employers liable for both forms of sexual harassment, arguing that employers are responsible for employees' on-the-job actions.

The notion of the hostile work environment recognizes that employers have the responsibility to create workplaces free of sexual harassment. For example, in response to a Stroh's Brewery advertising campaign featuring a "Swedish bikini team," women employees accused Stroh's of harassment due to a hostile work environment. The court ruled that the campaign constituted sex discrimination.

The 1986 Supreme Court ruling on hostile work environments (*Meritor Savings Bank v. Vinson* 1986) is murky, so the lower courts make decisions on a case-by-case basis. Is a pinup facing one person's desk harassment, or would a demand to remove it violate the civil liberties of the person who owns the pinup? What is the effect of ten pinups facing everyone? What is an unwanted sexual advance? Employers' legal liability in sexual harassment cases is forcing them to reexamine the assumption that sexual harassment occurs because of a few abusive individuals and to explore the effects of a sexualized workplace.

Intentional Actions

Managers and supervisors are key players in the business of gendering, partly because gender is a tool that enables them to better control workers and because in some cases gender attributes are marketable assets. Because they are in positions of authority, bosses have the power to implement their beliefs and stereotypes and thereby organize jobs in ways that make the jobs gendered.

Creating the gender designation of a job. In this section we discuss studies of how three particular jobs became gendered: Marine, cocktail waitress, and executive secretary. In all three cases, organizational leaders deliberately defined jobs as "belonging" to one sex or the other.

Until recently, the Marines recruited soldiers by promising to make men out of boys. When faced with women recruits, the Corps responded by gendering Marines—that is, by heightening the distinctions between women and men Marines (Williams 1989). For example, the Corps required that female Marines wear makeup and allowed female but not male Marines to carry umbrellas. Such forms of differentiation send the message that, first and foremost, female Marines are women. By claiming that Marines should not adorn themselves (but that women should) and by claiming that Marines are not vulnerable (but that women are), the Corps created contradictory role requirements for being a Marine and being a woman. In effect, the Corps told female Marines that when the roles conflicted, they were supposed to act like women, not Marines.

Most important, the Corps barred female Marines from the most "manly" job—combat. Women are capable of combat; they have filled such positions elsewhere in the world, including Greece, the Netherlands, Norway, Israel, and other countries (Seager and Olson 1986). During World War II, American women flew refueling planes in combat zones, although the no-girls-in-combat rule meant that they could not defend themselves when attacked. By denying female Marines combat roles and by enforcing sex-differentiated dress codes, the Corp reaffirmed the maleness of Marines and women's marginal role.

Another example of how employers gender a job was unearthed by examining how serving drinks became women's work. Before 1940, jobs involving liquor were considered corrupting for women, and few employers would hire women to mix alcoholic drinks or serve them (Detman 1990). Nowadays most servers are women, and employers often design the job with female workers in mind. For example, many cocktail waitresses are required to wear uniforms that accentuate their sex, if not their sexuality. Cocktail waitresses at the now defunct Playboy Clubs had to wear skimpy bunny costumes that included a corset and high heels. They were instructed to tell patrons who touched them, "The customers are not allowed to touch the bunnies" rather than the less feminine "Stop that!" or "Keep you hands to yourself!" (Steinem 1986). Less extreme versions of employers' gendering of the cocktail waitress job exist in many establishments, marking it as women's work.

Employers have also molded the job of executive secretary along gendered lines, according to Rosabeth Moss Kanter (1977). Executive secretary positions rarely have formal job descriptions, formal performance standards, or objective evaluations. Executive secretaries are sometimes termed their boss's "office wife," because their duties include such personal services as doing their boss's holiday gift shopping or making his personal appointments. Their career advancement depends on their social skills and attractiveness rather than their technical skills (p. 76). The small number of men employed as executive secretaries signals the success with which employers have gendered the job. Few men want to or would be hired for such thoroughly gendered work.

Using gender to meet organizational goals. Employers sometimes use gender to control workers and to increase profit. Sociologist Robert Thomas

(1985), who worked alongside Mexican and Mexican-American workers in the California lettuce fields, described how supervisors drew on pre-existing gender practices—such as the cultural acceptability of directing violence toward women—to enforce work discipline. Supervisors got women workers to work harder through anger, physical force, and threats of firing, but they never used these tactics on men. According to one male lettuce cutter, "to a man that would be a challenge to fight" (p. 180). Supervisors also flirted with women workers to get what they wanted. One supervisor, for example, charmed and complimented a woman to talk her out of rotating into a different job. As we noted in Chapter 1, U.S. firms in Southeast Asia have drawn heavily on gender to control their workers. By sponsoring beauty pageants, "guess whose legs these are" contests, and makeup classes, these employers distract women from poor working conditions. Managers around the world commonly use flirting to divide young, more attractive workers from older ones and to distract workers from poor working conditions (Hossfeld 1990).

Firms have also found gender a useful selling tool, and in the process they used gender to control workers. According to Arlie Hochschild (1983:104–14) about half the jobs that American women do and about a quarter of the jobs that men do involve **emotion work**. In doing emotion work, employees must manage their feelings in order to create certain feelings in customers. For example, bill collectors steel themselves to feel no sympathy in order to make people feel humiliated. Retail clerks try to project warmth, good feeling and a willingness to serve—stereotypically womanly qualities—in an attempt to make customers feel good about the company. Gender enters into emotion work because women are more likely to be in jobs that demand it and because most of the emotion work is about making other people feel good—a task that society has largely given to women.

To make passengers feel good about Delta Airlines, the company regulated flight attendants' display of their own feelings—in addition to making flight attendants keep their weight down (other crew members were exempt) and establishing rules about dress. Delta gave attendants intensive training in the control of negative emotions toward passengers. Attendants were instructed to hide their anger and "smile, smile, smile" regardless of the circumstances. Trainers taught flight attendants that they should convert annoyance at a passenger into empathy by pretending that the flight cabin is their living room and that the passenger is a customer or a friend—or a needy child. In other words, flight attendants were taught to view impersonal relations "as if they were personal" (Hochschild 1983:106). One trainer grilled her class by asking, "What are we selling?" When a student answered, "We're selling Delta," the teacher corrected her: "No, you're selling yourself!" This Delta training manager, like other managers, drew on stereotypically female traits to market Delta. And thus the gendered workplace benefited the employer.

Actions by Workers

Workers also have a hand in gendering work. Workers who work together day in and day out create shared values and ideologies, which constitute a **workplace culture**. They develop shared perceptions of the world; shared values, symbols, and languages; and shared ways of behaving that separate work-group members from nonmembers. This section shows how workplace culture can gender work.

Workplace culture serves several purposes. First, it socializes new workers to the informal work codes, which typically operate to protect worker' specialized knowledge and to help workers get around management. Another important function of workplace culture is to imbue jobs with dignity, often by preserving workers' rights in the face of disrespectful managers or customers. Third, a shared workplace culture helps work groups exclude unwelcome outsiders. Finally, in oppressive, exploitive work systems, workplace culture may embrace ideologies that denounce the oppressive aspects of the job and celebrate workers' skills.

The pervasiveness of sex segregation at work means that many people work in same-sex groups. Although all the functions of workplace culture—socializing, dignifying, excluding, and resisting—are pervasive in both men's and women's work groups, these functions sometimes operate differently. For example, both men's and women's work cultures socialize newcomers to the informal rules of the workplace. One of the most important rules is to resist pressure from managers to raise output. People who violate this rule of staying within the production boundaries set by the work group are labeled ratebusters. Men's and women's work cultures tend to treat ratebusters differently. In a factory of the 1930s, men workers would "bing" (punch in the arm with force) a ratebuster: "Worker 8: 'If you don't quit work I'll bing you.' . . . [He] struck Worker 6 and finally chased him around the room" (Roethlisberger and Dickson 1975:94). Similarly, in a machine shop in the 1970s, male workers planned to beat up a ratebuster or hide his tools (Burawoy 1979:170). Compare this type of response to an example from a group of women retail salesclerks in a turn-of-the-century department store. The salesclerks set informal sales quotas that they would not exceed (Benson 1986). Store managers tried to break this system by instituting bonuses. The salesclerks' main strategy was to agree among themselves to cooperate instead of compete: If someone was not making her sales quota, another clerk would share some of her own sales, and they would split their commissions (Benson 1986:257). The women also subverted the bonus plan by refusing to do tasks that would not increase their sales (for example, ignoring customers who appeared to be "just looking," refusing to restock shelves, and actively promoting only expensive items). A clerk who chose to participate in management's bonus plan—a ratebuster—was dealt with harshly. Other salesclerks banged her shins with drawers, ridiculed her, messed up her stock, and ostracized her. Because men's and women's work groups develop different cultures, here we examine them separately.

Women's Work Groups

One notable characteristic of women's groups is their tendency to celebrate private life at work. In many workplaces, female workers hold parties for birthdays, engagements, pregnancies, weddings, and retirements. A British garment-factory worker described bridal celebrations involving both East-Asian and English women who would "dress you up to look like clowns, put flour in your hair, on your face—it gets everywhere. And then everyone gets drunk at lunch-time. . . No one does any work all day" (Westwood 1985:118).

Female workers celebrate personal events at work for several reasons. First, celebrations provide a way to take time off work. One office supervisor for the city government of Seattle admitted that she frequently permitted women employees to extend lunch hours for birthday parties to make up for poor pay. Workplace celebrations also allow women to create community. Western societies have traditionally assigned women the task of forging ties. Women do it at home by mediating disputes, for example, and they bring the skill of community-building to work as well. A third reason that women's work groups perform celebrations is to create bridges. Consider the case of an ethnically diverse New England garment factory. Yankee and Portuguese women diffused ethnic tension by emphasizing commonalities in their family roles and in life-cycle events. For example, at a Yankee woman's baby shower, the Portuguese-speaking women contributed to buying gifts and stood by to admire the gifts (Lamphere 1984:256–7). The two groups of women also shared photographs of their families, thereby bringing family life into the workplace, "making connections with others, making strangers into acquaintances, and making acquaintances into friends" (Lamphere 1984:259).

Accommodation versus resistance? Do these distinctively female work cultures lead women to accept poor working conditions or to resist them? Some social scientists have argued that celebrating domesticity is fundamentally conservative, because it encourages women to escape from a difficult work situation into marriage instead of fighting for justice at work (see, for example, Tentler 1979:180–5). Indeed, some employers may encourage female factory workers to think of themselves as women first and as workers second for just this reason, as we discussed earlier.

On the other hand, in having parties at work, women can resist their bosses by reducing their output and by overcoming divisions based on race, class, and ethnicity. The Portuguese- and American-born textile workers described earlier forged connections strong enough to enable them to stage a wildcat strike (Lamphere 1984). Mexican-American workers in a California cannery used family ties to organize against both their company and an indifferent union (Zavella 1987). African-American ward secretaries and other mostly white hospital employees opened up communication channels and bridged differences through wedding and baby showers and potluck dinners. So successfully did they forge a common culture that they were able to organize and stage a walkout to protest the hospital's treatment of them (Sacks 1984). Celebrating family life at work, then, can unite workers by creating community.

Women's work cultures can also create a sense of identity that helps them resist domination at work and at home. Their culture at work can acknowledge women's skills, thereby nourishing self-respect. Through their work groups, for example, some waitresses have been able to disregard society's evaluation of their jobs as menial labor and instead recognize the judgment and memory their jobs require and the dignity of expertly providing an important service (Cobble 1991:53). Moreover, self-respect learned on the job can influence gender relations off the job, helping women redefine the home as a workplace where a women may appropriately demand a more egalitarian division of labor (Costello 1985). Indeed, one study found that female hospital workers who had organized a union and waged a strike became more insistent about the division of labor at home (Fantasia 1988:166).

Unions. In discussing the role of women's workplace culture in accommodation and resistance, we must also examine why women are less likely than men to be in unions. In 1990 unions represented 14 percent of female workers and 22 percent of male workers (Amott 1993). Three factors explain women's low levels of unionization. First, until recently, few unions had recruited women, and many had actively excluded women because they were seen as competitors for men's jobs. Second, unions have often failed to address women's concerns. For example, the United Auto Workers devised a pension plan that disallowed pensions for female members who had spent some time home with their children; after World War II, the United Auto Workers cooperated with car manufacturers to force women out of their wartime jobs (Milkman 1987). And the first union contract at Philco established job ladders that granted workers seniority rights but locked women into dead-end, customarily female jobs (Cooper 1991).[1] A third reason for women's low levels of unionization is their concentration in industries that are hard to organize. The traditionally female industries tend to invest in labor rather than in equipment, so they can easily move to nonunionized areas if workers threaten to form a union.

With the recent employment declines in traditionally unionized industries, unions increasingly have courted women's occupations. Between 1960 and 1990, the number of female union members doubled. Women are now 37 percent of the unionized workforce but account for two out of every three new union members (Eaton 1992).

Unions that address women's issues—such as equal opportunity, age discrimination, and pay equity—are more likely to win union representation elections than unions that do not have such an emphasis (Milkman 1985:310). One union that has used this strategy successfully is 9to5, an independent working women's organization that is affiliated with the Service Employees' International Union. It organized clerical workers by emphasizing women's issues, downplaying union hierarchies in favor of rank-and-file participation, and rallying support through skillful use of the media. Among 9to5's strategies have been the popular 1980 film *9 to 5*, rallies on National Secretaries Day, and publicity about the hazards of video display terminals.

---

[1] The union newspaper tried to involve women by publishing a separate women's page, which featured the column "Our Own Beauty Shoppe: A Page for Our Girls." The union did nothing, however, to fight for women who left work because of a pregnancy and thus lost all seniority rights (Cooper 1991).

Men's Work Groups

Forging bonds among workers is just as important to men's groups as it is to women's groups. And like women, men use gender to create their own workplace culture. However, men use such mechanisms as gender displays and jokes demeaning homosexuals and women to establish their bonds.

Male workers establish camaraderie and goodwill among group members for many reasons. One reason is that, through solidarity and collective strength, male workers are better able to stand up for their rights (Fantasia 1988:109). For example, the managers of a power plant divided a group of 11 male workers into small subgroups based on their work status, wage rate, and race. These differences drove workers apart and hampered their struggle with management over work rules. But by finding ways to forge bonds with each other, the workers broke down status barriers. For example, they took turns buying doughnuts or rounds of beer; each man—regardless of race or rank—could thereby raise his status by exhibiting generosity (Padavic 1991). Men also built solidarity by highlighting their masculinity: All men could share in conversations disparaging women or flaunting their own sexual prowess.

Men also build camaraderie through the use of gender displays, language or rituals so characteristic of one sex (as Chapter 1 explained) that they mark the workplace as belonging to that sex. Male gender displays highlight manliness—a trait that men share by virtue of not being women—and thus heighten male workers' sense of unity.[2] In one example of a gender display, a student in an automotive electrical course

> proceeded without recourse to wiring diagrams. . . . He also shunned customary safety precautions, taking electrical shocks rather than disconnecting the negative battery cable or using the insulated tools available. Finally, he made great shows of physical strength, by, for instance, supporting a [heavy automotive] component with one hand while examining wires located behind it with the other." (Weston 1990:144–45)

Other examples of male gender displays observed among skilled blue-collar tradespeople include electricians working on live circuits instead of throwing the circuit breaker, plumbers sawing through asbestos without masks, and tool-crib attendants hand-carrying very heavy items when dollies were available (Weston 1990). None of these practices saved time,

---

[2]Women also engage in gender displays—for example, by competing to see who can bring the best food to an office party. But female gender displays seem to play a smaller role in building worker solidarity than men's gender displays do.

but they did enhance these men's reputations as "hard" workers. Gender displays occur too among professionals and managers. In Chapter 1 we referred to a best-selling book about stockbrokers that reported the use of the honorific nickname "big, swinging dicks." First-year Harvard Business School students assigned to the "D section" dubbed themselves the "big, swinging D's," despite the fact that over a third were female.[3]

Another way that men's work groups forge bonds is by collectively affirming heterosexuality. David Halle (1984) described an incident in a chemical factory that he interpreted as a ritual affirmation of heterosexuality:

> A group of four workers are sitting and talking. One gets up and goes to the bathroom. A minute or so later a second, Freddy, also moves toward the bathroom. . . . A friend comments: "Hey, Freddy, got your knee pads with you?" (Halle 1984:182)

The working conditions of blue-collar workers often place men in intimate physical proximity. Jokes about homosexuality reassure them that their close relationships are only friendships (Halle 1984:183).

Sometimes male workers magnify the importance of their gender in order to enhance the status of a job in their own eyes. Robin Leidner (1991) showed how male sales agents and managers at an insurance company labored to demonstrate to themselves and others that certain jobs were appropriate only for men, even when there was no objective reason for the designation. To do the job well, these male workers had to take the role of "interactive inferior," allowing the customer to dominate the interaction:

> They were supposed to paste on smiles when they did not feel like smiling and to behave cheerfully and deferentially to people of every status and with every attitude. The workers . . . had to try to remain pleasant even in the face of insult. (Leidner 1991:171)

To help the agents redefine this behavior as masculine, trainers taught them that passively accepting mistreatment was manly, not womanly. Screaming back at a customer, the men were told, would be letting the customer get the best of you rather than standing up for yourself in a masculine way. The company taught agents to "play up" potential customers by using what society usually labels as feminine wiles. Agents

---

[3]The fact that these students are the future managers of the top corporations in the United States suggests that the managers of the future will not necessarily be more sensitive to gender issues than today's managers are.

interpreted these more "feminine" aspects of the job in such a way that they were protected from feeling degraded when performing the tasks. By construing these behaviors as part of a campaign to outwit prospective customers, the insurance agents could view their roles as so thoroughly masculine that only an exceptionally tough woman could handle insurance sales. According to one agent, "most girls don't have what it takes. They don't have the killer instinct" (Leidner 1993:202). A sales manager said he would not hire a woman unless "she had a kind of bitchy attitude." Thus, in order to make their jobs more acceptable to themselves, male workers may exaggerate the importance of their gender.

What happens when a woman is hired into a men's work group? Dominant groups often exaggerate the differences that set off the token, a practice that Rosabeth Moss Kanter (1977:221) termed **boundary heightening**. For example, white workers in a setting they dominate might tell racial jokes in front of African-American workers, or heterosexual workers might tell jokes about homosexuals in front of gay or lesbian workers. An emphasis on any commonality that men share—an interest in sports or in sexual banter, for example—can indicate that women are out of place. Of course, male group members may have talked about sports or women's bodies before any women arrived on the scene and could just be continuing their normal behavior. They are engaging in boundary heightening, however, if they emphasize their commonality more than they did before the woman arrived or make a point of not doing it because of the woman's presence. For example, men who pointedly refuse to swear in front of a woman call attention to her presence, marking her as an outsider who is disrupting men's normal behavior.

In sum, male camaraderie creates solidarity among work-group members, but at the same time it can exclude women. However, men's work cultures are not invariably hostile to women. In some instances, men unionists have supported women workers' collective actions. For example, when Yale University's clerical workers, who were mostly women, struck for 10 weeks, the mostly male service and maintenance workers' local financially supported the clerical workers' union and honored the women workers' picket lines (Ladd-Taylor 1985).

As influential as work groups are, it is important to remember that some gendered actions in the workplace are performed by individuals—for example, a man who constantly talks about his macho exploits or a woman who regularly takes up collections in the office for baby showers. Much of the behavior intended to drive out women, in fact, comes from individuals and not from the whole work group. Sometimes these individuals introduce gender in an attempt to maintain a single-sex workplace or to remind women that they do not belong. For example, a female real estate attorney reported that after she won an important case, a male coworker awarded her a set of brass balls (Ely in press). This gift sent the message that although a woman can sometimes perform as well as a man, women are still different and lacking something. A similar message was sent by the male engineer who dubbed female engineers as "performing seals" who must have been taught by a man behind the scenes (Cockburn 1991). Although a single worker's views may not be representative of the group, one person invoking gender can have a substantial impact. Often only one man is reminding a woman that she does not belong, while the rest of the work group is treating her well. Whether that one man succeeds in driving the woman out depends to a large extent on how much she needs the job. If the income it provides is higher than the income for alternative jobs, the odds are that woman will stay and find ways to deal with the problem (Padavic 1989).

Summary

Both employers and workers socially construct gender at work. Gender is embedded in organizations because of employers' past practices and current assumptions—for example, that only men or women belong in certain jobs. Employers encourage "appropriate" gender behavior and use gender distinctions to control workers or to meet organizational goals. Workers, too, enact gender in their jobs. Both men and women workers use gender to socialize new workers or to forge ties with one another—but they tend to have different styles. Some men also use work groups to assert masculine dominance. The result of both workers' and employers' actions is a gendered work setting that reinforces the traditional sexual division of labor and exaggerates the importance of people's sex in the work they do.

8

Paid Work and Family Work

The relationship between family and work has changed dramatically over the years. The first big change occurred with the Industrial Revolution and the rise of capitalism, which shifted most production from households to factories, drastically altering the work patterns of men, women, and children. The last 50 years, however, have brought another equally dramatic "revolution": women's rising participation in the labor force. Today, the typical married woman works for pay in the labor force in addition to working at home as a homemaker. Combining paid work and family work has been difficult for women of all classes. In the early industrial period, the doctrine of separate spheres kept middle- and upper-class women out of the workforce, and the task of combining paid work and family responsibilities fell largely on working-class and poor women. But today, a family's economic level no longer determines whether a woman works outside the home. Thus work/family conflict spans the entire economic spectrum. However, now that more privileged women—who tend to have more political clout—are concerned about blending their work lives and family lives, employers and the American government have begun to address the problem of work/family conflict. Nevertheless, individual women bear the brunt of the problem.

This chapter discusses the effects of women's labor force participation on their family work, and vice versa, and examines employers' and governments' attempts to help people cope with the need to combine paid work and family work.

The Decline of the Stay-at-Home Wife and Mother

At the turn of the century, fewer than 4 percent of married women were in the labor force; by 1992, 57.8 percent were (U.S. Women's Bureau 1993). Mothers' rising labor force participation is as dramatic as married women's. Today women are less likely to interrupt their labor force participation for children, statistics show. The more recently women were born, the more likely they are to be in the labor force at every age (see Figure 8.1). Among women born before 1951, labor force participation dropped when they were in their late 20s, but few women born after 1950 are leaving the labor force to have children. In 1976, 31 percent of mothers with a child under 1 year old were in the labor force; that percentage had grown to 53 percent in 1990 and to 68 percent for college graduates (O'Connell and Bachu 1992).

In 1992 both parents were employed in 42 percent of families with children, compared to 35 percent in 1975 (Hayghe 1990, 1993). As Figure 8.2 shows, family-work patterns have changed considerably in the last 50 years. Families with employed husbands and stay-at-home wives accounted for only 18 percent of all families in 1992, compared to 67 percent in 1940. In addition, the skyrocketing divorce rate and huge increases in the number of unmarried mothers have increased the number of families maintained solely by employed women. As Figure 8.2

FIGURE 8.1

Labor Force Participation by Age for U.S. Men and Women, 1950 and 1991

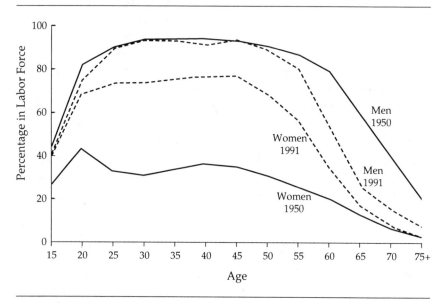

Source: Bloom and Brender 1993:figure 2.

FIGURE 8.2

Work Patterns of Families, 1940 to 1992

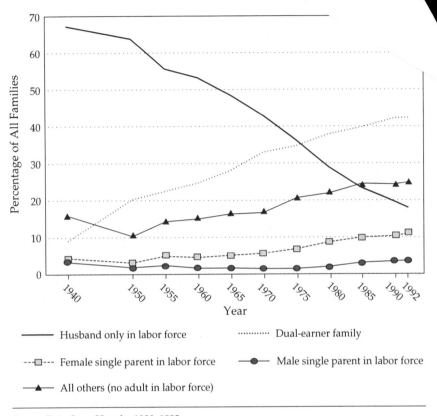

Source: Data from Hayghe 1990, 1993.

shows, the proportion of female single-parent families in the workforce grew from about 5 percent in 1965 to a little over 11 percent in 1992; meanwhile, the proportion of father-only families has remained stable at around 3 percent.[1]

Women's labor force participation has increased during the twentieth century for all women, regardless of their race or ethnicity. However, as

---

[1]The diverse group of "other families" includes persons who maintain their families without being in the labor force. The growth in the percentage of such families since 1940 has stemmed primarily from the increasing popularity of early retirement.

saw in Chapter 2, in 1900 African-American women were more likely to be in the labor force than white women were, a situation that persisted for decades. Only in the 1990s did white women catch up with black women in labor force participation. By 1993, 57.9 percent of white women and 57.1 percent of African-American women were in the labor force. Hispanic women are less likely to be in the labor force—52 percent in 1993. The Census Bureau classifies several groups as Hispanic, however. Of these, Cuban women have the second highest rate of labor force participation among U.S. women; Puerto Rican women have the lowest rate. Mexican-American women's likelihood of being in the labor force is quite low, resembling that of American-Indian women's. Among men, the pattern differs: 79.4 percent of men of Hispanic origin, 76.3 percent of Anglos, and 69.1 percent of African Americans were employed in 1993 (U.S. Bureau of Labor Statistics 1993b).

The differences in labor force participation among these racial and ethnic groups reflect both employers' demand for workers of a particular sex and race or ethnicity and the economic situations of their families. Black women have always been in the labor force in great numbers, both because employers sought low-wage labor and because discrimination against black men heightened black women's need to work for pay. Puerto Rican women's labor force participation is lower because they have finished fewer years of school on average (which makes them less desirable to employers) and because they are more likely to be single parents (which impedes labor force participation). Mexican-American and American-Indian women also lack the education that would make them more attractive to employers; in addition, both groups are concentrated in the Southwest, where fewer jobs are available, and both groups face discrimination. On the other hand, Hispanic men are four percentage points more likely than Anglo men to participate in the labor force, because they have been concentrated in service and farm jobs, where there is a demand for their labor for at least part of the year. The majority of Cuban Americans—who tend to be better educated than other Hispanics—live in the Southeast, especially Florida, where job prospects are better (Smith and Tienda 1988:65–7).

Overall, race and ethnicity do affect the likelihood of belonging to the labor force, but they have different effects for women and men. Among women, the long-run trend is toward convergence, minimizing differences across racial and ethnic groups. Among men, however, the trend has been toward divergence: The differences among black, white, and Hispanic men have been increasing.

Work/Family Conflict

Dramatic changes in family structure and women's labor force participation have not brought substantial changes to the sexual division of labor. Today, most married women share responsibility for the breadwinner role; but men, by and large, have been slower to share domestic responsibilities. Furthermore, no other institution in society, neither public nor private, has stepped in to help working women. As a result, women have shouldered the responsibilities of work and family largely on their own.

Jobs and families both demand enormous commitments of time and energy, especially during the peak years of family formation and career growth. Jobs usually consume about a third of a person's day, not including time spent commuting and preparing for work. In addition, many working women are responsible for caring for four groups: themselves, their husbands, their children, and their elderly parents or in-laws. Children require considerable time, frequently during their parents' paid work hours; children's sicknesses and school events cannot be scheduled around work hours.

In sum, although women enjoy the status, satisfaction, and power that a paid job provides, they also experience the stress of coping with a double day. Many also face logistical problems. Most men with families do not experience these stresses. Indeed, some resent the pressure from their wives to provide more help with family chores. But as you will see, some men also have trouble with their confinement to the breadwinner role.

The Gendering of Work/Family Conflict

"Man may work from sun to sun, but a woman's work is never done." Although employed women must do housework, many married men can simply choose not to (Hochschild 1989). Even wealthy women in high-level jobs do not escape all household labor. Alice M. Rivlin, deputy director of the Office of Management and Budget during the Clinton administration, noted that she often runs into people at the supermarket who are surprised to see her there. "How else do they think I'm going to get food? Do they think I have a staff?" (Burros 1993). Zoe Baird and Kimba Wood were forced to withdraw from consideration as U.S. Attorney General because of improprieties in hiring immigrant workers as housekeepers. In their case, a double standard seemed to be operating: Society has never condemned male appointees who have employed immigrant workers to clean their houses, fix their meals, and tend their children—presumably because the domestic realm was their wives' responsibility, not theirs.

Some Marxist historians of capitalism predicted that industrialization would lead governments or private entrepreneurs to take over the family's domestic functions. These historians believed that either government or business could provide services like cooking and laundry more efficiently than the family could, thereby freeing women and children to work in the marketplace. As we know, this shift did not occur. In the upheaval of early capitalism, when all other social relations were being renegotiated, why did the family remain the site of housework? One answer is that everyone—except women—benefits from this arrangement. It satisfies employers because it relieves them of the cost of maintaining and reproducing the labor force they depend on. It satisfies men because it saves them from packing their own lunches or laundering their own work clothes.

But this arrangement does not often satisfy women, because bearing sole responsibility for running family affairs is a considerable burden. At home they are responsible for taking care of the needs of all family members, even at the expense of their own needs. In fact, when she marries, a woman adds nine hours a week, on average, to her household labor (Shelton 1992:66). At work, employers often give women fewer opportunities than men because employers assume that women's paid work is less important to women than their family responsibilities, making them less committed to paid work. In the rest of this chapter, we examine how this social construction of housework as women's responsibility affects women's and men's lives.

Problems for Women

In the following sections, we focus on the ways that women and men respond to the competing demands of work and family. For women, the main problem is managing their time efficiently so as to fulfill both their age-old obligations as homemakers and their newer obligations as paid workers. The expressions "double day" and "second shift" were coined to describe employed women's dual responsibilities for paid and unpaid work (Hochschild 1989).

Nevertheless, we should note, being employed benefits women and their families. First, women's employment is essential for most families' economic well-being; often it makes the difference between household self-sufficiency and poverty. Jobs and income are also crucial to the 26 million unmarried women who were in the labor force in 1993. In married couples, when both members work full time, year-round, wives contribute over 40 percent of the total household income (Crispell 1993). Combining work and family has positive emotional effects as well. Success in one role—for example, a promotion at work—can buffer a woman from difficulties in another role, such as a divorce (Thoits 1983; Reskin and Coverman 1985). Even for women in dead-end jobs that offer few opportunities for success, employment still brings satisfactions that can complement family work. As sociologist Myra Ferree stated,

> Some of the worst difficulties in full-time housework, such as isolation or lack of recognition, may be relieved by certain rewards in the work force, such as ties with coworkers and a paycheck, while some of the problems of paid employment, such as close supervision and fragmentation of the work, can be balanced by rewards at home, such as autonomy and an undivided work process. (1987a:297)

Housework. A major problem for women is finding the time for both housework and paid work. When a woman enters the labor force, each extra hour she puts into her paid job reduces her housework efforts by a half hour (Schor 1991:36). She cooks less, cleans less, and spends less time with her children. Working women substitute daycare centers, fast-food restaurants, and laundries for home-provided services (Bergmann 1986).[2] Women may also be able to employ a childcare or domestic worker to do some tasks. However, if that worker fails to show up, women must do the work themselves.

Women also cut the amount of time spent on domestic obligations by reducing the number of dependents at home. Many women in professional jobs either wait to have children until after their careers are established, have fewer children than they would prefer, or forgo children or marriage. Among the highest-paid officers and directors of Fortune 500 companies, for example, few of the men but 40 percent of the women were childless (University of California at Los Angeles/Korn-Ferry 1993).[3]

---

[2]Some researchers argue that the amount of housework has increased because it now includes some tasks that used to be performed by others for pay. Until World War II, for example, people telephoned their neighborhood grocer, who would fill and deliver the grocery order. Today consumers do this labor without pay: We go to supermarkets, push carts through crowded aisles, stand in line to pay for our purchases, and then haul them home (Glazer 1984, 1988).

[3]The causal relationship between childlessness and career success is impossible to establish. Employers that practice statistical discrimination may have weeded out many women with children because they think women's families may interfere with job performance.

Most men and women profess to believe that working couples should share household responsibilities (Schor 1991:104). Yet family demands remain mostly women's responsibility, even among women who work full time. Fully employed women spent an estimated 33 hours a week on housework in 1987, compared to men's 20 hours a week (Shelton 1992:83). A conservative estimate is that women average 65 hours a week in paid and unpaid work (Schor 1991), but other studies report as many as 84 hours a week for married mothers, 79 hours for unmarried mothers, and 72 hours for fathers (Burden and Googins 1987). Women with young children, those in professional jobs, and those who must hold two paid jobs work even longer hours (Schor 1991:21; Shelton 1992). The price of this time crunch for women is less leisure and too little sleep (Hochschild 1989; Schor 1991). Working mothers whom Arlie Hochschild interviewed talked about sleep "the way a hungry person talks about food" (1989:9).

Some women respond to the pressure of the double day by prodding their husbands or partners to do more housework. Interviews with working wives have revealed that many are unsuccessful (Hochschild 1989). One couple avoided divorce over the issue of housework by assigning the downstairs to the husband and the upstairs to the wife. The upstairs included the living room, kitchen, two bathrooms, and two bedrooms; the downstairs included the garage, car, and dog. Men often exaggerate their contributions, as did this man who was asked what he did to share the work of the home:

> He answered, "I make all the pies we eat." He didn't have to share much responsibility for the home; "pies" did it for him. Another man grilled fish. Another baked bread. In their pies, their fish, and their bread, such men converted a single act into a substitute for a multitude of chores. (Hochschild 1989:43)

Table 8.1 shows how couples in which both partners hold full-time jobs divide the housework. Two things stand out: Women and men do different tasks,[4] and women clearly spend more time than men on domestic tasks. Moreover, many of the tasks done mostly by men—such as auto maintenance and outdoor tasks—are weekly or monthly chores and can be scheduled; women's tasks customarily must be done daily. A man

---

[4]Women and men also did different household tasks in the past. In the nineteenth century, middle-class men did some yard work, were responsible for certain purchases (wine, books, pictures, wheeled vehicles), and helped to paint and paper rooms (Davidoff and Hall 1987:387).

TABLE 8.1

Time Spent on Household Tasks by Full-Time Workers, Measured in Hours per Week, 1987

Household Tasks	Men	Women	Men as a Percentage of Women
Preparing meals	3.0	8.0	37.5
Washing dishes	2.3	5.2	44.2
House cleaning	2.1	6.6	31.8
Outdoor tasks	4.9	2.1	42.8*
Shopping	1.7	2.9	58.6
Washing, ironing	1.0	3.8	26.3
Paying bills	1.6	2.0	80.0
Auto maintenance	2.0	0.4	20.0*
Driving	1.2	1.7	70.6

*Women as a percentage of men.

Source: Beth Anne Shelton, *Women, Men, and Time: Gender Differences in Paid Work, Housework, and Leisure*. New York: Greenwood Press (an imprint of Greenwood Publishing Group, Inc., Westport, CT), 1992, p. 83. Reprinted with permission.

can postpone changing the car's oil for a week if something else comes up, but a woman cannot postpone washing the dishes for a week or making an emergency trip to the pediatrician.

Men in the United States are doing more housework than they used to, but not much more (Hochschild 1989:278; Shelton 1992:75). In 1978, 76 percent of wives who were employed full time did the majority of housework (Ross 1986). In 1987, 66 percent of employed wives still reportedly did most or all of the housework (Harris 1987). Whether their wives work outside the home or not has little effect on how much housework men do. However, men who are better educated or have a young child at home do slightly more than other men (Shelton 1992; Thompson and Walker 1991), as do African-American and Hispanic men (Shelton and John 1993).

The bottom line is that women do much more housework than men. This pattern is likely to continue in the next generation: Daughters of mothers who work full time spend 10.2 hours a week on housework, in contrast to sons' 2.7 hours (Exter 1991). The unequal division of household labor is much the same around the world, although the size of the gap varies. For example, Swedish and Japanese women spend the same number of hours on housework (31 per week), but Swedish men spend about 15 hours more per week on housework than Japanese men do (Blau and Ferber 1990). Even in Sweden, whose citizens hold liberal gender-role attitudes, women perform three-quarters of the housework (Kalleberg and Rosenfeld 1990).

As women's earnings approach parity with men's, the household division of labor may become more equitable. Cross-national research shows a slight tendency for the division of household labor between the sexes to become a little more equal as women's opportunities to earn money in the labor force expand (Blau and Ferber 1990). In the United States, relative equality between women's and men's earnings leads to men's doing more housework (Ferree 1987b). In "macho" cultures, however, it is not how much women earn, but how much husbands earn, that affects the amount of domestic work husbands do. For example, in Greece, Honduras, and Kenya, low-earning men do not perform housework, apparently because they feel threatened by their wives' earnings; only women in these countries whose husbands earn a relatively high income are able to gain some equality in the family (Safilios-Rothschild 1990).

Childcare. Not surprisingly, the responsibility for finding accessible, affordable childcare usually falls to mothers.[5] Data from 1991 for households in which mothers worked showed that fathers cared for 20 percent of preschoolers,[6] other relatives cared for 23 percent, nonrelatives cared for another 23 percent, organized facilities such as daycare centers and nursery schools cared for another 23 percent, and mothers cared for about 9 percent in their workplaces (O'Connell 1993).

Obtaining adequate childcare is the primary source of stress among employed mothers (Ross and Mirowsky 1988). Women's increasing participation in the paid workforce has reduced the number of relatives available for childcare, so parents increasingly rely on organized facilities. However, organized childcare is often inadequate to meet working mothers' needs. First, most centers operate only during standard business hours and offer no care for sick children. In one survey, half the respondents whose child had been sick in the previous month had missed at least a day of work (Hofferth et al. 1991). Second, childcare is seldom

---

[5]Women also predominate among paid childcare providers. In 1990 almost half a million women and 234 men were paid to care for children in someone else's home. Another 188,419 women and 22,932 men worked as providers of childcare in organized setting (U.S. Bureau of the Census 1992a).

[6]This figure is a marked increase; it had hovered around 15 percent since 1977.

cheap; it constitutes one of the largest work-related costs. Single mothers and poor families are particularly hard hit by childcare costs. In 1990 poor mothers of preschoolers spent 23 percent of their family income on childcare, compared to 6 percent of family income for high-income mothers (Hofferth et al. 1991). Third, not enough affordable facilities exist to meet the demand. One study found that inadequate childcare prevented almost 14 percent of young mothers from working for part or all of the previous year (Cattan 1991). The high cost and inaccessibility of childcare force some parents to leave their children home alone. According to a 1990 study, one out of nine children under age 13 whose mothers were employed were left without any childcare at all (Hofferth et al. 1991).

Despite media scare stories, most experts agree that out-of-home care is not harmful to children. Indeed, out-of-home care appears to enhance children's social skills and learning abilities (Lamb 1992; O'Connell and Bachu 1992). Moreover, high-quality childcare often raises poor children's test scores (Piotrkowski and Katz 1982). The real problem is not whether only mothers can provide good care but where to find affordable, accessible, and reliable childcare.

Care of elderly relatives. Working women increasingly face another family demand: care of elderly relatives. Although most of the rapidly growing elderly population care for themselves, of the 22 percent who were disabled in 1985, most relied on family and friends for care. In 1985, 20 to 30 percent of IBM's and The Travelers' Companies' employees over age 30 cared for an elderly person (Creeden 1989). In 1989 only 3 percent of full-time employees received any kind of help from employers in caring for elderly relatives (Hyland 1990). As the number of elderly increases, a growing number of workers must somehow fit caretaking into their days—by forgoing sleep, leisure, and in some cases full-time employment.

Relocation for a job. Gender stereotypes influence decisions about moving when one partner's career would benefit from geographic relocation. In many managerial and professional occupations, workers advance their career by moving. In the past, employers assumed that committed workers would make these moves, and the workers did. Today, however, geographic moves present serious problems for dual-career couples.

Husbands' and wives' concerns do not carry equal weight in family decisions about whether to move. Usually it is the wives who sacrifice their careers and their earnings so the husband can advance. In 1992, men accounted for 82 percent of all corporate moves (Employee Relocation Council 1992). Mainstream economists would explain that families maximize their total income by following the best-paying job and that this job is usually the man's. But most families favor moving if the husband wants to, even if losing the wife's income will set back her career or reduce the household's income (Bielby and Bielby 1992b). Cultural beliefs support this arrangement. In 1985 a majority of both women and men in a national sample believed that a wife should give up a "good and interesting" job if her husband were offered a better one elsewhere (Simon and Landis 1989). Findings like these highlight men's greater power in decisions that affect the family.

Problems for Men

The conflicts that men experience between their work and family roles differ greatly from those women face. Since industrialization, men's primary family role has been breadwinner.[7] Thus, men's primary work/family problems occur when they are unable to perform the breadwinner role, are discontented with the role's limits, or view their wives as competitors for the role.

Unemployment. Men's traditional role as primary breadwinner has led researchers to assume that unemployment is particularly problematic for men. Until recently, most research showed more emotional distress among unemployed men than unemployed women, although this is no longer the case (Kessler et al. 1987). These ill effects are worst for men whose wives are employed (Turner 1992). The erosion of their family power presumably heightens men's distress at losing their breadwinner role. Indeed, interviews with families during the Great Depression showed that unemployed men lost their wives' and children's respect. An unemployed father said, "When a father cannot support his family, supply them with clothing and good food, the children are bound to lose respect" (Komarovsky 1940:98). His employed 17-year-old son added, "He is not the same father, that's all. You can't help not looking up to him like we used to" (Komarovsky 1940:100–1).

In societies where men are defined solely as earners, male unemployment is associated with family violence. If society decrees that a man's sole contribution to family life is his paycheck, he will feel worthless if

---

[7]Society has given men—but never women—permission to escape from their family obligations. Indeed, only half the women with legal orders for child support receive the full amount. The rest are about evenly divided between those who receive partial payments and those who receive none (Lester 1991).

he cannot live up to that obligation, and feelings of worthlessness can lead to violence. Research for the United States has shown that unemployment increases the likelihood that a man will abuse his wife (Straus et al. 1980:129).

Discontent with the breadwinner role. Many men resent bearing the entire financial responsibility for their families. This responsibility can limit men's options both at work and at home. A cabinetmaker during the Great Depression, for example, wanted to learn radio mechanics, but because he was the sole provider for his family, he could not afford to quit his job to retrain.

Some men acutely feel the disconnection that arises between themselves and their children when work requires that they sacrifice time with their family. One father in a recent study was disturbed by how little he saw his children:

> In the past year, I've been lucky to get home on weekends and am often away for six weeks at a time without seeing my kids. A new child was born six months ago, and she doesn't even recognize me. (Andrews and Bailyn 1993:265)

In contrast, one man who took advantage of his company's generous family-leave policy enjoyed the experience: "I got one of the best months [to be home], three months old. It's a great time to inherit a kid" (Fried 1993).

The proportion of men who still believe that the provider role belongs exclusively to men has been falling. In 1988, only 30 percent of a national sample of men agreed that it is best for men to hold the provider role while women take care of the home, down from 69 percent in 1977 (National Opinion Research Corporation 1990; Wilkie 1993).

Power struggles with wives. The traditional division of labor that kept women from contributing financially to the family also preserved men's dominance in the family and kept men from seeing their wives as competitors. Earning wages gives women higher status and more power in family decisions (Blumstein and Schwartz 1983). Men feel the difference: One study found that the more income women earned, the more their husbands felt underpaid (Mirowsky 1987). When women outearn their husbands, relations between the couple can become even more tense.

Families try to avoid such power struggles in various ways. In Ghana, where women have traditionally earned money by selling fish, women reduce tension by keeping their income secret from their husbands. As one woman explained,

We never discussed matters having to do with his or my income and work. Once a husband gets to know about the finances of his wife, the man begins to be tight with money. He will not be willing to take some of the financial responsibility [for the children] that he previously was shouldering. Therefore a safe practice is to keep the man in the dark. (C. Robertson 1984:71)

Women's growing labor force participation is difficult for men who fear that it will erode their importance in the family, and families struggle to reduce the tension this change creates.

Responses to Work/Family Conflicts

Attempts to resolve work/family conflicts tend to center on the practical problems of juggling work and family life, particularly the childcare problem. In this country, individual women have been largely responsible for finding ways to accommodate both work and family roles. Only when the problems have become so severe that they spill over into the workplace or affect politicians have governments and private employers stepped in. Some employers have instituted such programs as home work, flexible schedules, and help with childcare. The U.S. government, however, has done little to help families cope. Even when employers or the government have acted, they have addressed mainly childcare issues. Rarely has either looked for innovative ways to assist with day-to-day domestic chores. Thus these chores remain in the family or are turned over to paid providers. In this section we examine the programs that employers have implemented; then we turn to those that European and U.S. governments have initiated.

Employer-Sponsored Programs

Employers have devised some strategies to accommodate family responsibilities—although far fewer than employers provide in other industrialized countries—mainly in order to improve recruitment and to reduce turnover among women workers. Employers with the most far-reaching programs are those, such as hospitals, that depend on a female workforce. When Kaiser Shipbuilding Company sought to recruit women workers during the labor shortage brought on by World War II, it provided on-site, around-the-clock childcare, facilities for sick children, and even cheap carryout dinners for working mothers to take home (Sidel 1986:119). But at war's end, when Kaiser no longer needed to retain women, it abolished these programs. Almost half a century later, a few employers provide benefits similar to those that Kaiser provided. For example, Riverside Hospital in Columbus, Ohio, which has a female chief executive officer, provides on-site childcare (including care for sick children) and eldercare. More revolutionary is its practice of allowing any employee to fax a shopping list to a nearby grocery store, which then delivers the groceries to a pickup site in the staff parking lot. This section discusses some of the employer-sponsored programs that have been implemented to keep costs down or to retain valued women workers; these programs are now helping some workers cope with work/family conflict.

Assistance with childcare. Over half of employers provide workers with some kind of help with childcare (U.S. Bureau of Labor Statistics 1988). Employers institute childcare-assistance programs to address problems of recruitment, absenteeism, and turnover (Ferber and O'Farrell 1991:133).[8] Figure 8.3 shows the most common forms of assistance. But the most common forms—scheduling policies that make it easier for parents to be home when their children are and childcare counseling and referral services—tend to be the least helpful. Only 5.2 percent of employers provided the most helpful benefit, which is on-site childcare.

Just because most employers offer some kind of assistance with childcare, it does not follow that most workers get help. As Figure 8.3 shows, large companies are more likely than small ones to provide benefits; however, small companies employ the majority of workers. In 1989, 5 percent of all full-time employees were eligible for childcare assistance, and 11 percent were eligible for flexible scheduling (Hyland 1990). By and large, high-status workers receive far more childcare benefits than other workers. In 1990, 39 percent of female professionals had access to at least one childcare-related employment benefit, but only 11 percent of service workers did (Kleiman 1993a). In the same year, college-educated women were three times more likely to have access to such benefits than high-school graduates were. As economist Heidi Hartmann observed, "Employers care more about the better-educated, higher-skilled workers and try harder to recruit and retain them" (Kleiman 1993a).

Flexible scheduling. Employers in industrial societies traditionally have organized work so that all workers are present during the same hours. This

---

[8]One study showed that failures in childcare arrangements had caused between 6 and 15 percent of mothers to lose time from work in the previous month (Hofferth et al. 1991:346).

FIGURE 8.3

Percentage of Employers Offering Selected Childcare Benefits, 1987

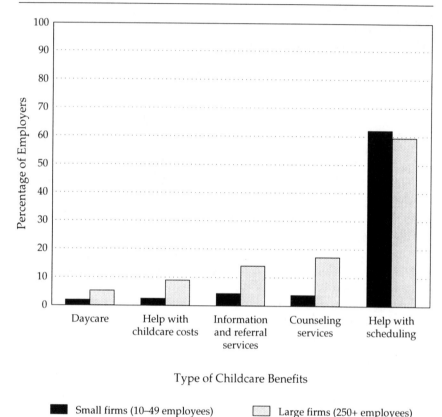

Type of Childcare Benefits

■ Small firms (10–49 employees)   ☐ Large firms (250+ employees)

Source: Data from U.S. Bureau of Labor Statistics 1988:table 1.

tradition is changing, however. In 1991, among full-time, year-round workers, 15.5 percent of men and 14.5 percent of women worked evenings, nights, rotating shifts, or other irregular schedules (U.S. Bureau of Labor Statistics 1992d). A government survey found that in 1987, 35 percent of firms offered some workers part-time work and 43 percent offered some leeway in scheduling working hours (U.S Bureau of Labor Statistics 1988). Far fewer firms allowed two people to share a full-time job (16 percent) or let employees work at home some or all of the time (8 percent).

Such policies accommodate workers' family burdens only when workers have a choice about them. Flexibility at McDonald's restaurants, for example, means that workers are supposed to be flexible about working late or leaving early depending on how busy the outlet is (Leidner 1993:51). Employers in the British baking industry hired women part time to increase employers' flexibility in dealing with the fluctuating demand for baked goods (Beechey and Perkins 1987).

Workers who have a say in their hours of work, however, find flexible schedules useful in arranging childcare. In fact, a 1992 poll found that, although the majority of women prefer full-time over part-time work (or no work), they want flexible scheduling to be a condition of full-time work (N. Collins 1993a).

Catalyst (1986), an organization interested in improving women's access to high-level jobs, has put forward a controversial proposal to create a new career path for professionals who want to combine career and family. Workers on this proposed career path would have less demanding work schedules but would be promoted more slowly. Although the proposed slow track would be available to both sexes, the media dubbed it the "mommy track," and past experience suggests that most men would avoid it. If so, Catalyst's proposal would reinforce the traditional sexual division of labor at home while perpetuating sex differences in promotions and authority at work. Although we know of no employers that have formally implemented the "mommy track," an informal separate mobility track for women has long been in operation, as Chapter 5 showed.

Home work. **Home work** refers to paid jobs that workers do at home. Home workers include two distinct groups: professional workers and clerical or blue-collar workers (Leidner 1988; Tomaskovic-Devey and Risman 1993). Employers typically pay clerical and blue-collar home workers on a piecework basis for such tasks as knitting sweaters on a machine, making costume jewelry, or entering insurance claims on a computer. Moreover, the volume and scheduling of work are unsteady, the pay is low, and workers receive few or no benefits (Costello 1989). Such home work is reminiscent of preindustrial cottage industry in some ways. For example, home work has historically used child labor. This practice continues today when the home-working parent must produce a certain number of units or is paid on a piecework basis (Leidner 1988). In the 1940s, the U.S. Department of Labor outlawed most cottage industry, but it became legal again during the Reagan administration. Employers have reintroduced home work for clerical and blue-collar workers to reduce labor costs by avoiding fringe benefits (such as sick leave and health insurance).

Caring for children while doing another job is a problem for home workers (Christensen 1989:193). Although home work may appeal to women without affordable childcare, many find that working near their children does not necessarily make childcare easier. One home worker who processed insurance claims complained about the company's irregular scheduling of the work load: "If you'd [unexpectedly] get six hours of work someday and you have two little kids at home and you only have three hours worth of TV, when are you going to get the work done?" (Costello 1989:207). Home work is therefore often not a satisfactory solution to work/family conflict for working-class women.

The other large group of home workers consists of high-status professionals. Employers' main reasons for instituting home work for professionals are to enhance their productivity, satisfaction, and retention (Tomaskovic-Devey and Risman 1993). Like clerical workers, professional workers often use computer hookups to do their work. In contrast to clerical home workers, however, professional workers receive the same pay and benefits that they would in the office. Yet they too may experience a cost: Working from home renders them less visible in their organization and thus may reduce their promotion chances.[9]

Summary. Labor shortages predicted for the end of the century may force corporations to take more responsibility for helping employees reconcile family and work. But two problems arise in leaving the hope for change with corporations. First, as we will discuss in Chapter 9, the workforce is polarizing into two groups: privileged workers (managers and professionals) and contingent workers (those with no job security, often in temporary or part-time jobs) who are hired and fired according to employers' labor needs. Employers tend to make family benefits available only to privileged workers. Second, most people work for small companies that cannot afford costly changes. To meet the needs of the majority of workers, the government must become more involved.

Government-Sponsored Programs

Some governments have addressed work/family conflicts by offering services that help both women and men accommodate their dual responsi-

---

[9]Both sexes do home work; in fact, more men than women work at home. But whereas female home workers spend more time on housework than do comparable women who travel to a worksite, male home workers spend no more time on housework or childcare than their male counterparts do (Silver 1993).

bilities. But the United States has provided fewer such benefits than the governments of many other advanced industrial countries. There are two reasons for this disparity. First, this country has not faced the persistent labor shortages that prompted other countries to encourage women's labor force participation. Only during wartime have labor shortages led the United States to institute such policies. In World War II, for example, when the United States desperately needed women to fill war-related jobs vacated by men, federal and state governments established 3,012 childcare centers (Sidel 1986:119). The second reason that the United States provides fewer benefits is ideological. Whereas European societies place a premium on social welfare, American ideology values individual freedom above all else. The American tradition of individualism is at odds with the notion that a country has a stake in raising the next generation. In contrast, Europeans believe that society bears some responsibility for family well-being and will gain from investing in the next generation.

Neither labor shortages nor ideology are enough to ensure that governments will address the family needs of workers. Consider the Soviet Union, which was the first country to make a public commitment to providing family services—partly because it badly needed women laborers and partly because the country's governing ideology mandated equality between the sexes. Beyond providing childcare, however, the Soviet government did nothing to aid women in their dual roles. In 1984 Soviet women had the highest rate of labor force participation in the world (90 percent) but were still responsible for all domestic labor except childcare (Attwood and McAndrew 1984).

The attempt to provide relief from women's double day has also failed in postrevolutionary Cuba. After offering free childcare for years to draw women into the labor force, the Cuban government decided that incorporating men into domestic work would be cheaper. A 1975 law made men and women equally responsible for family work (Nazzari 1986). However, inequalities in the power of women and men doomed the law to fail. In 1982 women still did virtually all the housework in most households (Catasus et al. 1988)

Are market economies more successful than nonmarket ones in helping women with the double day? In the Western hemisphere, except for childcare, the answer is no. Western European governments offer a wide range of social-insurance programs that cover many basic human needs, including family care (we discuss these later). But none of these countries has devised mechanisms to spare working women from the daily drudgery of cooking, cleaning, and marketing. Instead, they have devised ways to allow women to do these things and still work for pay. Part-time work in Scandinavia, for instance, comes with guaranteed health-care benefits, which are rare in the United States. As a result, Scandinavian women are less likely than American women to work full time: 50 percent of Norwegian and Swedish women are employed part time, compared to only 25 percent of U.S. women (Kalleberg and Rosenfeld 1990; U.S. Bureau of Labor Statistics 1993a).

Although Western industrialized nations have not relieved women of other domestic duties, many nations do require employers to provide leave for giving birth, rearing small children, and caring for elderly relatives. Mandated maternity or parental leave is now common, as Table 8.2 shows. Sweden's plan is the most extensive: 270 days of leave at 90 percent of pay after a child's birth, another 90 days at a lower rate of pay, and 18 months of unpaid leave.

In comparison, parental leave in the United States is paltry. Until recently, the United States had no federal laws requiring employers to provide any kind of leave (including sick leave), and few employers voluntarily offered it. Although 21 states required employers to provide some form of family leave for some employees (Ferber and O'Farrell 1991:148) in 4 of those states, which were studied in depth, 24 percent of the employers failed to meet the mandated minimum requirements (Families and Work Institute 1991). Then in 1993 President Clinton signed into law the Family and Medical Leave Act. The act, which applies only to establishments with 50 or more employees, requires employers to provide up to 12 weeks of unpaid leave and job protection

TABLE 8.2

Parental Leave Policies for Selected Western Industrialized Countries

Country	Duration of Leave (in weeks)	Percenage of Pay	Recipient
Sweden	12–52	90 for 38 weeks	Mother or father
West Germany	52	100 for 14–18 weeks	Mother of father
Austria	16–52	100 for 20 weeks	Mother
Italy	22–48	80 for 22 weeks	Mother
Chile	18	100 for 18 weeks	Mother
Canada	17–41	60 for 15 weeks	Mother
United States	12	0	Mother or father

Source: Adapted from John J. Sweeney and Karen Nussbaum, *Solutions for the New Workforce*. Cabin John, MD: Seven Locks Press, 1989, p. 108. Reprinted with permission.

after a pregnancy or other family emergency. The act covers both fathers and mothers and both biological and adopting parents (although it excludes same-sex domestic partners). Because most U.S. workers work in small businesses, as we noted earlier, most are not covered. Also, the law is of no value to parents who cannot afford unpaid leave. According to one study, fewer than 40 percent of working women have benefits or income protection that would allow them to take a six-week unpaid leave (9to5 1992).

Maternity- and family-leave policies can help reduce the work/family conflict that women experience, but the policies pose a risk for their beneficiaries. Family leave may reinforce the existing sexual division of labor. Traditional gender roles and men's higher pay mean that wives, not husbands, will usually take the leave. A 1990 survey of the 1,000 largest U.S. companies found that although 31 percent offered paternity leave, only about 1 percent of eligible employees took it (Robert Half International, 1990). Many fathers fear that family leave will cost them a promotion, and they may be right. Catalyst (1986) found that 63 percent of all employers, and 41 percent of employers with a leave policy, disapproved of fathers' taking any leave for the birth of a child. One Oregon employer, for example, worried that men employees would use the leave to go elk hunting (Larson 1993). Even with all their shortcomings, however, family-leave policies are a significant step forward. They force employers to acknowledge workers' nonwork lives. But workers need to be vigilant to ensure that family leaves do not perpetuate women's inequality.

In childcare policies, as in family-leave policies, the vast majority of European countries offer more comprehensive options than the United States does, although the United States offers more than developing nations. Care for preschoolers in Europe is considered a government responsibility, regardless of parents' employment status. In Belgium and France, publicly funded institutions care for 95 percent of children between the ages of 3 and 5; Italy cares for 90 percent; and Denmark cares for 85 percent (Ferber and O'Farrell 1991:168). Swedes have a strong public commitment to childcare, which they express in high taxes for quality childcare centers, in-home care for younger children, and recreation centers for older children (Sidel 1986). The passage in 1990 of the Early Childhood and Education Act moved the United States closer to the European model. Through expanded tax credits for working parents and increased funding for Head Start programs, the law gives low- and moderate-income families more access to childcare.

In conclusion, any nation's policies to provide family leave, guaranteed benefits for part-time work, and publicly funded childcare help women manage their work and family responsibilities. But if the policies are gendered, they can also hurt women by reinforcing women's subordinate position in the labor market and in the home (Bergmann 1986). Mandatory leave can discourage employers from hiring women for some jobs and confine women to jobs with routine duties, where they can be replaced easily. Mandatory family leave may also keep pay low in customarily women's jobs to offset the cost of leave. Finally, family-leave policies—if men reject them—reinforce the idea that caring for family members is exclusively women's responsibility. The gendered effects of part-time work are also a concern. By making part-time work more available to women, the Swedish and Norwegian governments have helped women cope with the work/family burden; however, they have reinforced the sexual division of labor at home and reduced women's pay and promotion opportunities. Obviously, policymakers must examine such policies carefully to make sure they will encourage sex equality in the home and in the workplace.

Summary

As we noted in Chapter 1, society devalues unpaid domestic work and thus allocates it to the lower-status group: women. If there were a Nobel Prize for dishwashing, women would not be allowed near the sink. Although childcare and family-leave policies are becoming more common, nowhere have employers or governments attempted to relieve women's domestic burdens of cooking, cleaning, laundry, marketing, and dishwashing. Some women can afford to buy these services, but for the most part, these domestic tasks remain thoroughly in women's hands within the private sphere. Labeling these tasks as women's work forces women, not men, to reconcile domestic work with paid work. If fairness is a goal in restructuring the relationship between family and work, inequalities in the sexual division of labor must be addressed. The alternative—women shouldering the entire burden of the double day—will preserve inequality at home and in the workplace for another generation.

Women, Men, and Work in the Twenty-First Century

In this chapter we ask what changes we can expect in women's and men's work lives at the turn of the twenty-first century. What trends will affect employment in general, and how are these trends likely to affect the topics raised in this book? We conclude by speculating on what the future holds for women and men at work.

Trends in Work at the End of the Twentieth Century

Four major workplace changes are currently underway in America: the restructuring of the economy toward decreased employment in manufacturing and increased employment in services; the polarization of jobs into simpler, deskilled jobs and upgraded, more complex ones; the increasing importance of part-time and temporary workers; and the growing diversity in the workforce. The first three trends—economic restructuring, upgrading and deskilling, and increasing part-time and temporary work—are occurring as a result of employers' attempts to compete profitably in an increasingly global economy. The increasing diversity in the workplace is a result of changes in this country's demography.

Economic Restructuring

Economic restructuring is the ongoing transformation of a nation's economy, in which some industries and jobs grow and others decline. For several decades, the proportion of U.S. workers employed in production industries has been dropping and the proportion employed in services has been growing. The manufacturing sector is projected to employ only about 13 percent of workers by the year 2005, down from a high of 24 percent in 1940 (Kutscher 1991:7). Many U.S. firms have been exporting manufacturing jobs to lower-wage parts of the world, such as Asia and Mexico.[1] The loss of these jobs has contributed to the decline in American men's earnings which we discussed in Chapter 6.

While the U.S. industrial base has been crumbling, the growth of the service sector has created millions of new jobs. This trend, too, will continue. Experts project that almost 90 percent of new jobs created between 1988 and the year 2000 will be in the service sector (National Commission on Working Women 1990) and that 81 percent of all jobs in the year 2005 will be in service industries (Carey and Franklin 1991).

The decline of the manufacturing sector and explosion of the service sector matter because these sectors provide very different kinds of jobs. Wages tend to be substantially lower in the service sector: For every dollar an employer paid in manufacturing wages in 1991, a retail-trade worker or personal-services worker earned 63 cents (U.S. Bureau of the Census 1992d). In addition, service-sector jobs have twice the turnover rate of those in manufacturing and are substantially more likely to be part time, hence lacking benefits.

Many of the fastest-growing service occupations are in well-paying fields like law, medicine, and computers. However, the occupations predicted to supply the most new jobs (with the exceptions of registered nurses and general managers) are low-skilled, low-paying ones such as waiter, janitor, and food-counter worker (see Table 9.1). In fact, low-skilled, low-paying jobs are predicted to employ eight times more workers than highly skilled service-sector jobs are (Silvestri and Lukasiewicz 1987).

Upgrading and Deskilling

The second trend is change in the level of skills that jobs demand. Economic restructuring is **upgrading** some jobs and **deskilling**—or reducing the complexity, skill, and knowledge—of others. The decline in manufacturing jobs has cost the economy many skilled and semiskilled blue-collar jobs. At the same time, the growth of the service sector has created both skilled and unskilled jobs. As Table 9.1 shows, however, low-skill service-sector jobs will predominate.

One way that employers have deskilled jobs is through new technologies (Levin and Rumberger 1987). This sort of deskilling has occurred in

---

[1]Many of these jobs in developing countries go to women, drawing them into the labor force and providing them with pay and autonomy that they would not otherwise have. But this employment also subjects women to sweatshop working conditions, extremely low pay, and hazardous jobs.

TABLE 9.1

Occupations with the Largest Projected Job Growth, 1990 to 2005

Occupation	Number of Projected New Jobs	Percent Female (1992)	Median Weekly Wages for Both Sexes (1992)
Retail sales clerks	887,000	54.5	$270
Registered nurses	767,000	93.5	662
Cashiers	685,000	75.7	219
General office clerks	670,000	84.1	356
Truck drivers	617,000	3.3	418
Managers and administrators	598,000	43.6	650
Janitors and cleaners	555,000	22.0	291
Nursing aides, orderlies	552,000	87.9	266
Food-counter and related workers	550,000	60.9	204
Waiters, waitresses	449,000	72.9	222
Secondary school teachers	437,000	53.9	610
Information clerks and receptionists	422,000	88.6	319

Source: Data from Silvestri and Lukasiewicz 1991:table 4; U.S. Bureau of Labor Statistics 1992a:table 5.

secretarial work, bookkeeping, printing, and insurance adjusting and underwriting, to name a few occupations. According to Randy Hodson and Robert Parker (1988:25), "Increasingly, whether the context is manufacturing or the automated office, control and discretion are being removed from workers and placed directly in automated equipment." The occupation of butcher, for example, has been deskilled by the introduction of boxed beef (in which central processing plants do many of the early stages of processing); as a result, cutters need less technical competence (Walsh 1989). Deskilling is also common at fast-food restaurants. Burger King can now train workers to operate the cash register with nine minutes of training, and it is trying to cut two minutes off this time (Hodgkinson 1988). Twenty years ago, a McDonald's counter worker needed the ability to work a cash register and make change; today counter workers need only identify the picture of a hamburger on the register. Moreover, many modern cash registers now are programmed to take over part of the selling job: When a McDonald's counter worker punches the keys for a hamburger and a shake, the keys for apple pie, cookies, and ice cream light up to remind the worker to suggest them (Leidner 1991). In clerical work, the secretary of 20 years ago was a generalist, performing a wide variety of tasks; that worker has been replaced by the word-processing operator, whose sole task is to manually strike a keyboard, often under electronic surveillance (Sweeney and Nussbaum 1989).

At the same time, new technology—especially computerization—is upgrading some jobs (Zuboff 1988). Some innovative companies have re-designed jobs to provide workers with more autonomy, because autonomy is critical for a quick response to a rapidly changing business environment. These upgraded jobs tend to offer high wages and advancement potential. Workers in upgraded jobs can also develop their skills and expertise in a variety of areas.

Researchers are debating whether deskilling or upgrading predominates in today's workplace. They agree, however, that advanced technology in itself does not determine the skill level of a job. Instead, employers and workers determine what effect new technology has on work: If workers have no power and if employers do not seek the advantages of a more skilled workforce, then new technology is likely to lead to deskilling (Hodson and Parker 1988).

The Rise of the Contingent Workforce

The third trend is the expansion of the contingent workforce. **Contingent work** is any job in which workers lack an explicit or implicit contract for long-term employment or in which the minimum hours vary unsystematically (Polivka and Nardone 1989:11). In short, contingent workers lack job security and income security. Their jobs depend on the employer's need for workers. Contingent workers include temporary workers, many part-time workers, and some independent contractors.

Employers rely on contingent workers so they can expand and contract their workforce in response to changing circumstances. The economic rationale behind a contingent workforce is cost savings. Not having to pay for health insurance, sick leave, unemployment insurance, workers' compensation, Social Security, pensions, and vacations saves employers 20 to 40 percent of the cost of regular employees (Sweeney and Nussbaum 1989; Callaghan and Hartmann 1991). The same factors that make contingent work attractive to employers—the lack of job security and benefits—make it unattractive to workers. Not surprisingly, con-

tingent employment has been concentrated in industries where workers
have little power to combat the practice through unions (Cornfield 1987).
Contingent workers include three groups:

- *Temporary workers.* Temporary employment grew 3 to 10 times faster
than overall employment between 1982 and 1992 (Ansberry 1993;
Hartmann 1993). In 1992, two-thirds of new private-sector jobs were
temporary (Ansberry 1993). Many of these contingent workers hold
a series of jobs punctuated by unemployment; they often find jobs
through temporary-employment agencies, which have burgeoned in
recent years. Clerical work has been the mainstay of temporary
work, but increasingly employers are hiring professional and technical workers on this basis (Christensen 1989). For example, some
computer programmers, accountants, and managers now work on a
contingent basis.

- *Part-time workers.* Part-time employment has been growing fastest in
the retail-trade and service sectors (Tilly 1991). Among all employed
nonagricultural workers, 18.9 percent worked part time in 1992, but
the proportion of part-time workers in services was 23.6 percent
(U.S. Bureau of Labor Statistics 1993a). Most part-time jobs provide
few fringe benefits and no opportunity for advancement. Their
greatest disadvantage, however, is the low pay. The average part-
time worker earned only 58 percent of the hourly pay of a full-time
worker in 1989 (Tilly 1991:12); the hourly pay was even less for
workers employed part time and for part of the year (Institute for
Women's Policy Research 1993a). As you might guess, turnover is
high. The U.S. Bureau of Labor Statistics classifies part-time employment as being either voluntary or involuntary. Between 1970 and
1990, almost 90 percent the growth in part-time employment was
due to the growth of involuntary part-time employment (Callaghan
and Hartmann 1991). Thus it seems that the growth of part-time
employment is largely driven by employer needs, not workers'
choices.

- *Independent contractors.* As Chapter 5 explained, independent
contractors are workers whom employers hire on a freelance basis
to do work that regular employees otherwise would do in-house
(Christensen 1989). According to the Internal Revenue Service, the
number of independent contractors grew by over 50 percent
between 1985 and 1988, to 9.5 million workers (U.S. General Accounting Office 1991). Employers have switched many workers to
independent-contractor status to save on fringe benefits, reduce the

permanent payroll, and reduce tax requirements. Many textbook editors, real estate agents, and building cleaners, for example, now work on this basis, whereas in the past they were regular employees. Even professionals are subject to becoming independent contractors (Zachary and Ortega 1993). Aetna Life & Casualty Company cut 2,600 jobs in 1992 and then rehired many laid-off workers to do the same job as independent contractors, at lower pay and without benefits (Zachary and Ortega 1993).

The numbers of independent contractors, temporary workers, and part-time workers—the contingent workforce—are growing and undoubtedly will continue to grow. It is difficult to measure contingent employment, because some contingent workers fall in more than one category, but one estimate is that in 1988 about 25 to 30 percent of the workforce was made up of contingent workers (Belous 1989).

Workforce Diversity

According to the U.S. Bureau of Labor Statistics, women, minorities, and immigrants make up a growing segment of the workforce, and their share is predicted to continue growing at least through the year 2005 (Kutscher 1991). Whites are expected to remain the majority of workers, but their share of the labor force is expected to drop from 78.6 percent in 1990 to 73 percent in 2005. African Americans will expand their share of the workforce from 10.7 percent in 1990 to 11.6 percent in 2005. Hispanics will increase even more rapidly, from 7.7 percent of the workforce to 11.1 percent, exceeding the projected growth in labor force participation of African Americans. Asians and others are expected to increase from 3.1 percent of the labor force to 4.3 percent.

Immigration has fueled recent population growth in the United States. Whereas in the 1960s immigration was responsible for only 11 percent of population growth, in the 1970s it accounted for 33 percent, and in the 1980s it accounted for 39 percent (Johnston and Packer 1987). Legal and undocumented immigrants are also likely to be the fastest-growing group in the labor market. Recent immigrants, most of whom are from Asia and Latin America, tend to be either high-skilled, well-educated workers or low-skilled, little-educated ones ("Immigrants" 1992). The rising number of immigrants and their historical tendency to be active in the labor force means that they will make up an increasing share of the labor force.

Implications for Working Women and Men

These economic changes will have a substantial effect on progress toward equality between women and men in the workforce. The impact will be felt in five areas: labor force participation, sex segregation, the pay gap, the gendering of work, and the relationship between work and family.

Labor Force Participation

Society has come to take women in the work force for granted. Women will account for 62 percent of net labor force growth between 1990 and 2005, and men's labor force participation will decline slightly. As a result, in 2005, 47.4 percent of the civilian labor force will be female (U.S. Women's Bureau 1992). The labor force participation rates of women of color are projected to outpace white women's: Hispanic and Asian women's participation rate will grow 80 percent between 1900 and 2005, African-American women's will grow 34 percent, and white women's will grow 23 percent (U.S. Women's Bureau 1992).

By the turn of the twenty-first century, 61 percent of all working-age women are projected to be in the labor force (Fullerton 1987), up from 57.8 percent in 1992 (U.S. Women's Bureau 1993). Just 30 years ago, researchers were asking whether working mothers caused juvenile delinquency. Now most young women college graduates expect to work full time. As a result, researchers and federal agencies are asking how society can accommodate women's labor force participation, and employers are exploring ways to facilitate their increasing dependency on women workers.

Sex Segregation

The preface to this book described a prospective employer's unequal treatment of male and female applicants for the position of manager for a lawn-care firm. Can we expect prospective employers in the year 2005 to treat women and men more equally than the Cincinnati employer did in the summer of 1993? In this section we consider the ways in which economic restructuring and the changing nature of work may indeed affect the degree of sex segregation at the beginning of the twenty-first century.

The overall level of segregation in the future will depend partly on trends in the occupations that are already heavily segregated. The growth of female-dominated jobs—such as information clerk, nurses' aide, and food-counter worker—will tend to increase sex segregation in the workplace.[2] On the other hand, the loss of heavily male skilled and semiskilled manufacturing jobs will help offset the segregative effect of the growth of predominantly female jobs. Obviously, segregation that stems from the loss of desirable jobs is not in anyone's interest. The kind of integration that will benefit women and society will result from women's expanded access to all jobs—the good ones and the not-so-good ones.

Two factors point to the continuation of a sex segregated workforce. Although the trend toward upgrading will help highly educated, computer-literate women, minorities, and immigrants, deskilling is likely to consign others to low-skill jobs. Moreover, as economic restructuring shrinks the number of well-paying, male-dominated jobs, men are likely to resist women's entry into customarily male jobs.

On the bright side, the credentials and lifetime work expectations that women bring to the job increasingly resemble men's, so employers may be more likely to treat the sexes similarly. Additionally, as employers gain more experience with competent women in nontraditional jobs, competitive pressure to hire the best available workers may induce employers to hire more women.

In the workplace of the year 2000, the increased presence of women, nonwhites, and immigrants in the labor force may mean that the good jobs will not be reserved for "people with white skins . . . and wing tips" (White 1992:35). For example, if a lawn-care service seeks to hire 10 people and women are 6 of the 10 best-qualified applicants, the chances are good that the company will hire some women. Given the present concentration of women, minorities, and immigrants in the lower echelons of the labor market, however, a great deal of change will be necessary for them to move to the top.

The increased numbers of ethnic minorities in the labor force does not mean that they will find enhanced employment opportunities. These

---

[2]Part of the increase in sex segregation will be due to the growth of contingent jobs that are female-dominated (Callaghan and Hartmann 1991). Employers seeking contingent workers rely heavily on groups concentrated at the bottom of the labor hierarchy: women, minorities, youth, and the elderly (Sweeney and Nussbaum 1989). Consider temporary and part-time workers: In the late 1980s, women were about 45 percent of total workers but about two-thirds of all temporary and part-time workers (Tilly 1991). African Americans are also overrepresented among temporary workers: In the mid 1980s, they were 10.4 percent of the labor force but 12 percent of temporary workers (Howe 1986).

workers are concentrated in declining occupations and are under-represented in rapidly growing skilled occupations (Kutscher 1991:9; Silvestri and Lukasiewicz 1991:92). In addition, minorities' relative disadvantages in education and training—along with discrimination—will restrict their access to the higher-paying new jobs. In 1990, for example, African Americans made up only 7 percent and Hispanics only 3 percent of workers in the fast-growing occupation of mathematical and computer scientist (Silvestri and Lukasiewicz 1991). Yet these two minority groups were each 14 percent of the workers in the declining occupation of machine operators, assemblers, and inspectors.

The promotion gap. Will economic restructuring enhance women's chances of promotion? Not likely. Employers are eliminating many middle-management jobs as part of the retrenchment that has accompanied growing international competition. This economizing is likely to hamper women's and minorities' promotion chances for three reasons. First, the glass ceiling has trapped many women and minorities in exactly those midlevel management jobs that are slated for elimination, putting them at risk of unemployment; similarly, women's and minorities' concentration in staff positions that are not central to the organization's primary mission—such as personnel, public relations, and affirmative action—puts them at greater risk of unemployment. Second, the elimination of middle-management jobs will destroy job ladders out of the lower-level jobs in which women and minorities have been concentrated. Third, because higher-level jobs will require up-to-date training and skills, employers are likely to prefer newly trained graduates from outside the firm over current employees (Acker 1992).

The authority gap. The changing economy is not likely to improve women's and minorities' access to authority on the job either. Of course, some women will be found in those new upgraded, autonomous jobs where workers can exercise authority. Currently, however, the service-sector jobs that most women hold are the type that employers are most likely to deskill or shift to contingent status (Eitzen and Baca-Zinn 1992). Most female workers are unlikely to overcome the authority gap unless the government enforces laws designed to protect women's and minorities' access to jobs with authority. The U.S. Department of Labor's recent initiative to enforce the Glass Ceiling Act of 1991 provides a basis for cautious optimism.

Polarization between jobs that offer considerable decision-making authority and those that offer little may be under way within traditionally female jobs (Acker 1992). This split is between routine, low-wage, closely supervised jobs and relatively nonroutine, high-paying, autonomous jobs. Within nursing, for example, nurses and nurses' aides are moving further apart (Glazer 1991). New technology has upgraded the jobs of registered nurses, whereas the work of nurses' aides is low skilled and is paid at near-minimum wage. Women of color are concentrated disproportionately in the least desirable of the traditionally female occupations, so that polarization within these jobs is likely to raise yet another barrier to minority women's chances to exercise authority on the job.

Computerization is another force that may exacerbate the authority gap. Computerization allows bosses to more closely supervise lower-level workers, who disproportionately are women and ethnic minorities. In 1987, one study showed, employers used computers to monitor the work of 4 million to 6 million workers (Sweeney and Nussbaum 1989:155). One telephone company, for example, allowed operators 20 seconds per call. An employee claimed that operators have so little time to assist customers that they sometimes give out wrong numbers just to get customers off the line (Sweeney and Nussbaum 1989:155).

Research hints that the trend toward upgrading workers' skills and responsibilities benefits women less often than men. When Swedish banks assigned female tellers to tasks that managers had formerly done, such as approving loans and providing customers with investment and tax advice, they did not recognize the change as increasing the tellers' skill levels (Acker 1992). Whether skill upgrading increases authority depends partly on employers' willingness to acknowledge work as skilled when women perform it.

The pay gap. Economic and demographic trends may improve the pay gap, although the gap is likely to shrink mostly because of men's declining pay rather than women's increasing pay. Five of ten jobs predicted to expand most by the year 2000 pay below-poverty wages (Silvestri and Lukasiewicz 1987). Thus, according to many observers, the overall impact of restructuring on the wages of ordinary working people has been negative and is likely to remain so (Harrison and Bluestone 1988; Phillips 1990). The risk of unemployment has also increased in the new economy as jobs have been exported overseas to countries where workers command much lower pay than U.S. workers.

The decline in industrial jobs has been particularly destructive for people of color, some of whom had succeeded in moving into the middle class through unionized jobs in heavy industry (Wilson 1991; Higginbotham 1992). These jobs are being replaced by lower-paying jobs or no jobs (Higginbotham 1992:187). Women who had found jobs in traditionally male blue-collar industries have watched their jobs disappear. In general, though, white men have suffered greater earnings losses from industrial decline than women, because men had more to lose in the first place. They earned higher pay than women and minorities and were more likely to work in heavy industry, the sector hardest hit by the transformation of the economy (Acker 1992).

At the same time, the service sector has grown. If you look back at Table 9.1, you can see that some of the growth in the service sector will continue to be in higher-level professional, managerial, and technical fields where salaries are high (Acker 1992). But a great deal of the growth will be in low-wage service-sector jobs, where women, minorities, and immigrants are currently concentrated.

Overall, then, the pay gap should shrink as women increase their work experience. It will shrink further if women increase their representation in male jobs. The decline of men's average wages, through the loss of industrial jobs and the shift to a service economy, will help to narrow the pay gap but will not improve women's or men's economic condition.

The Gendering of Work

Employers and female and male workers all contribute to the gendered nature of work. One particularly troublesome outcome of gendered work is sexual harassment. The future on this score looks promising. Most large companies have implemented sexual harassment policies and training programs. Most important, however, are court decisions that have held employers responsible for workplace harassment. A unanimous 1993 ruling by the U.S. Supreme Court (*Teresa Harris v. Forklift Systems*) now gives workers a basis for claiming sexual harassment without having to prove that they have suffered psychological damage. Forcing employers to examine how workplace environments foster sexual harassment and holding them accountable is a major step forward.

We note with dismay, however, indications of how deep-seated the gendering of jobs is. Arthur Ochs Sulzberger, Jr., of *The New York Times*, a supporter of equal opportunities for women, has said that he wants to leave his son a more egalitarian paper than the one he inherited. From someone who will shape public opinion in the next century, this statement is encouraging—until we learn that Sulzberger also has a daughter (N. Robertson 1992:252). Even well-intentioned men may have difficulty seeing their own gender biases—in this case, the belief that sons, not daughters, inherit family businesses.

The fact remains that workers gender jobs both because gender is an important element of the larger culture and because those workers want to protect their material interests. To the extent that the four work trends discussed in this chapter—particularly deskilling and the decline of the manufacturing sector—hurt men as a group, male workers will continue to use gendering to preserve their stake in traditionally male jobs and their grip on authority.

The Relationship Between Work and Family

Chapter 8 mentioned that employers have organized work based on the presumption that workers are men who have few, if any, outside demands on their time. Implicitly, in conflicts between work and family, employers have long assumed that the family should take the back seat. Will the workplace of the future assume that work has absolute primacy in workers' lives? We think not.

For several years, employers have been gradually—and often grudgingly—accommodating to the reality of workers' lives, and momentum for more change is building. Some employers instituted family policies as early as 1965, and many such policies have been incorporated into workplace bureaucracies. Although government policies on family are not as far-reaching in the United States as in other industrialized nations, over 60 percent of employers now have personnel policies that help some workers juggle work and family. Few employers, however, have family policies that provide the most useful kinds of help. Congress took a step toward addressing the conflict between family and work by passing the 1993 Family and Medical Leave Act. This law requires employers to give some workers, both female and male, the right to keep their jobs when family crises or normal life events compel workers to take time from paid work. The Family and Medical Leave Act thus formally recognizes that workers have a right to meet family demands without sacrificing their jobs.

Employers' growing reliance on home workers and the growth of small home-based businesses are likely to perpetuate the unequal sexual division of labor between husbands and wives. Expectations that women should have near-exclusive responsibility for housework and childcare have not changed substantially. In 1975, among employed people, men spent 46 percent as much time as women on housework; in 1987 they spent 57 percent as much time. However, most of the improvement was due to couples' leaving tasks undone or hiring others to do them rather than men's doing more (Shelton 1992:74–5). The speed with which the domestic division of labor becomes more equal will depend on women's ability and willingness to insist that their partners share housework. And their ability to insist on more equal sharing will in turn depend on how fast women catch up to men in their paychecks and job status.

Conclusion

Women have made enormous progress in the last 30 years. Many employers treat the sexes more fairly than in the past. Consider the story of one organization. In 1993 the National Institutes of Health commissioned a self-study to learn if it treated its female and male employees equally. The study revealed that men outearned women at almost every rank and that women were less likely than men with the same credentials to be promoted. The director and her subordinates immediately took action: They instituted a formal policy regarding sex discrimination in job ladders, implemented a family-leave policy, vowed to bring women's salaries in line with men's, and formed a commission to recommend ways to discipline employees who engaged in discrimination or sexual harassment (Watson 1993:889). Both the self-study and the agency's response would have been inconceivable 30 years ago. Today the organization takes equality seriously. But the passage of time is not the only explanation for this agency's concern with sex inequality. Note that a woman was at the helm when the self-study was undertaken and when the agency reacted to the study's findings.

Few organizations have women at the top with the power to implement such change. Therefore, how quickly women achieve equality with men at work will largely depend on how much pressure ordinary working women put on employers, legislators, and policymakers. Not until the late 1960s, with the huge influx into the labor force of highly educated women who sought both careers and families, did women mount an attack on sex inequality at work. They sued employers for discrimination and pressured federal agencies to enforce laws against sex discrimination. They demanded and sometimes won flexible work schedules and led the appeal for accessible and affordable childcare. And they organized for pay equity, a concept—like sexual harassment—that was not even in the dictionary 20 years ago.

Opponents to sex equality have not taken these gains lying down, and the 1980s brought an effective counteroffensive. Conservative politicians tried to dilute federal affirmative action regulations, derailed efforts to enforce discrimination rules, and for a time made it harder to prove discrimination in court. They replaced appellate and Supreme Court judges who supported equal rights with opponents of equality. A series of Supreme Court decisions relieved employers of the obligation to desegregate jobs, although the Civil Rights Act of 1991 will help undo the courts' actions.

This backward march has taught us that constant enforcement is crucial in reducing inequality in the workplace. The important laws are in place: Compared to other industrialized countries, our antidiscrimination laws stand alone in providing for serious financial penalties (Bergmann 1986). The challenge is ensuring that regulatory agencies enforce them. Laws like Title VII of the 1964 Civil Rights Act are only as strong as the muscle behind them. Moreover, prohibitive costs of litigation prevent most discrimination victims from turning to the courts. Even a victory in court does not guarantee change. Court decisions that require employers to pay money damages often leave intact underlying discriminatory policies and practices (Bergmann 1986).

Enforcement is crucial, because it can make the cost of discrimination prohibitively high for employers. An attorney offered an analogy between the cost of discrimination and business costs:

> The only reason why we have seat belts or airbags in cars, the only reason why we have protectors on [industrial] presses for people who work on the assembly line is because it was costing the manufacturer of those goods too much money in payments stemming from successful lawsuits by injured people. (White 1992:201)

The prognosis for equality in the workplace depends on what Americans demand of their employers and government. It is encouraging to note that women and men workers have allied to further their rights as citizens and workers, as when the township of Ypsilanti, Michigan, sued General Motors in 1993 for accepting community incentives to remain in the town and then moving to a lower-wage area. Women workers at U.S.-owned factories just over the border in Mexico have organized the *Comite Fronterizo de Obreras* (Border Committee of Women Workers), which has fought successfully to gain higher pay, to protect workers from industrial chemicals, and to force employers to obey the Mexican labor laws. These workers have broadened their influence by forming alliances with churches and sympathetic unions in the United States. They are now investigating ways to permanently change their factories. These examples show that workers who fight can win.

The media and employers often claim that sex discrimination is all but dead. They insist that the barriers are gone: Women, like men, can now succeed through their own individual efforts. If pushed, these authorities may admit that women lag behind men in access to good jobs, promotions, and equal pay. But, they remind us, the American Dream says that if you are number two, like Avis Car Rental, you simply have to try harder. If you are Avis, this strategy may work, because Hertz is not making the rules. Women, however, are still competing in an economic world where men make the rules. Hard work pays off only for some fortunate women with the right class background, educational credentials, skin color, weight—and with good luck. For most women, however, hard work is not enough, because the system of sex inequality has beneficiaries as well as victims and those beneficiaries have a stake in not seeing the problem and minimizing real change.

To work for progress, we must see through the media's message. In a society that applauds its commitment to justice, recognizing injustice is the first step for the social pressure that progress requires. New regulations and better enforcement of existing ones are essential to reducing inequities in work processes and outcomes. Equally important, however, are policies that will improve the overall quality of work. The trends discussed in this chapter indicate the possibility of a deteriorating future, with a growing proportion of workers in low-paid and contingent jobs. Many analysts argue that our society is at a critical juncture where we must consciously break with past policies. A number of these analysts call for federal industrial policies that give employers tax incentives to create good jobs, for workplace policies that promote greater worker control, and for employment policies that provide equal opportunities and rewards regardless of workers' color or sex (see, for example, Harrison and Bluestone 1988; Reich 1991; Thurow 1992). For a better social and economic future, in which greater equity in employment accompanies better jobs for all workers, we must choose a new direction.

References

Acker, Joan. 1990. "Hierarchies, Jobs, Bodies: A Theory of Gendered Organizations." *Gender & Society* 4:139–58.

———. 1992. "The Future of Women and Work: Ending the Twentieth Century." *Sociological Perspectives* 35:53–68.

Adler, Marina A. 1993. "Gender Differences in Job Autonomy: The Consequences of Occupational Segregation and Authority Position." *Sociological Quarterly* 34:449–66.

Adler, Nancy J. 1984. "Women Do Not Want International Careers: And Other Myths About International Management." *Organizational Dynamics* 13:66–79.

———. 1988. "Pacific Basin Managers: A Gaijin, Not a Woman." Pp. 226–49 in Nancy J. Adler and Dafna N. Izraeli (eds.), *Women in Management Worldwide.* New York: M. E. Sharpe.

Administrative Office of the U.S. Courts. 1994. Unpublished report (January).

Alexander, Keith L. 1990. "Minority Women Feel Racism, Sexism Are Blocking the Path to Management." *Wall Street Journal* (July 25):B1.

Ames, Lynda J. 1990. "Equity at the End of the Day: Analyzing the Effects of Pay Equity Legislation Provisions." Presented at the American Sociological Association meeting, Washington, DC.

———. 1993. *Erase the Bias: A Pay Equity Guide to Eliminating Race and Sex Bias from Wage Setting Systems.* Washington, DC: National Committee on Pay Equity.

Amott, Teresa. 1993. *Caught in the Crisis: Women and the U.S. Economy Today.* New York: Monthly Review Press.

Amott, Teresa L. and Julie A. Matthaei. 1991. *Race, Gender, and Work: A Multicultural Economic History of Women in the United States.* Boston: South End Press.

Anderson, Karen Tucker. 1982. "Last Hired, First Fired: Black Women Workers During World War II." *Journal of American History* 69:82–97.

Andrews, Amy and Lotte Bailyn. 1993. "Segmentation and Synergy: Two Models of Linking Work and Family." Pp. 238–61 in Jane Hood (ed.), *Men, Work, and Family.* Newbury Park, CA: Sage.

Ansberry, Claire. 1993. "Workers Are Forced to Take More Jobs With Few Benefits." *Wall Street Journal* (March 11):A1.

Antal, Ariane B. and Dafna N. Izraeli. 1993. "A Global Comparison of Women in Management: Women Managers in Their Homelands and as Expatriates."

Pp. 52–96 in Ellen A. Fagenson (ed.), *Women in Management: Trends, Issues and Challenges in Managerial Diversity*. Newbury Park, CA: Sage.

Astrachan, Anthony. 1986. *How Men Feel: Their Response to Women's Demands for Equality*. Garden City, NY: Anchor Press.

Attwood, Lynne and Maggie McAndrew. 1984. "Women at Work in the USSR." Pp. 269–304 in Marilyn J. Davidson and Carly L. Cooper (eds.), *Working Women: An International Survey*. New York: Wiley.

Baker, Ross K. 1977. "Women Finally Break Into Government Jobs in the 1800s, but the Pay Is Poor, the Jobs Menial, and Men Hostile." *Smithsonian* 8:82–91.

Baxandall, Rosalyn, Linda Gordon, and Susan Reverby. 1976. *America's Working Women*. New York: Vintage Books.

Becker, Gary S. 1957. *The Economics of Discrimination*. Chicago: University of Chicago Press.

———. 1964. *Human Capital*. New York: National Bureau of Economic Research.

Beechey, Veronica and Tessa Perkins. 1987. *A Matter of Hours: Women, Part-Time Work and the Labour Market*. Cambridge, UK: Polity Press.

Beller, Andrea H. 1984. "Occupational Segregation and the Earnings Gap." Pp. 23–33 in *Comparable Worth: Issues for the 80's. A Consultation of the U.S. Commission on Civil Rights, June 67. Volume 1*. Washington, DC.

Belous, Richard S. 1989. *The Contingent Economy: The Growth of the Temporary, Part-Time, and Subcontracted Workforce*. McLean, VA: National Planning Association.

Benditt, John. 1993. "Gender and the Culture of Science: Women in Science '93." *Science* 260:383–430.

Bennett, Amanda. 1993. "Path to Top Jobs Now Twists and Turns." *Wall Street Journal* (March 15):D1, D6.

Bennett, Claudette E. 1992. *The Asian and Pacific Islander Population in the United States: March 1991 and 1990*. U.S. Bureau of the Census, Current Population Survey, Population Characteristics. Washington, DC: U.S. Government Printing Office.

Benson, Susan P. 1986. *Counter Cultures: Saleswomen, Managers, and Customers in American Department Stores, 1890–1940*. Urbana: University of Illinois Press.

Berg, Maxine. 1985. *The Age of Manufactures: Industry, Innovation, and Work in Britain, 1700–1820*. Oxford: Basil Blackwell.

Bergmann, Barbara R. 1986. *The Economic Emergence of Women*. New York: Basic Books.

Bergmann, Barbara R. and William Darity, Jr. 1981. "Social Relations, Productivity, and Employer Discrimination." *Monthly Labor Review* 104:47–9.

Berheide, Catherine W. 1992. "Women Still 'Stuck' in Low-Level Jobs." *Women in Public Services: A Bulletin for the Center for Women in Government* 3 (Fall).

Bielby, William T. and James N. Baron. 1984. "A Woman's Place Is With Other Women: Sex Segregation Within Organizations." Pp. 27–55 in Barbara F. Reskin (ed.), *Sex Segregation in the Workplace*. Washington, DC: National Academy Press.

———. 1986. "Men and Women at Work: Sex Segregation and Statistical Discrimination." *American Journal of Sociology* 91:759–99.

Bielby, Denise D. and William T. Bielby. 1988. "She Works Hard for the Money: Household Responsibilities and the Allocation of Work Effort." *American Journal of Sociology* 93:1031–59.

———. 1992a. "Cumulative Versus Continuous Disadvantage in an Unstructured Labor Market." *Work and Occupations* 19:366–87.

———. 1992b. "I Will Follow Him: Family Ties, Gender Role Beliefs, and Reluctance to Relocate for a Better Job." *American Journal of Sociology* 97:1241–67.

Blau, Francine D. and Marianne Ferber. 1986. *The Economics of Women, Men, and Work.* Englewood Cliffs, NJ: Prentice-Hall.

———. 1990. "Women's Work, Women's Lives: A Comparative Economic Perspective." National Bureau of Economic Research Working Paper No. 3447. Cambridge, MA: National Bureau of Economic Research, Inc.

Bloom, David E. and Adi Brender. 1993. "Labor and the Emerging World Economy." *Population Bulletin* (October).

Blum, Linda M. 1991. *Between Feminism and Labor: The Significance of the Comparable Worth Movement.* Berkeley: The University of California Press.

Blumstein, Phillip and Pepper Schwartz. 1983. *American Couples.* New York: William Morrow.

Boserup, Ester. 1970. *Women's Role in Economic Development.* London: Allen and Unwin.

Bovee, Tim. 1991. "Pay Gap Worsens for Women as They Age." *Los Angeles Times* (November 14):D2.

Boyd, Monica, Mary Ann Mulvihill, and John Myles. 1991. "Gender, Power, and Postindustrialism." *Canadian Review of Sociology and Anthropology* 28:407–36.

Braddock, Jomills Henry and James M. McPartland. 1987. "How Minorities Continue to Be Excluded from Equal Employment Opportunities: Research on Labor Market and Institutional Barriers." *Journal of Social Issues* 43:5–39.

Bradwell v. Illinois. 1873. 83 U.S. (16 Wall.) 130.

Brooks, Nancy Rivera. 1993. "Gender Pay Gap Found Among Top Executives." *Los Angeles Times* (June 30):D1, D3.

Burawoy, Michael. 1979. *Manufacturing Consent.* Chicago: University of Chicago Press.

Burden, Diane S. and Bradley Googins. 1987. *Balancing Job and Homelife Study: Managing Work and Family Stress in Corporations.* Boston: Boston University School of Social Work.

Burros, Marian. 1993. "Even Women at the Top Still Have Floors to Do." *New York Times* (May 31):A1, A11.

Callaghan, Polly and Heidi Hartmann. 1991. *Contingent Work: A Chart Book On Part-Time and Temporary Employment.* Washington, DC: Economic Policy Institute.

Callahan, Colleen R. 1992. "Dressed for Work: Women's Clothing on the Job, 1900–1990." *Labor's Heritage* 4:28–49.

Carey, Max and Alan Eck. 1984. "How Workers Get Their Training." *Occupational Outlook Quarterly* (Winter):3–21.

Carey, Max L. and James C. Franklin. 1991. "Industry Output, Job Growth Slowdown Continues." *Monthly Labor Review* 114:45–63.

Carney, Judith and Michael Watts. 1991. "Disciplining Women? Rice, Mechanization, and the Evolution of Mandinka Gender Relations in Senegambia." *Signs* 16:651–81.

Catalyst. 1986. *Report on a National Study of Parental Leaves.* New York: Catalyst.

Catasus, S., A. Farnos, F. Gonzalez, R. Grove, R. Hernandez, and B. Morejon. 1988. *Cuban Women: Changing Roles and Population Trends.* Geneva, Switzerland: International Labor Office.

Cattan, Peter. 1991. "Childcare Problems: An Obstacle to Work." *Monthly Labor Review* 114:3–9.

Chira, Susan. 1993. "Census Data Show Rise in Child Care by Fathers." *New York Times* (September 22):A10.

Christensen, Kathleen. 1989. "Flexible Staffing and Scheduling in U.S. Corporations." *Research Bulletin No. 240.* New York: The Conference Board.

Clement, Wallace and John Myles. 1994. *Relations of Ruling: Class and Gender in Postindustrial Societies.* Montreal: McGill-Queens University Press.

Cobble, Dorothy Sue. 1991. *Dishing It Out: Waitresses and Their Unions in the Twentieth Century.* Urbana: University of Illinois Press.

Cockburn, Cynthia. 1991. *In the Way of Women: Men's Resistance to Sex Equality in Organizations.* Ithaca: New York State School of Industrial and Labor Relations, Cornell University.

Cohen, Isaac. 1985. "Workers' Control in the Cotton Industry: A Comparative Study of British and American Mule Spinning." *Labor History* 26:53–85.

Cohn, Samuel. 1985. *The Process of Occupational Sex-Typing: The Feminization of Clerical Labor in Great Britain.* Philadelphia: Temple University Press.

Collins, Nancy. 1993a. "New IWPR Study Examines the Economic Benefits of Alternative Employment Patterns for Male and Female Workers." *Research-in-Brief.* Washington, DC: Institute for Women's Policy Research.

———. 1993b. "Self-Employment Versus Wage and Salary Jobs: How Do Women Fare?" *Research-in-Brief.* Washington, DC: Institute for Women's Policy Research.

Collins, Randall. 1974. *Conflict Sociology.* New York: Academic Press.

Collins, Sharon. 1989. "The Marginalization of Black Executives." *Social Problems* 36:317–31.

———. 1993. "Blacks on the Bubble: The Vulnerability of Black Executives in White Corporations." *Sociological Quarterly* 34:429–48.

Cooper, Patricia. 1991. "The Faces of Gender: Sex Segregation and Work Relations at Philco, 1928–1938." Pp. 320–50 in Ava Baron (ed.), *Work Engen-*

dered. Ithaca: New York State School of Industrial and Labor Relations, Cornell University.

Corcoran, Mary, Linda Datcher, and Greg Duncan. 1980. "Information and Influence Networks in Labor Markets." Pp. 1–37 in Greg Duncan and James Morgan (eds.), *5000 American Families*, Volume 8. Ann Arbor: Survey Research Center, Institute for Social Research, University of Michigan.

———. 1984. "The Economic Fortunes of Women and Children: Lessons From the Panel Study of Income Dynamics." *Signs* 10:232–8.

Cornfield, Daniel. 1987. *Workers, Managers, and Technological Change*. New York: Plenum Press.

Costello, Cynthia. 1985. "WEA're Worth It!: Work Culture and Conflict at the Wisconsin Education Association Insurance Trust." *Feminist Studies* 11:497–518.

———. 1989. "The Clerical Homework Program at the Wisconsin Physicians Service Insurance Corporation." Pp. 198–214 in Eileen Boris and Cynthia R. Daniels (eds.), *Homework: Historical and Contemporary Perspectives on Paid Labor at Home*. Urbana: University of Illinois Press.

Creeden, Michael A. 1989. "The Corporate Response to the Working Caregiver." *Aging Magazine* No. 358:16–9.

Crew, Spencer R. 1987. *Field to Factory*. Washington, DC: Smithsonian Institution.

Crispell, Diane. 1993. "Odds and Ends." *Wall Street Journal* (September 13):B1.

Crompton, Rosemary and Kay Sanderson. 1990. *Gendered Jobs and Social Change*. Boston: Unwyn Hyman.

Davidoff, Leonore and Catherine Hall. 1987. *Family Fortunes*. London: Hutchinson.

Davies, Margery W. 1982. *Woman's Place Is at the Typewriter: Office Work and Office Workers, 1870–1930*. Philadelphia: Temple University Press.

Davis, Patricia. 1993. "Fairfax Hospital to Pay $604,000 in Sex Bias Study." *Washington Post* (October 1):D1, D5.

Detman, Linda A. 1990. "Women Behind Bars: The Feminization of Bartending." Pp. 241–56 in Barbara F. Reskin and Patricia A. Roos (eds.), *Job Queues, Gender Queues: Explaining Women's Inroads Into Male Occupations*. Philadelphia: Temple University Press.

Diaz v. Pan American World Airways, Inc. 1971. 442F. 2d 385 (5th Cir.), cert. den. 404 U.S. 950.

Earle, Alice Morse. 1896. *Colonial Dames and Good Wives*. Boston: Houghton Mifflin.

Eaton, Susan C. 1992. "Women Workers, Unions, and Industrial Sectors of North America." IDP (Interdepartmental Project) Women Working Paper. Geneva, Switzerland: International Labor Organization.

EEOC v. Sears, Roebuck & Co. 1988. 628F. Supp. 1264 (N.D. Ill. 1986), affirmed 839 F. 2d 302 (7th Cir.).

Eitzen, D. Stanley and Maxine Baca-Zinn. 1992. "Structural Transformation and Systems of Inequality." Pp. 178–82 in Margaret L. Anderson and Patricia Hill Collins (eds.), *Race, Class, and Gender*. Belmont, CA: Wadsworth.

Ely, Robin J. In press. "The Social Construction of Relationships Among Professional Women at Work." In Marilyn Davidson and Ronald Burke (eds.), *Women in Management: Current Research Issues*. London: Paul Chapman Publishers.

Employee Relocation Council. 1992. "Relocation Trends Survey." Washington, DC: Employee Relocation Council.

England, Paula. 1992. *Comparable Worth: Theories and Evidence*. New York: Aldine de Gruyter.

England, Paula, Marilyn Chassie, and Linda McCormack. 1982. "Skill Demands and Earnings in Female and Male Occupations." *Sociology and Social Research* 66:147–68.

Epstein, Cynthia F. 1993. *Women in Law*. Urbana: University of Illinois Press.

Equal Employment Opportunity Commission. 1993. "National Database Fiscal Year 1983 to Fiscal Year 1992." Washington, DC: Equal Employment Opportunity Commission.

Exter, Thomas. 1991. "Everybody Works Hard Except Junior." *American Demographics* 13(May):14.

Faludi, Susan. 1987. "I Paid a Price for Wanting to Earn a Living: You Always Pay a Price." *West* (September 27):18–26.

———. 1988. "Diane Joyce." *MS* (January):62–5, 90–2.

———. 1991. *Backlash: The Undeclared War Against American Women*. New York: Crown.

Families and Work Institute. 1991. *Beyond the Parental Leave Debate*. New York: Families and Work Institute.

Fantasia, Rick. 1988. *Cultures of Solidarity: Consciousness, Action, and Contemporary American Workers*. Berkeley: University of California Press.

Farley, Jennie. 1993. "Commentary." Pp. 97–102 in Ellen A. Fagenson (ed.), *Women in Management: Trends, Issues and Challenges in Managerial Diversity*. Newbury Park, CA: Sage.

Ferber, Marianne A. and Brigid O'Farrell. 1991. *Work and Family: Policies for a Changing Work Force*. Washington, DC: National Academy Press.

Fernandez-Kelly, Maria P. 1983. *For We Are Sold, I and My People: Women and Industry in Mexico's Frontier*. Albany, NY: SUNY Press.

Ferree, Myra M. 1987a. "Family and Job for Working Class Women: Gender and Class Systems Seen From Below." Pp. 289–301 in Naomi Gerstel and Harriet E. Gross (eds.), *Families and Work*. Philadelphia: Temple University Press.

———. 1987b. "She Works Hard for a Living: Gender and Class on the Job." Pp. 322–47 in Beth B. Hess and Myra M. Ferree (eds.), *Analyzing Gender: A Handbook of Social Science Research*. Newbury Park, CA: Sage.

Fierman, Jaclyn. 1990. "Why Women Still Don't Hit the Top." *Fortune* (July 30):40,42,46,50,54,58,62.

Fine, Gary A. 1987. "One of the Boys: Women in Male-Dominated Settings." Pp. 131–47 in Michael S. Kimmel (ed.), *Changing Men: New Directions in Research on Men and Masculinity.* Newbury Park, CA: Sage.

Folbre, Nancy. 1991. "The Unproductive Housewife: Her Evolution in Nineteenth-Century Economic Thought." *Signs* 16:463–84.

Fox, Mary Frank and Sharlene Hesse-Biber. 1984. *Women at Work.* Mountain View, CA: Mayfield.

Fried, Mindy. 1993. "From Maternity to Parental Leave: Challenging the Gender Balance." Presented at the Sociologists for Women in Society meeting, Raleigh, NC.

Fullerton, Howard N. 1987. "Labor Force Projections: 1986–2000." Monthly Labor Review 110:10–29

Glass, Jennifer. 1990. "The Impact of Occupational Segregation on Working Conditions." *Social Forces* 68:779–96.

Glazer, Nona Y. 1984. "Servants to Capital: Unpaid Domestic Labor and Paid Work." *Review of Radical Political Economics* 16:61–87.

———. 1988. "Overlooked, Overworked: Women's Unpaid and Paid Work in the Health Services' 'Cost Crisis.'" *International Journal of Health Services* 18:119–37.

———. 1991. "'Between a Rock and a Hard Place': Women's Professional Organizations in Nursing and Class, Racial, and Ethnic Inequalities." *Gender & Society* 5:351–72.

Glenn, Evelyn Nakano and Charles M. Tolbert, II. 1987. "Technology and Emerging Patterns of Stratification for Women of Color: Race and Gender Segregation in Computer Occupations." Pp. 318–31 in Barbara Drygulski Wright (ed.), *Women, Work, and Technology.* Ann Arbor: University of Michigan Press.

Goldin, Claudia. 1990. *Understanding the Gender Gap.* New York: Oxford University Press.

Goode, William J. 1982. "Why Men Resist." Pp. 131–47 in Barrie Thorne and Marilyn Yalom (eds.), *Rethinking the Family.* New York: Longman.

Goozner, Merrill. 1991. "$3 Million Sex-Bias Accord at Marriott." *Chicago Tribune* (March 6):sec. 3, p. 3.

Greenhouse, Linda. 1993. "Plain Talk Puts Ginsburg at Fore of Court Debates." *New York Times* (October 14):A1, A9.

Grimm, James W. 1978. "Women in Female-Dominated Professions." Pp. 293–315 in Ann Stromberg and Shirley Harkess (eds.), *Women Working: Theories and Facts in Perspective.* Palo Alto, CA: Mayfield.

Gross, Edward. 1968. "Plus Ça Change: The Sexual Segregation of Occupations Over Time." *Social Problems* 16:198–208.

Grossman, Rachel. 1979. "Women's Place in the Integrated Circuit." *Southeast Asia Chronicle—Pacific Research.* SRC No.66/PSC 9(5):2–17.

Gutek, Barbara. 1981. *Sex and the Workplace.* New York: Praeger.

————. 1988. "Women in Clerical Work." Pp. 225–40 in Ann H. Stromberg and Shirley Harkess (eds.), *Women Working: Theory and Facts in Perspective.* Mountain View, CA: Mayfield.

Halle, David. 1984. *America's Working Man.* Chicago: University of Chicago Press.

Harlan, Sharon. 1991. "Number of Women in Government Increasing." *Women in Public Services: A Bulletin for the Center for Women in Government* 1 (Summer).

————. 1992. "Women Face Barriers in Top Management." *Women in Public Services: A Bulletin for the Center for Women in Government* 2 (Winter 1991/92).

Harris, Louis. 1987. *Inside America.* New York: Vintage.

Harrison, Bennett and Barry Bluestone. 1988. *The Great U-Turn.* New York: Basic Books.

Hartmann, Heidi. 1993. "Profits and Losses of Temps in the Workplace." *Washington Times* (June 6):B4.

Hayghe, Howard V. 1990. "Family Members in the Work Force." *Monthly Labor Review* 113:14–19.

————. 1993. Telephone conversation with Michelle Fondell (September).

Henley, Nancy and Jo Freeman. 1975. "The Sexual Politics of Interpersonal Behavior." Pp. 391–401 in Jo Freeman (ed.), *Women: A Feminist Perspective.* Mountain View, CA: Mayfield.

Herlihy, David. 1990. *Opera Muliebria: Women and Work in Medieval Europe.* Philadelphia: Temple University Press.

Higginbotham, Elizabeth. 1987. "Employment for Professional Black Women in the Twentieth Century." Pp. 73–99 in Christine Bose and Glenna Spitze (eds.), *Ingredients for Women's Employment Policy.* Albany, NY: SUNY Press.

————. 1992. "We Were Never on a Pedestal: Women of Color Continue to Struggle With Poverty, Racism, and Sexism." Pp. 183–90 in Margaret L. Anderson and Patricia Hill Collins (eds.), *Race, Class, and Gender.* Belmont, CA: Wadsworth.

Hochschild, Arlie. 1983. *The Managed Heart.* Berkeley: University of California Press.

Hochschild, Arlie with Anne Machung. 1989. *The Second Shift.* New York: Viking.

Hodgkinson, Harold. 1988. Presentation to the Florida Task Force on Improving Math, Science, and Computer Education, Orlando, FL. (May 14).

Hodson, Randy and Robert E. Parker. 1988. "Work in High Technology Settings: A Review of the Empirical Literature." *Research in the Sociology of Work* 4:1–29.

Hofferth, Sandra L., April Brayfield, Sharon Deich, and Pamela Holcomb. 1991. *National Child Care Survey, 1990.* Washington, DC: The Urban Institute.

Hoffmann, Carl and John Shelton Reed. 1981. "Sex Discrimination?—The XYZ Affair." *Public Interest* 62:21–39.

Hooks, Janet M. 1947. *Women's Occupations Through Seven Decades.* Women's Bureau Bulletin No. 218. U.S. Department of Labor. Washington, DC: U.S. Government Printing Office.

Hossfeld, Karen J. 1990. "'Their Logic Against Them': Contradictions in Sex, Race, and Class in Silicon Valley." Pp. 149–78 in Kathryn Ward (ed.), *Women Workers and Global Restructuring.* Ithaca: New York State School of Industrial and Labor Relations, Cornell University.

Howe, Wayne. 1986. "Temporary Help Workers: Who They Are, What Jobs They Hold." *Monthly Labor Review* 109:45–7.

Howell, Martha C. 1986. "Women, the Family Economy, and Market Production." Pp. 198–222 in Barbara Hanawalt (ed.), *Women and Work in Pre-Industrial Europe.* Bloomington: Indiana University Press.

Hubler, Shawn and Stuart Silverstein. 1992. "Women's Pay in State Lags 31% Behind Men's." *Los Angeles Times* (December 29):A1, A18–9.

Humphrey, John. 1985. "Gender, Pay, and Skill: Manual Workers in Brazilian Industries." Pp. 214–31 in Haleh Afshar (ed.), *Women, Work, and Ideology in the Third World.* New York: Tavistock.

Hyland, Stephanie L. 1990. "Helping Employees With Family Care." *Monthly Labor Review* 113:22–6.

Hymowitz, Carol and Timothy D. Schellhardt. 1986. "The Glass Ceiling: Why Women Can't Seem to Break the Invisible Barrier That Blocks Them From Top Jobs." *Special Report on the Corporate Woman. Wall Street Journal* (March 24: sec. 4, pp. 1D, 4D, 5D.

"The Immigrants: How they're Helping to Revitalize the U.S. Economy." 1992. *Business Week* (July 13): 114, 116–120, 154.

Institute for Women's Policy Research. 1993a. "State Pay Equity Programs Raise Women's Wages." News release, May 20. Washington, DC: Institute for Women's Policy Research.

———. 1993b. "The Wage Gap: Women's and Men's Earnings." *Research-in-Brief.* Washington, DC: Institute for Women's Policy Research.

Jackman, Mary R. 1994. *The Velvet Glove: Paternalism and Conflict in Gender, Class, and Race Relations.* Berkeley: University of California Press.

Jacobs, Jerry A. 1989a. "Long-Term Trends in Occupational Segregation by Sex." *American Journal of Sociology* 95:160–73.

———. 1989b. *Revolving Doors.* Palo Alto, CA: Stanford University Press.

———. 1992. "Women's Entry Into Management: Trends in Earnings, Authority, Values, and Attitudes Among Salaried Managers." *Administrative Science Quarterly* 37:282–301.

Jacobs, Jerry A. and Brian Powell. 1985. "Occupational Prestige: A Sex-Neutral Concept?" *Sex Roles* 12:1061–71.

Jacobs, Jerry A. and Ronnie J. Steinberg. 1990. "Compensating Differentials and the Male-Female Wage Gap: Evidence From the New York State Comparable Worth Study." *Social Forces* 69:439–68.

Jencks, Christopher, Lauri Perman, and Lee Rainwater. 1988. "What Is a Good Job? A New Measure of Labor-Market Success." *American Journal of Sociology* 93:1322–57.

Johnston, David. 1993. "FBI Agent to Quit Over Her Treatment in Sexual Harassment Case." *New York Times* (October 11):A7.

Johnston, William B. and Arnold H. Packer. 1987. *Workforce 2000: Work and Workers for the 21st Century.* Indianapolis: Hudson Institute.

Jones, Jacquelyn. 1985. *Labor of Love, Labor of Sorrow.* New York: Vintage.

Kalleberg, Arne and Rachel Rosenfeld. 1990. "Work in the Family and in the Labor Market: A Cross-National, Reciprocal Analysis." *Journal of Marriage and the Family* 52:331–46.

Kanter, Rosabeth Moss. 1976. "The Policy Issues: Presentation VI." Pp. 282–91 in Martha Blaxall and Barbara Reagan (eds.), *Women and the Workplace.* Chicago: University of Chicago Press.

———. 1977. *Men and Women of the Corporation.* New York: Basic Books.

———. 1983. "Women Managers: Moving Up in a High Tech Society." Pp. 21–36 in Jennie Farley (ed.), *The Woman in Management: Career and Family Issues.* Ithaca: New York State School of Industrial and Labor Relations, Cornell University.

Kessler, Ronald C., James S. House, and J. Blake Turner. 1987. "Unemployment and Health in a Community Sample." *Journal of Health and Social Behavior* 28:51–9.

Kessler-Harris, Alice. 1986. "Women's History Goes to Trial: EEOC vs. Sears, Roebuck, and Co." *Signs* 11(Summer):767–79.

———. 1990. *A Woman's Wage: Historical Meanings and Social Consequences.* Lexington, KY: University Press of Kentucky.

Kidwell, Claudia Brush and Valerie Steele (eds.). 1989. *Men and Women: Dressing the Part.* Washington, DC: Smithsonian Institution.

Kim, Marlene. 1989. "Gender Bias in Compensation Structures: A Case Study of Its Historical Basis and Persistence." *Journal of Social Issues* 45:39–50.

King, Mary C. 1992. "Occupational Segregation by Race and Sex, 1940–88." *Monthly Labor Review* 115:30–6.

———. 1993. "Black Women's Breakthrough Into Clerical Work: An Occupational Tipping Model." Presented at the Society for the Advancement of Socioeconomics meeting, New York.

Kleiman, Carol. 1993a. "Study Shows Job Status Skews Family Benefits." *Chicago Tribune* (February 8):C3.

———. 1993b. "Women End Up Sacrificing Salary for Children." *Tallahassee Democrat* (March 3):D8.

Komarovsky, Mirra. 1940. *The Unemployed Man and His Family.* New York: Dryden.

Kondo, Dorinne K. 1990. *Crafting Selves.* Chicago: University of Chicago Press.

Kowaleski, Maryanne and Judith M. Bennett. 1989. "Crafts, Guilds, and Women in the Middle Ages: Fifty Years After Marian K. Dale." *Signs* 14:474–88.

Kraut, Karen and Molly Luna. 1992. *Work and Wages: Facts on Women and People of Color in the Workforce.* Washington, DC: National Committee on Pay Equity.

Kutscher, Ronald E. 1991. "New BLS Projections: Findings and Implications." *Monthly Labor Review* 114:3–12.

"Labor Letter." 1992. *Wall Street Journal* (October 27):A1.

Ladd-Taylor, Molly. 1985. "Women Workers and the Yale Strike." *Feminist Studies* 11:465–89.

Lamb, Michael. 1992. "Nonmaternal Care and the Security of Infant-Mother Attachment: A Reanalysis of the Data." *Infant Behavior and Development* 15:71–83.

Lamphere, Louise. 1984. "On the Shopfloor: Multi-Ethnic Unity Against the Conglomerate." Pp. 247–63 in Karen B. Sacks and Dorothy Remy (eds.), *My Troubles Are Going to Have Trouble With Me.* New Brunswick, NJ: Rutgers University Press.

Larson, Carolee. 1993. "Discourse and Feminist Power: The Parental Leave Debate in Congress." Presented at the Sociologists for Women in Society meeting, Raleigh, NC.

Lehrer, Jim. 1992. *A Bus of My Own.* New York: Putnam's.

Leidner, Robin. 1988. "Homework: A Study in the Interaction of Work and Family Organization." *Research in the Sociology of Work* 4:69–94.

———. 1991. "Serving Hamburgers and Selling Insurance: Gender, Work, and Identity in Interactive Service Jobs." *Gender & Society* 5:154–77.

———. 1993. *Fast Food, Fast Talk: Service Work and the Routinization of Everyday Life.* Berkeley: University of California Press.

Lerner, Gerda. 1979. "The Lady and the Mill Girl." Pp. 182–96 in Nancy F. Cott and Elizabeth H. Pleck (eds.), *A Heritage of Her Own.* New York: Simon and Schuster.

Lester, Gordon H. 1991. *Child Support and Alimony: 1989.* U.S. Bureau of the Census Current Population Reports, Series P-60 (September). Washington, DC: U.S. Government Printing Office.

Levin, Henry M. and Russell W. Rumberger. 1987. "Educational Requirements for New Technologies: Visions, Possibilities and Current Realities." *Educational Policy* 1:333–54.

Lewis, Michael M. 1989. *Liar's Poker: Rising Through the Wreckage on Wall Street.* New York: Norton.

Lochner v. New York. 1905. 198 U.S. 45.

Lorber, Judith. 1992. "Gender." Pp. 748–65 in Edgar F. Borgatta and Marie L. Borgatta (eds.), *Encyclopedia of Sociology. Volume 2.* New York: Macmillan.

———. 1994. *The Paradoxes of Gender,* New Haven, CT: Yale University Press.

Mackey, Sandra. 1987. *The Saudis.* New York: Houghton Mifflin.

Major, Brenda. 1989. "Gender Differences in Comparisons and Entitlement: Implications for Comparable Worth." *Journal of Social Issues* 45:99–115.

Major, Brenda and Blythe Forcey. 1985. "Social Comparisons and Pay Evaluations: Preferences for Same-Sex and Same-Job Wage Comparisons." *Journal of Experimental Social Psychology* 21:393–405.

Major, Brenda, Dean B. McFarlin, and Diane Gagnon. 1984. "Overworked and Underpaid: On the Nature of Gender Differences in Personal Entitlement." *Journal of Personality and Social Psychology* 47:1399–412.

Markham, William T., Sharon Harlan, and Edward J. Hackett. 1987. "Promotion Opportunity in Organizations." *Research in Personnel and Human Resource Management* 5:223–87.

Marsden, Peter V., Arne L. Kalleberg, and Cynthia R. Cook. 1993. "Gender Differences in Organizational Commitment: Influences of Work Positions and Family Roles." *Work and Occupations* 20:368–90.

Matthaei, Julie A. 1982. *An Economic History of Women in America: Women's Work, the Sexual Division of Labor, and the Development of Capitalism.* New York: Schocken.

McGuire, Gail M. and Barbara F. Reskin. 1993. "Authority Hierarchies at Work: The Impacts of Race and Sex." *Gender & Society* 7:487–506.

McNeil, John. 1992. *Workers With Low Earnings: 1964–1990.* U.S. Bureau of the Census Current Population Reports, Consumer Income, Series P-60, No. 178. Washington, DC: U.S. Government Printing Office.

Mead, Margaret. 1949. *Coming of Age in Samoa.* New York: New American Library.

Meritor Savings Bank, FSB, v. Mechelle Vinson et al. 1986. 477 U.S. 57, 91 (June 19).

Merton, Robert K. 1972. "Insiders and Outsiders." *American Journal of Sociology* 78:9–47.

Meyer, Herbert H. and Mary D. Lee. 1978. *Women in Traditionally Male Jobs: The Experiences of Ten Public Utility Companies.* U.S. Dept. of Labor, Employment and Training Administration. Washington, DC: U.S. Government Printing Office.

Milkman, Ruth. 1985. "Women Workers, Feminism and the Labor Movement Since the 1960s." Pp. 300–22 in Ruth Milkman (ed.), *Women, Work, and Protest.* New York: Routledge and Kegan Paul.

———. 1987. *Gender at Work.* Urbana: University of Illinois Press.

Mincer, Jacob and Solomon Polachek. 1974. "Family Investments in Human Capital: Earnings of Women." *Journal of Political Economy* 82:76–108.

Mirowsky, John. 1987. "The Psycho-Economics of Feeling Underpaid: Distributive Justice and the Earnings of Husbands and Wives." *American Journal of Sociology* 92:1404–34.

Moran, Stahl & Boyer, Inc. 1988. *Status of American Female Expatriate Employees: Survey Results.* Boulder, CO: International Division, Moran, Stahl & Boyer, Inc.

Morrison, Ann M., Randall P. White, Ellen Van Velsor, and the Center for Creative Leadership. 1987. *Breaking the Glass Ceiling.* New York: Addison-Wesley.

———. 1992. *Breaking the Glass Ceiling.* Rev. ed. New York: Addison-Wesley.

National Commission on Working Women. 1990. *Women and Work: Workforce 2000 Trends.* Washington, DC: Wider Opportunities for Women.

National Committee on Pay Equity. 1989. *Work & Wages: Facts on Women and People of Color in the Workforce.* Washington, DC: National Committee on Pay Equity.

———. 1991. "After 28 Years, Equal Pay for Equal Work Still Not Achieved." *Newsnotes* 12(1):3.

National Opinion Research Corporation. 1990. *General Social Survey.* Chicago: University of Chicago Press.

Nazzari, Muriel. 1986. "The 'Woman Question' in Cuba." Pp. 65–82 in Barbara C. Gelpi, Nancy C. M. Hartsock, Claire C. Novak, and Myra H. Strober (eds.), *Women and Poverty.* Chicago: University of Chicago Press.

9to5. 1992. *Wage Replacement and Family Leave: Is It Necessary? Is It Feasible?* Cleveland: Working Women Education Fund.

Northrup, Herbert R. and John A. Larson. 1979. *The Impact of the AT&T-EEO Consent Decrees.* Labor Relations and Public Policy Series, No. 20. Philadelphia: Industrial Research Unit, University of Pennsylvania.

O'Connell, Martin. 1993. *Where's Papa: Father's Role in Child Care.* Population Trends and Public Policy No. 20. Washington, DC: Population Reference Bureau.

O'Connell, Martin and Amara Bachu. 1990. *Who's Minding the Kids? Childcare Arrangements, 1986–87.* U.S. Bureau of the Census, Current Population Reports, Series P-70, No. 20. Washington, DC: U.S. Government Printing Office.

———. 1992. *Who's Minding the Kids? Childcare Arrangements: Fall 1988.* U.S. Bureau of the Census, Current Population Reports, Series P-70, No. 30. Washington, DC: U.S. Government Printing Office.

Office of the Inspector General. 1993. *The Tailhook Report: The Official Inquiry Into the Events of Tailhook '91.* New York: St. Martin's Press.

Ong, Aihwa. 1986. *Spirits of Resistance and Capitalist Discipline: Factory Women in Malaysia.* Albany, NY: SUNY Press.

Oppenheimer, Valerie Kincade. 1968. "The Sex-Labeling of Jobs." *Industrial Relations* 7:219–34.

Padavic, Irene. 1987. *Staying or Switching: The Effect of Experience in Blue-Collar Jobs on White-Collar Women's Aspirations.* Unpublished dissertation. University of Michigan.

———. 1989. "Attractions of Male Blue-Collar Jobs for Black and White Women: Economic Need, Exposure, and Attitudes." *Social Science Quarterly* 72:33–49.

————. 1991. "The Re-Creation of Gender in a Male Workplace." *Symbolic Interaction* 14:279–94.

Papanek, Hanna. 1973. "Purdah: Separate Worlds and Symbolic Shelter." *Comparative Studies in Society and History* 15:289–325.

Phillips, Kevin. 1990. *The Politics of Rich and Poor.* New York: Random House.

Pinchbeck, Ivy. 1930. *Women Workers and the Industrial Revolution, 1750–1850.* London: Virago.

Piotrkowski, Chaya S. and Mitchell H. Katz. 1982. "Indirect Socialization of Children: The Effects of Mothers' Jobs on Academic Behavior." *Child Development* 53:409–15.

Pleck, Elizabeth. 1976. "Two Worlds in One." *Journal of Social History* 10:178–95.

Polachek, Solomon. 1981. "A Supply Side Approach to Occupational Segregation." Presented at the American Sociological Association meeting, Toronto.

Polivka, Anne E. and Thomas Nardone. 1989. "On the Definition of 'Contingent Work.'" *Monthly Labor Review* 112:9–16.

Presser, Harriet B. 1989. "Can We Make Time for Children? The Economy, Work Schedules, and Child Care." *Demography* 26:523–43.

Reich, Robert B. 1991. *The Work of Nations: Preparing Ourselves for 21st Century Capitalism.* New York: Knopf.

Reskin, Barbara F. 1988. "Bringing the Men Back In: Sex Differentiation and the Devaluation of Women's Work." *Gender & Society* 2:58–81.

————. 1991. "Labor Markets as Queues: A Structural Approach to Changing Occupational Sex Composition." Pp. 170–92 in Joan Huber (ed.), *Macro-Micro Interrelationships in Sociology.* Newbury Park, CA: Sage.

————. 1994. "Segregating Workers: Occupational Differences by Race, Ethnicity, and Sex." Presented at the meeting of the Industrial Relations Research Association, Boston.

Reskin, Barbara F. and Shelly Coverman. 1985. "Sex and Race Interactions in the Determinants of Psychological Distress: A Reappraisal of the Sex-Role Hypothesis." *Social Forces* 63:1038–59.

Reskin, Barbara F. and Heidi Hartmann. 1986. *Women's Work, Men's Work: Sex Segregation on the Job.* Washington, DC: National Academy Press.

Reskin, Barbara F. and Arne L. Kalleberg. 1993. "Sex Differences in Promotion Experiences in the United States and Norway." R.C. No. 28, Presented at the International Sociological Association meeting, Durham, NC.

Reskin, Barbara F. and Deborah J. Merritt. 1993. "Sex Segregation Among Law Faculty Members." Unpublished paper.

Reskin, Barbara F. and Irene Padavic. 1988. "Supervisors as Gatekeepers: Male Supervisors' Response to Women's Integration in Plant Jobs." *Social Problems* 35:401–15.

Reskin, Barbara F. and Patricia A. Roos. 1990. *Job Queues, Gender Queues: Explaining Women's Inroads Into Male Occupations.* Philadelphia: Temple University Press.

Reskin, Barbara F. and Catherine E. Ross. 1992. *"Jobs, Authority, and Earnings Among Managers: The Continuing Significance of Sex."* Work and Occupations 19:342–65.

Rigdon, Joan E. 1993. "Three Decades After the Equal Pay Act, Women's Wages Remain Far From Parity." *Wall Street Journal* (June 9):B1, B8.

Robert Half International. 1990. *Parent Track Survey.* Menlo Park, CA: Robert Half International.

Robertson, Claire. 1984. *Sharing the Same Bowl.* Bloomington: Indiana University Press.

Robertson, Nan. 1992. *The Girls in the Balcony.* New York: Random House.

Roethlisberger, F. J. and William J. Dickson. 1975. "A Fair Day's Work." Pp. 85–94 in Paul V. Crosby (ed.), *Interaction in Small Groups.* New York: Macmillan.

Roos, Patricia A. and Barbara F. Reskin. 1984. "Institutionalized Barriers to Sex Integration in the Workplace." Pp. 235–60 in Barbara F. Reskin (ed.), *Sex Segregation in the Workplace.* Washington, DC: National Academy Press.

Rosenfeld, Rachel A. and Arne L. Kalleberg. 1991. "A Cross-National Comparison of the Gender Gap in Income." *American Journal of Sociology* 96:69–106.

Ross, Catherine. 1986. "The Division of Labor at Home." *Social Forces* 64:816–33.

Ross, Catherine and John Mirowsky. 1988. "Child Care and Emotional Adjustment to Wives' Employment." *Journal of Health and Social Behavior* 29:127–38.

Rubin, Gayle. 1975. "The Traffic in Women: Notes on the 'Political Economy' of Sex." Pp. 157–209 in Rayna Reiter (ed.), *Toward an Anthropology of Women.* New York: Monthly Review Press.

Ryan, Mary P. 1983. *Womanhood in America.* 3rd ed. New York: Franklin Watts.

Sacks, Karen B. 1984. "Computers, Ward Secretaries, and a Walkout in a Southern Hospital." Pp. 173–92 in Karen B. Sacks and Dorothy Remy (eds.), *My Troubles Are Going to Have Trouble With Me.* New Brunswick, NJ: Rutgers University Press.

Safa, Helen I. 1990. "Women and Industrialization in the Caribbean." Pp. 72–97 in Sharon Stichter and Jane L. Parpart (eds.), *Women, Employment, and the Family in the International Division of Labour.* Philadelphia: Temple University Press.

Safilios-Rothschild, Constantina. 1990. "Socio-Economic Determinants of the Outcomes of Women's Income-Generation in Developing Countries." Pp. 221–8 in Sharon Stichter and Jane L. Parpart (eds.), *Women, Employment, and the Family in the International Division of Labour.* Philadelphia: Temple University Press.

Salaff, Janet W. 1990. "Women, the Family, and the State: Hong Kong, Taiwan, Singapore—Newly Industrialized Countries in Asia." Pp. 98–136 in Sharon Stichter and Jane L. Parpart (eds.), *Women, Employment and the Family in the International Division of Labour.* Philadelphia: Temple University Press.

Schor, Juliet B. 1991. *The Overworked American: The Unexpected Decline of Leisure.* New York: Basic Books.

Schrijvers, Joke. 1983. "Manipulated Motherhood: The Marginalization of Peasant Women in the North Central Province of Sri Lanka." *World Quarterly* 14:185–209.

Schroedel, Jean Reith. 1985. *Alone in a Crowd: Women in the Trades Tell Their Stories.* Philadelphia: Temple University Press.

Schultz, Vicki. 1991. "Telling Stories About Women and Work: Judicial Interpretation of Sex Segregation in the Workplace in Title VII Cases Raising the Lack of Interest Argument." Pp. 124–43 in Katharine Bartlett and Rosanne Kennedy (eds.), *Feminist Legal Theory.* Boulder: Westview.

Schur, Edwin M. 1983. *Labeling Women Deviant: Gender, Stigma, and Social Control.* Philadelphia: Temple University Press.

Scott, Joan Wallach. 1982. "The Mechanization of Women's Work." *Scientific American* 247:167–87.

Scott, Joan Wallach and Louise A. Tilly. 1975. "Women's Work and the Family in Nineteenth Century Europe." *Comparative Studies in Society and History* 17:36–64.

Seager, Joni and Ann Olson. 1986. *Women in the World: An International Atlas.* New York: Simon and Schuster.

Segal, Amanda T. with Wendy Zellner. 1992. "Corporate Women." *Business Week* (June 8):74–8.

Segura, Denise. 1992. "Chicanas in White-Collar Jobs: 'You Have to Prove Yourself.'" *Sociological Perspectives* 35:163–82.

Shaeffer, Ruth G. and Edith F. Lynton. 1979. *Corporate Experiences in Improving Women's Job Opportunities.* Conference Board Report No. 755. New York: The Conference Board.

Sharma, Ursula. 1979. "Segregation and Its Consequences in India: Rural Women in Himachal Pradesh." Pp. 259–83 in Patricia Caplan and Janet Bujra (eds.), *Women United, Women Divided.* Bloomington: Indiana University Press.

Shellenbarger, Sue. 1993. "Work and Family: Women Start Younger at Own Businesses." *Wall Street Journal* (March 15):B1.

Shelton, Beth Anne. 1992. *Women, Men, and Time: Gender Differences in Paid Work, Housework, and Leisure.* New York: Greenwood.

Shelton, Beth Anne and Daphne John. 1993. "Ethnicity, Race, and Difference: A Comparison of White, Black, and Hispanic Men's Household Labor Time." Pp. 131–50 in Jane Hood (ed.), *Men, Work, and Family.* Newbury Park, CA: Sage.

Shorter, Edward. 1975. *The Making of the Modern Family.* New York: Basic Books.

Sidel, Ruth. 1986. *Women and Children Last: The Plight of Poor Women in Affluent America.* New York: Viking.

Silver, Hilary. 1993. "Homework and Domestic Work." *Sociological Forum* 8:181–204.

Silvestri, George and John Lukasiewicz. 1987. "A Look at Occupational Employment Trends to the Year 2000." *Monthly Labor Review* 110:46–63.

———. 1991. "Occupational Employment Projections." *Monthly Labor Review* 114:64–94.

Simon, Rita J. and Jean M. Landis. 1989. "Women's and Men's Attitudes About a Woman's Place and Role." *Public Opinion Quarterly* 53:265–76.

Skolnick, Arlene. 1991. *Embattled Paradise: The American Family in an Age of Uncertainty.* New York: Basic Books.

Smith, Joan. 1984. "The Paradox of Women's Poverty: Wage-Earning Women and Economic Transformation." *Signs* 19:291–310.

Smith, Shelley A. and Marta Tienda. 1988. "The Doubly Disadvantaged: Women of Color." Pp. 61–80 in Ann H. Stromberg and Shirley Harkess (eds.), *Women Working: Theories and Facts in Perspective.* 2nd ed. Mountain View, CA: Mayfield.

Smith, Shirley J. 1985. "Revised Worklife Tables Reflect 1979–80 Experience." *Monthly Labor Review* 108:23–30.

Sokoloff, Natalie J. 1992. *Black Women and White Women in the Professions.* New York: Routledge.

Sorensen, Elaine. 1989. "Measuring the Effect of Occupational Sex and Race Composition on Earnings." Pp. 49–69 in Robert T. Michael, Heidi I. Hartmann, and Brigid O'Farrell (eds.), *Pay Equity: Empirical Inquiries.* Washington, DC: National Academy Press.

Spaeth, Joe L. 1989. *Determinants of Promotion in Different Types of Organizations.* Unpublished manuscript. Urbana: University of Illinois.

Spitze, Glenna. 1988. "Women's Employment and Family Relations: A Review." *Journal of Marriage and the Family* 50:595–618.

———. 1991. "Women's Employment and Family Relations." Pp. 381–404 in Alan Booth (ed.), *Contemporary Families: Looking Forward, Looking Back.* Minneapolis: National Council on Family Relations.

Starobin, Robert S. 1970. *Industrial Slavery in the Old South.* New York: Oxford University Press.

Starr, Tama. 1991. *The Natural Inferiority of Women.* New York: Poseidon.

"A Statistical Portrait of the Nation: Education and Income." 1993. *New York Times* (January 28):A14.

Steiger, Thomas and Barbara F. Reskin. 1990. "Baking and Baking Off: Deskilling and the Changing Sex Make-Up of Bakers." Pp. 257–74 in Barbara F. Reskin and Patricia A. Roos, *Job Queues, Gender Queues: Explaining Women's Inroads Into Male Occupations.* Philadelphia: Temple University Press.

Steinberg, Ronnie J. 1990. "The Social Construction of Skill." *Work and Occupations* 17:449–82.

Steinberg, Ronnie J. and Jerry A. Jacobs. 1993. "Invisible Work in a Feminized World: Pay Equity in Non-Profit Organizations." Unpublished paper. Philadelphia: Temple University.

Steinem, Gloria. 1986. "I Was a Playboy Bunny." Pp. 29–69 in Gloria Steinem, *Outrageous Acts and Everyday Rebellions.* New York: NAL-Dutton.

Steinhoff, P. G. and T. Kazuko. 1988. "Women Managers in Japan." Pp. 103–21 in Nancy J. Adler and Dafna N. Izraeli (eds.), *Women in Management Worldwide.* New York: M. E. Sharpe.

Stender et al. v. Lucky. 1992. "Findings of Fact and Conclusion of Law," *Federal Reporter,* vol. 803, Fed. Supplement, p. 259.

Stichter, Sharon. 1990. "Women, Employment, and the Family: Current Debates." Pp. 11–71 in Sharon Stichter and Jane L. Parpart (eds.), *Women, Employment, and the Family in the International Division of Labour.* Philadelphia: Temple University Press.

Straus, Murray A., Richard J. Gelles, and Suzanne K. Steinmetz. 1980. *Behind Closed Doors: Violence in the American Family.* New York: Anchor.

Strober, Myra H. and Carolyn L. Arnold. 1987. "The Dynamics of Occupational Segregation Among Bank Tellers." Pp. 107–47 in Clair Brown and Joseph A. Pechman (eds.), *Gender in the Workplace.* Washington: Brookings Institute.

Subich, Linda M., Gerald V. Barrett, Dennis Doverspike, and Ralph A. Alexander. 1989. "The Effects of Sex-Role Related Factors on Occupational Choice and Salary." Pp. 91–104 in Robert T. Michael, Heidi I. Hartmann, and Brigid O'Farrell (eds.), *Pay Equity: Empirical Inquiries.* Washington, DC: National Academy Press.

Sweeney, John J. and Karen Nussbaum. 1989. *Solutions for the New Work Force.* Cabin John, MD: Seven Locks.

Swerdlow, Marian. 1989. "Men's Accommodations to Women Entering a Nontraditional Occupation: A Case of Rapid Transit Operatives." *Gender & Society* 3:373–87.

Szafran, Robert F. 1982. "What Kinds of Firms Hire and Promote Women and Blacks? A Review of the Literature." *Sociological Quarterly* 23:171–90.

Tentler, Leslie Woodcock. 1979. *Wage-Earning Women: Industrial Work and Family Life in the United States, 1900–1930.* New York: Oxford University Press.

Teresa Harris v. Forklift Systems, Inc. U.S. Supreme Court Slip Opinion 92–1168. Unpublished.

Thoits, Peggy. 1983. "Multiple Identities and Psychological Well-Being: A Reformulation and Test of the Social Isolation Hypothesis." *American Sociological Review* 48:174–87.

Thomas, Robert J. 1985. *Citizenship, Gender, and Work: Social Organization of Industrial Agriculture.* Berkeley: University of California Press.

Thompson, Linda and Alexis J. Walker. 1991. "Gender in Families." Pp. 76–102 in Alan Booth (ed.), *Contemporary Families: Looking Forward, Looking Back.* Minneapolis: National Council on Family Relations.

Thurow, Lester C. 1992. *Head-to-Head: The Coming Economic Battles Among Japan, Europe, and America.* New York: Morrow.

Tilly, Chris. 1991. "Reasons for the Continuing Growth of Part-Time Employment." *Monthly Labor Review* 114:10–18.

Tilly, Chris and Charles Tilly. 1994. "Capitalist Work and Labor Processes." In Neil J. Smelser and Richard Swedberg (eds.), *Handbook of Economic Sociology.* Princeton, NJ: Princeton University Press.

Tomaskovic-Devey, Donald. 1993a. "The Gender and Race Composition of Jobs and the Male/Female, White/Black Pay Gap." *Social Forces* 72:45–76.

———. 1993b. *Gender and Racial Inequality at Work.* Ithaca: New York State School of Industrial and Labor Relations, Cornell University.

Tomaskovic-Devey, Donald and Barbara Risman. 1993. "Telecommuting Innovation and Organization: A Contingency Theory of Labor Process Change." *Social Science Quarterly* 74:367–85.

Treiman, Donald J. and Heidi I. Hartmann. 1981. *Women, Work, and Wages.* Washington, DC: National Academy Press.

Turner, J. Blake. 1992. "Economic Context and the Health Effects of Unemployment." Presented at the Society for the Study of Social Problems meeting, Pittsburgh, PA.

Ullman, Joseph P. and Kay Deaux. 1981. "Recent Efforts to Increase Female Participation in Apprenticeship in the Basic Steel Industry in the Midwest." Pp. 133–49 in Vernon M. Briggs, Jr., and Felician Foltman (eds.), *Apprenticeship Research: Emerging Findings and Future Trends.* Ithaca: New York State School of Industrial and Labor Relations, Cornell University.

United Nations. 1991. *The World's Women: Trends and Statistics, 1970–1990.* New York: United Nations Publications.

University of California at Los Angeles/Korn-Ferry International. 1993. *Decade of the Executive Woman.* Los Angeles: University of California at Los Angeles.

U.S. Bureau of the Census. 1961. *Historical Statistics of the United States: Colonial Times to 1957.* Washington, DC: U.S. Government Printing Office.

———. 1975. *Historical Statistics of the United States: Colonial Times to 1970. Part I.* Washington, DC: U.S. Government Printing Office.

———. 1981. *Money Income of Families and Persons in the United States: 1979.* Current Population Reports, Series P-60, No. 129 (November). Washington, DC: U.S. Government Printing Office.

———. 1983. *Money Income of Families and Persons in the United States: 1981.* Current Population Reports, Series P-60, No. 137 (March). Washington, DC: U.S. Government Printing Office.

———. 1986. *Earnings in 1983 of Married Couple Families by Characteristics of Husband and Wife.* Current Population Reports, Series P-60, No. 153 (March). Washington, DC: U.S. Government Printing Office.

———. 1988. *Money Income of Families and Persons in the United States: 1986.* Current Population Reports, Series P-60, No. 159 (June). Washington, DC: U.S. Government Printing Office.

———. 1991. *Money Income of Families and Persons in the United States: 1990.* Current Population Reports, Series P-60, No. 174 (August). Washington, DC: U.S. Government Printing Office.

————. 1992a. *Detailed Occupation and Other Characteristics From the EEO File for the United States.* 1990 Census of Population Supplementary Reports, 1990 CP-S-1-1. Washington, DC: U.S. Government Printing Office.

————. 1992b. *Money Income of Families and Persons in the United States: 1991.* Current Population Reports, Series P-60, No. 180 (August). Washington, DC: U.S. Government Printing Office.

————. 1992c. Poverty in the United States: 1991. Current Population Reports, Series P-60, No. 181 (August). Washington, DC: U.S. Government Printing Office.

————. 1992d. *Statistical Abstracts of the United States: 1992.* Washington, DC: U.S. Government Printing Office.

U.S. Bureau of Labor Statistics. 1988. *BLS Reports on Employer Child Care Practices.* News release 88-7 (January 15). Washington, DC: U.S. Department of Labor.

————. 1991. *Employment and Earnings* 38 (January). Washington, DC: U.S. Department of Labor.

————. 1992a. *Employment and Earnings* 39 (January). Washington, DC: U.S. Department of Labor.

————. 1992b. *Employment in Perspective: Minority Workers.* Report No. 840. Washington, DC: U.S. Department of Labor.

————. 1992c. *Usual Weekly Earnings of Wage and Salary Workers: Third Quarter, 1992.* Report No. USDL 92-673. Washington, DC: U.S. Department of Labor.

————. 1992d. *Workers on Flexible and Shift Schedules.* News release 92-491 (August 14). Washington, DC: U.S. Department of Labor

————. 1993a. *Employment and Earnings* 40 (January). Washington, DC: U.S. Department of Labor.

————. 1993b. *Employment in Perspective: Minority Workers.* Report No. 857. Washington, DC: U.S. Department of Labor.

————. 1993c. *Usual Weekly Earnings of Wage and Salary Workers: Fourth Quarter, 1992.* Report No. USDL 93–92. Washington, DC: U.S. Department of Labor.

————. 1993d. *Work Experience of the Population in 1992.* Report No. USDL 93-444. Washington, DC: U.S. Department of Labor.

U.S. General Accounting Office. 1991. *Workers at Risk: Increased Number in Contingent Employment Lack Insurance, Other Benefits.* GAO Report No. HRD-91–56. Washington, DC: U.S. Government Printing Office.

U.S. General Services Administration. 1990. *Code of Federal Regulations.* Washington, DC: U.S. Government Printing Office.

U.S. Merit Systems Protection Board. 1992. *A Question of Equity: Women and the Glass Ceiling in the Federal Government. A Report to the President and Congress by the U.S. Merit Systems Protection Board.* Washington, DC: U.S. Merit Systems Protection Board.

U.S. Small Business Administration. 1988. *Small Business in the American Economy.* Washington, DC: U.S. Government Printing Office.

U.S. Women's Bureau. 1992. *Facts on Working Women*. Report No. 92-1 Washington, DC: U.S. Government Printing Office.

———. 1993. *Facts on Working Women*. Report No. 93-2 Washington, DC: U.S. Government Printing Office.

Von Glinow, Mary Ann. 1988. "Women in Corporate America: A Caste of Thousands." *New Management* 6:36–42.

Walsh, John P. 1989. "Technological Change and the Division of Labor: The Case of Retail Meatcutters." *Work and Occupations* 16:165–83.

Watson, Traci. 1993. "Glossy Strategic Plan Hits the Streets." *Science* 260:888–9.

Weitzman, Lenore J. 1979. *Sex Role Socialization*. Palo Alto, CA: Mayfield.

West, Candace and Don H. Zimmerman. 1987. "Doing Gender." *Gender & Society* 1:125–51.

Weston, Kath. 1990. "Production as Means, Production as Metaphor: Women's Struggle to Enter the Trades." Pp. 137–51 in Faye Ginsburg and Anna Lowenhaupt Tsing (eds.), *Uncertain Terms: Negotiating Gender in American Culture*. Boston: Beacon.

Westover, Belinda. 1986. "'To Fill the Kids' Tummies': The Lives and Work of Colchester Tailoresses, 1880–1918." Pp. 54–75 in Leonore Davidoff and Belinda Westover (eds.), *Our Work, Our Lives, Our Words*. London: Macmillan.

Westwood, Sallie. 1985. *All Day, Every Day: Factory and Family in the Making of Women's Lives*. Urbana: University of Illinois Press.

White, Jane. 1992. *A Few Good Women: Breaking the Barriers to Top Management*. Englewood Cliffs, NJ: Prentice-Hall.

Whyte, William F. 1948. *Human Relations in the Restaurant Industry*. New York: McGraw-Hill.

Wilkie, Jane R. 1993. "Changes in U.S. Men's Attitudes Toward the Family Provider Role, 1972–1989." *Gender & Society* 7: 261–79.

Williams, Christine L. 1989. *Gender Differences at Work: Women and Men in Nontraditional Occupations*. Berkeley: University of California Press.

———. 1992. "The Glass Escalator: Hidden Advantages for Men in the 'Female' Professions." *Social Problems* 39:253–67.

Wilson, Franklin D. and Lawrence L. Wu. 1993. "A Comparative Analysis of Labor Force Activities of Ethnic Populations." Center for Demography and Ecology Working Paper No. 93-01. Madison: University of Wisconsin.

Wilson, William J. 1991. "Studying Inner-City Social Dislocations." *American Sociological Review* 56:1–14.

Working Women. 1981. *In Defense of Affirmative Action: Taking the Profit Out of Discrimination*. Cleveland.

Wright, Carroll D. 1892. "Why Women Are Paid Less Than Men." *The Forum* 13:629–39.

Yarrow, Michael. 1987. "Class and Gender in the Developing Consciousness of Appalachian Coal Miners." Presented to the 5th UMIST-ASTON Annual Conference on Organization and Control of the Labor Process, April 22–24, Manchester, England.

Zachary, G. Pascal and Bob Ortega. 1993. "Workplace Revolution Boosts Productivity at Cost of Job Security." *Wall Street Journal* (March 10):A1, A8.

Zavella, Patricia. 1987. *Women's Work and Chicano Families: Cannery Workers in the Santa Clara Valley.* Ithaca: New York State School of Industrial and Labor Relations, Cornell University.

Zelizer, Viviana A. 1989. "The Social Meaning of Money: 'Special Monies.'" *American Journal of Sociology* 95:342–77.

Zuboff, Shoshanna. 1988. *In the Age of the Smart Machine: The Future of Work and Power.* New York: Basic Books.

Glossary/Index